Mountain Biking
the Washington, D.C./
Baltimore Area

Mountain Biking the Washington D.C./ Baltimore Area

An Atlas of Northern Virginia, Maryland, and D.C.'s
Greatest Off-Road Bicycle Rides

Fifth Edition

Martín Fernández and Scott Adams

FALCONGUIDES

GUILFORD, CONNECTICUT
HELENA, MONTANA

FALCONGUIDES®

An imprint of Rowman & Littlefield
Falcon, FalconGuides, and Outfit Your Mind are registered trademarks of Rowman & Littlefield.

Distributed by NATIONAL BOOK NETWORK

Copyright © 2015 by Rowman & Littlefield
Photos by Martín Fernández unless otherwise noted.
Maps by Trailhead Graphics Inc. © Rowman & Littlefield

British Library Cataloguing-in-Publication Information available

Library of Congress Cataloging-in-Publication Data available

ISBN 978-1-4930-0601-4 (paperback)
ISBN 978-1-4930-1490-3 (e-book)

∞™ The paper used in this publication meets the minimum requirements of American National Standard for Information Sciences—Permanence of Paper for Printed Library Materials, ANSI/NISO Z39.48-1992.

The authors and Rowman & Littlefield assume no liability for accidents happening to, or injuries sustained by, readers who engage in the activities described in this book.

This edition is dedicated to the memory of "Uncle" Scott Scudamore. May his indomitable spirit live within all of us and his legacy endure forever. Learn more about Scott at scudfries.org.

Contents

The Rides

Western Maryland—Mountain Region
Garrett County and Deep Creek Lake

Honorable Mentions

Maryland Piedmont Region
Montgomery County (MoCo)

Overview

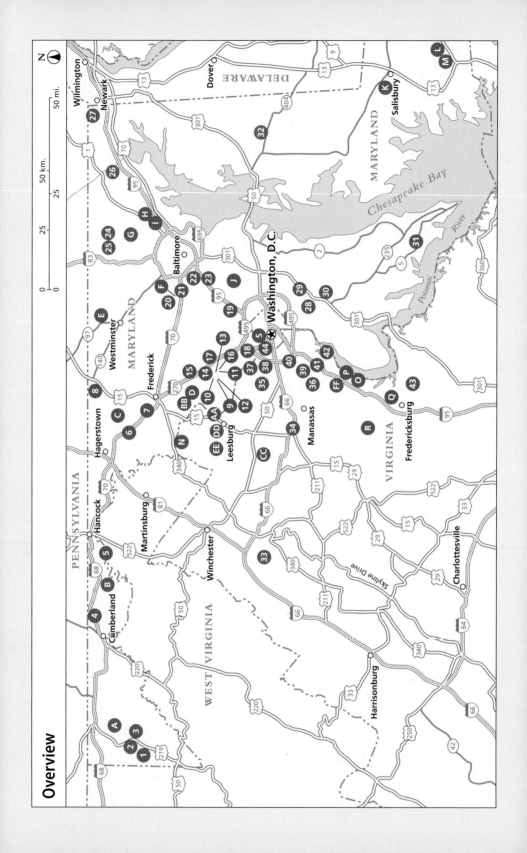

Howard County
Patapsco Valley State Park

Coastal Maryland

Northern Virginia

Acknowledgments

Without my wife, Courtney, this book would not be possible. Her encouragement and support have helped me every step of the way. To my *viejos*, my brother and sisters. To Ari, and all the rides ahead of us; I'm glad she's here for this fifth edition. A special thanks to MORE and all of the regional mountain bike groups and all of their volunteers for the efforts they make to ensure that we have places like these to enjoy our sport. And to you, the reader, for taking the plunge and getting this trail guide. See you on the trail!

—Martín Fernández

A special thanks to all the folks who have ever supported my efforts and desires to get to this point. It goes without saying that I would be hard-pressed to manage my ideas and dreams without all of the regular and unending encouragement, extra helping hands, and borrowed elbow grease from those around me and from those who believe in me. Thanks.

—Scott Adams

Preface

I am fortunate in my work for the International Mountain Bicycling Association (IMBA) to be able to sample trails all over the world. You might think my regular travel to Washington, D.C. would lack good mountain biking. But it's quite the opposite. The D.C. area has some very desirable mountain biking given the years of great advocacy and trails stewardship by IMBA's local chapter, the Mid-Atlantic Off-Road Enthusiasts (MORE).

Mountain Biking the Washington, D.C./Baltimore Area author Martin Fernandez has been an active volunteer for MORE for twenty years. And that means two things: first, he knows best where the choice riding is in the area, and second, he knows how to piece together the best trails in a manner that only a professional guide service could replicate. Martin's book is like having your own professional guide. And because MORE has helped to add and expand so many new trails in the area, this new edition ensures you have current quality trail information to make for a great ride for all abilities.

And remember as you are enjoying your next D.C.-area ride, there are no "Trail Fairies." Trails, especially quality trails like those featured in this book, are the result of ongoing advocacy and stewardship. And thanks to a very well-organized local group like MORE, the D.C. area can boast a continual expansion and addition of quality trails. I urge you to be a part of this stewardship effort. At IMBA we call it *Trail Love*.

—**Mike Van Abel,** President & USA Executive Director

I appreciate the opportunity to encourage your readers to join a local organization such as the Mid-Atlantic Off-Road Enthusiasts (MORE), the Fredericksburg Area Mountain Bike Enthusiasts (FAMBE), Eastern Shore IMBA (ESIMBA), and Southern Maryland Mountain Bike (SMMB). I encourage readers to join one of these organizations to continue working behind the scenes to assure we are able to ride our bikes on regional trails. I would also encourage readers to work with other organizations such as hikers, runners, equestrians, and "friends of" groups, as we all value and respect public lands and their availability for recreation.

It is our responsibility to be good stewards of our natural resources and provide recreational access to future generations. Please consider how you can give back.

—**Ernest "Ernie" Rodriguez,** MORE President

Introduction

You'll find that this guide contains just about everything you'll ever need to choose, plan for, enjoy, and survive a ride in Northern Virginia, Maryland, and Washington, D.C. Stuffed with useful Washington, D.C./Baltimore–specific information, this book features fifty mapped and cued rides and eighteen honorable mentions, as well as everything from advice on getting into shape to tips on getting the most out of cycling with your kids.

We've designed this FalconGuide to be highly visual, for quick reference and ease of use. This means that the most pertinent information rises quickly to the top, so you don't have to waste time poring through bulky ride descriptions to get mileage cues. They're set aside for you. Yet a FalconGuide doesn't read like a laundry list. Take the time to dive into a ride description and you'll soon realize that this guide is not just a good source of information; it's a good read. In the end you get the best of both worlds: a quick reference guide and an engaging look at a region.

How to Use This Guide

Mountain Biking Washington, D.C./Baltimore is divided into six sections, each representing one of the six major geographic regions in Maryland, Northern Virginia, and D.C. Within each section are the featured rides found in the region. Each ride is then subsequently divided into a variety of components. The Ride Specs are fairly self-explanatory. Here you'll find the quick, nitty-gritty details of the ride: where the trailhead is located, the nearest town, ride length, riding time, difficulty rating, trail surface, lay of the land, park schedules and fees, contact information for trail management, and what other trail users you may encounter. Our Getting There section gives you dependable directions from a nearby city, right down to where you'll want to park, as well as GPS coordinates for the trailhead. The Ride is the meat of the chapter. Detailed and honest, it's our carefully researched impression of the trail(s). While it's impossible to cover everything, you can rest assured that we won't miss what's important. In Miles and Directions, we provide mileage cues to identify all turns and trail name changes, as well as points of interest. Between this and the route map, you simply can't get lost. Where possible, we try to tell you how you can combine multiple rides to build your own "epic" outing. We'll also tell you where to eat after your ride, where to stay, and what else to see while you're in the area. The Honorable Mentions section details additional rides in each region that will inspire you to get out and explore on your own.

If you've owned past editions of this guidebook you'll notice some differences, particularly in the ride descriptions. When Scott and I set out to write this book more than twenty years ago, off-road riding opportunities in the Washington, D.C., and Baltimore regions were very limited. So much has changed since then, and today, our region is a virtual mecca for mountain biking. The George Washington National Forest alone would need a guidebook of its own. In order to fit as many trails as possible in this edition we've shortened and consolidated the ride descriptions. This has allowed us to offer you more destinations, fifty, to visit and explore. You'll also notice the new "You May Run Into" sidebars. We felt it was important to recognize many of the individuals who have tirelessly worked over the years to ensure we have these places to ride. Finally, we've built a detailed website, www.mtbdc.com, to provide you with additional information, including changes to any of the routes in the book, and maps and details about other rides not included here. Check it regularly for updates based on our most recent rides.

Route Map

This is your primary guide to each ride. It shows all the accessible roads and trails, points of interest, water, towns, landmarks, and geographical features. It also distinguishes trails from roads, and paved roads from unpaved roads. The selected route is highlighted, and directional arrows point the way.

The Maps

We don't want anyone, by any means, to feel restricted to just the roads and trails that are mapped here. We hope you will have an adventurous spirit and use this guide as a platform to dive into Washington's backcountry and discover new routes for yourself. One of the simplest ways to begin this is to just turn the map upside down and ride the course in reverse. The change in perspective is fantastic and the ride should feel quite different. With this in mind, it will be like getting two distinctly different rides on each map.

For your own purposes, you may wish to copy the directions for the course onto a small sheet to help you while riding, or photocopy the map and cue sheet to take with you. These pages can be folded into a bike bag, stuffed into a jersey pocket, or used with a map holder (Google "BarMap of the gods"). You can also take a snapshot of the book page on your smart phone for quick and easy access. Just remember to slow or even stop when you want to read the map.

Ride Finder

Best Rides for Sightseeing
  3. Deep Creek Lake State Park
  4. Rocky Gap State Park
 37. Great Falls National Park
CC. Middleburg Vineyard Tour

Best Rides for Seeing Historic Landmarks
  5. Woodmont Natural Resources Management Area
 37. Great Falls National Park
 44. Chesapeake & Ohio Canal

Best Rides for Seeing Birds and Wildlife
  3. Deep Creek Lake State Park
  5. Woodmont Natural Resources Management Area
 11. MoCo South
 16. Seneca Creek State Park
 27. Fair Hill Natural Resource Management Area
 30. Cedarville State Forest

Best Rides for Kids and Families
 19. Fairland Regional Park
 23. Rockburn Branch Regional Park
 24. Northern Central Rail-Trail
 29. Rosaryville State Park
 30. Cedarville State Forest
 34. Conway Robinson State Forest
 35. Lake Fairfax Park
 39. Burke Lake Loop
 40. Wakefield Park/Lake Accotink Trail

Best Rides for Camping
  1. 5.5-Mile Trail
  3. Deep Creek Lake State Park
  4. Rocky Gap State Park
  6. Greenbrier State Park
  7. Gambrill State Park
 26. Susquehanna River Ride
FF. Prince William State Forest

Best Rides with Technical Singletrack

1. 5.5-Mile Trail
7. Gambrill State Park: Yellow Trail
8. Emmitsburg—Rainbow Lake
21. Daniels Area
33. Elizabeth Furnace
36. Fountainhead Regional Park

Best Rides with Flowy Singletrack

8. Emmitsburg—Rainbow Lake
9. Seneca Bluffs Trail (SBT)
10. Seneca Ridge Trail (SRT)
11. MoCo South
12. Schaeffer Farms
19. Fairland Regional Park
29. Rosaryville State Park
36. Fountainhead Regional Park

Map Legend

Transportation

Interstate/Divided Highway	═══════
Featured U.S. Highway	═══════
U.S. Highway	═══════
Featured State, County, or Local Road	▬▬▬▬▬
Primary Highway	───────
County/Local Road	───────
Featured Bike Route	••••••••••••
Bike Route	••••••••••••
Featured Trail	------------
Dirt Road/Trail	------------
Railroad	⊢─┼─┼─┼─┤

Hydrology

Reservoir/Lake	⬭
River/Creek	∿

Land Use

State/Local Park, Open Space	▭
State Line	— · — · —

Symbols

Interstate	(95)
U.S. Highway	(15)
State Highway	(16)
Trailhead (Start)	🔟
Mileage Marker	17.1◆—
Small Park	🌲
Visitor Center	❷
Point of Interest/Structure	■
Parking	🅿
Campground	⛺
Picnic Area	⛱
Restroom	🚻
Boat Ramp	⊷
Marina	⚓
Bridge	⏜
Capital	✪
Town	○
Mountain/Peak	▲
Direction Arrow	→

Western Maryland– Mountain Region

Maryland is perhaps one of the most diverse states in the country. Composed of five distinct geographic provinces, Maryland offers a tremendous variety of off-road cycling destinations. The Blue Ridge creates a distinct division in the state's topography. To the east of the Blue Ridge, the Maryland Piedmont area gives way to the prolific shores of the Chesapeake Bay and Maryland's coastal region. To the west of the Blue Ridge, the majestic Appalachians rise to give Maryland's mountain region an extraordinary array of diversity. Within a couple of hours, one can be on the plains and shores of the Chesapeake and then in the hills of western Maryland.

The terrain in the western part of Maryland is well suited for mountain biking. Rocky, technical, and extremely changeable, the landscapes provide the perfect place to enjoy challenging East Coast riding. There are climbs that are long enough to test every muscle in your body, but the rewarding descents that follow will make it all worthwhile.

Fat-tire enthusiasts will find that there just isn't enough time in a single season to ride the countless number of trails and dirt roads open to cycling in the counties of western Maryland, made up of the Blue Ridge, Great Valley, Valley and Ridge, and Appalachian Plateau provinces. In this guide, we have selected what we think are some of the best examples of what this wonderful region has to offer.

The popularity of mountain biking has prompted many natural resource officials to reevaluate the way that lands in western Maryland are managed. While there are areas where cycling is still prohibited, the majority of state parks and forests allow bikers access to their trails. Many parks are starting specific programs to attract mountain bikers to the region.

Deep Creek Lake offers a vast network of trails bound to satisfy the most ardent cyclist. But if you prefer to mix activities, you can instead enjoy an array of water sports on Maryland's largest man-made body of water. Come winter, Deep Creek is transformed into a skier's paradise. Some of the very same trails you bike during the summer are used by snowmobiles and cross-country skiers during the winter. In short, if you love the outdoors you'll find that the mountain side of Maryland is a great place to visit.

Garrett County and Deep Creek Lake

Garrett County, the second-largest county (by land area) in Maryland, was founded in 1872 and is the westernmost county in the state. It is the only Maryland county that doesn't lie within the Chesapeake Bay's basin. Instead, Garrett County and its mountainous terrain forms part of the Mississippi River's drainage basin. The county is bordered to the north by the Mason-Dixon line with Pennsylvania, to the south by the Potomac River and West Virginia, and to the west by West Virginia. The county sits amid the highland zones of the Appalachian Mountains, and because of that is a prime destination for rugged and challenging mountain biking.

Named after John Work Garrett, president of the B&O Railroad at the time, the county opened up to economic development in the 1850s with the arrival of the railroad. During the railroad's heyday, the county saw great economic development and the areas around what is now Deep Creek and McHenry became large mining and timber centers. The railroad also opened up the county to tourism, and until the early 1900s it was a favorite destination for the rich and famous. With the decline of the railroad the county's industry took a hit, and both the mining and timber industries, along with the tourism trade, began to decline.

The damming of the junction of Deep Creek and the Youghiogheny River by the Youghiogheny Hydroelectric Company in the mid-1920s created Maryland's largest inland lake, Deep Creek Lake. It was then that the area began to take the shape we know today. In the mid-1950s Wisp Ski Resort opened for business, and tourism began to increase once again in the area. In the year 2000, the state of Maryland purchased the lake from the Pennsylvania Electric Company and opened it for public access. By 2011 Wisp had changed ownership, and an influx of cash improved the resort not only to offer winter recreational activities, but also summer fun opportunities. Since then, Deep Creek has become a regional vacationing destination for families who come to enjoy a variety of activities year-round, including boating, fishing, snowmobiling, hiking, road cycling, and now mountain biking.

Ride Information (Applies to Rides 1 to 3)

Local Information
Garrett County Chamber of Commerce
www.visitdeepcreek.com

Local Events and Attractions
Garrett County Chamber Office
(301) 387-4FUN
Contact the Deep Creek Lake Park office for various activities within the park.
(301) 387-5563

Bike Shops
High Mountain Sports
Oakland, MD
www.highmountainsports.com
(301) 387-4199

Accommodations
Deep Creek Lake is one of Maryland's most popular vacation destinations. There are campsites, bed-and-breakfasts, inns, hotels,

cottages, and more. Depending on the time of year you visit, reservations might be necessary. For a complete listing of accommodations online, visit www.visitdeepcreek.com.

Where to Eat

Mountain State Brewing Company
McHenry, MD
(301) 387-3360
www.mountainstatebrewing.com

1 5.5-Mile Trail

The 5.5-Mile Trail is an approximately 5.5-mile trail that connects Herrington Manor State Park with Swallow Falls State Park in Garrett County. This ride will take you along the singletrack trail and then around forest fire roads before delivering you back to the starting point. Although I have documented this ride as a loop, it can easily be ridden as an out-and-back by turning around at the youth group camping area of Swallow Falls State Park at mile 4.7.

Start: Parking area adjacent to Swallow Falls Road
Length: 10.9-mile loop
Ride time: About 1–2 hours
Difficulty: Easy to moderate
Trail surface: Singletrack, doubletrack, and gravel roads
Lay of the land: Wooded with slightly hilly terrain

Land status: State parks and forest
Nearest town: McHenry, MD
Other trail users: Hikers
Trail contacts: Swallow Falls State Park, Oakland, MD, (301) 387-6938; Herrington Manor State Park, Oakland, MD, (301) 334-9180; garretttrails.org
Schedule & fees: 8 a.m. to sunset; small vehicle fee

Getting there: From US 219 take Mayhew Inn Road for approximately 4.5 miles to Oakland Sang Run Road. Continue straight on Oakland Sang Run Road (left) and make your first left onto Swallow Falls Road. The trailhead will be approximately 2.3 miles on the left, shortly after the intersections of Mellott Road and Swallow Falls Road. GPS coordinates: 39.464295, -79.443960.

The Ride

The 5.5-Mile Trail follows portions of an old narrow-gauge tram road that was used by wagons in the old mining districts of Garrett County. The road was also used to haul logs out of the area during Garrett County's lumbering peak. If you look closely, you may even be able to see the old imprints of the cross ties along the trail.

The trail connects two of Garrett County's most picturesque state parks, Swallow Falls and Herrington Manor, via a 5.5-mile singletrack trail through mature, picturesque hemlock forests. The remaining part of the ride will take you along gently rolling gravel roads and snowmobile trails along the Snaggy Mountain area of Garrett State Forest. Popular both in the summer and winter months, the Snaggy Mountain section of the ride provides access to primitive camping sites.

Although we do not see it during our ride, I highly recommend you take some time to visit the spectacular Muddy Creek Falls at Swallow Falls State Park. Water from the Muddy Creek crashes down on the sandstone beds below for nearly 60 feet to create the state's highest free-falling waterfalls. During times of high water,

The trail connects two of Garrett County's most picturesque state parks, Swallow Falls and Herrington Manor.

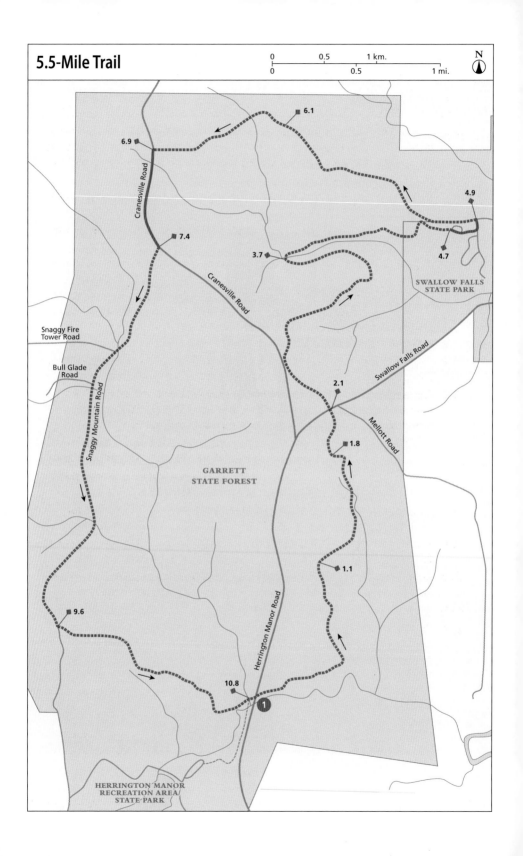

5.5-Mile Trail

the roaring falls are spectacular, and even in times of lower flow, the layered, cross-bedded sandstone walls unmasked by the water provide a breathtaking view.

Miles and Directions

0.0 Start from the parking area adjacent to Swallow Falls Road. The trailhead is immediately to the left as you face the trailhead sign. There is a green blaze at its entrance and a sign that reads Swallow Falls to Herrington State Park, 5.5 miles. We'll begin measuring from here. The trail is blazed white.

1.1 The trail continues to the right. You can see the remnants of an older trail straight ahead. Stay right.

1.8 Turn right at this intersection and continue following the white blazes. (The fork to the left will take you back toward marker 1.1.)

2.1 Cross Swallow Falls Road. (A left turn on the road will take you back toward the parking area.)

3.7 Cross the bridge that spans Toliver Run. Be careful since this bridge tends to be slippery when wet. A short, steep climb awaits you on the other side of the bridge. Immediately after the climb, turn right to continue on the white trail. (The red-blazed Toliver trail to the left will connect with Maple Glade Road.)

4.7 Cross into Swallow Falls State Park and reach the youth camping area. Continue straight through the camping area past the restrooms until you reach the stop/yield signs.

4.9 Turn left and head straight toward the Maryland Conservation Corps building. When you reach the building, turn left on and onto the gravel road, Maple Glade Road. Stay on Maple Glade for approximately 2 miles until you reach Cranesville Road.

6.1 Continue straight on Maple Glade Road. (Look left and you'll see the entrance to the red-blazed Toliver trail. Turn left here if you want to bail out and return along the 5.5-mile trail.)

6.9 Turn left on Cranesville Road. Exercise caution at this intersection since vehicle traffic is present in this area. Ride along Cranesville for approximately 0.5 mile.

7.4 Turn right into the clearly marked Garrett Forest Snaggy Mountain Area and continue straight along the gravel road.

9.6 Turn left at Shelter 8b. There is a small day-use area to the right. Begin a descent back to the starting point.

10.6 Turn left at the T intersection. Listen for vehicle traffic along Herrington Manor Road to the left.

10.8 Turn left to cross over Herrington Manor Road. Look for the parking area across the road.

10.9 The loop is complete!

2 Fork Run Recreation Area

The trails at Fork Run offer more experienced mountain bikers a challenging network of trails. If you've ridden Deep Creek Lake and tackled the distances of the 5.5-Mile Trail, then you're ready for the tight and technical trails of the Fork Run Area.

Start: Fork Run Trail Parking Area
Length: 8.1-mile lollipop
Ride time: About 1.5–3 hours
Difficulty: Moderate/difficult
Trail surface: Mostly singletrack
Lay of the land: Wooded hilly terrain with significant elevation changes

Land status: County property
Nearest town: McHenry, MD
Other trail users: Hikers, climbers
Trail contacts: www.garretttrails.org
Schedule: May to October

Getting there: From US 219 (Garrett Highway) turn onto Mayhew Inn Road. Continue on Mayhew Inn Road for a little over 4 miles and make a sharp right onto Oakland Sang Run Road. After 1 mile turn right onto Shingle Camp Road and then make an immediate left into the Fork Run Recreation Area. The entrance road dead-ends at the trail parking area. GPS coordinates: 39.524884, -79.403793.

The Ride

The Fork Run trails were conceived more than a decade ago, but it wasn't until 2010 that actual design and work on the system began in partnership with the nonprofit organization Adventure Sports Center International (ASCI) and the Garrett College Adventure Sports Institute. Paige Hull Teagarden, then executive director of Garrett Trails, also worked in partnership with Garrett County Community Action and secured a grant from Maryland Green Jobs to hire workers during the summer months to help with the build. With the help of IMBA, volunteers, and the labor provided by the Maryland Green Jobs grant, construction of the system began in earnest.

Shortly after work began, however, ASCI ran into financial troubles and the Fork Run Area and all of the nonprofit's assets were acquired by the county, including the trails and land at Fork Run. Today, the area at Fork Run is under a Maryland environmental trust, so enjoyment of the land by recreational users will continue in the future. ASCI continues to operate in the region under county ownership and still runs and manages a phenomenal Olympic whitewater rafting and canoe/kayak center on the mountaintop above Wisp Ski Resort. If you have time in your schedule and enjoy water sports, the center is a must-visit in the summer months.

The system has slowly, but consistently, expanded over the course of the last four years. Year one saw the completion of the red trail. Year two saw the construction and completion of the lower switchback loop, while the third year saw the construction

YOU MAY RUN INTO: STEVE GREEN

If you've been visiting the Deep Creek Lake area for any amount of time (summer or winter), then chances are you've already run into Steve at High Mountain Sports, *the* ski and bike shop in Deep Creek. If not, you'll likely see him riding the trails at Fork Run, his favorite off-road spot.

Steve has been living in the Deep Creek area since 1991 and riding for more than forty years. He puts in about 2,000 miles per year on his bike, mostly on the road, but a good chunk of it on the dirt and rocks of Garrett County. When there were few off-road riding opportunities available to mountain bikers, he set out to change things. "How hard can it be to build a trail?" he asked, and set off to find out the answer by forming the Garrett Association of Mountain Bike Operators (GAMBO), which later morphed into today's Garrett Trails organization. It turned out that building trail wasn't so easy after all, but despite that, he's forged on with an army of local volunteers to cut some of the finest trail in Maryland. For every mile of trail built he spends endless time in meetings ensuring things get done right. "I really don't like the meetings," he says, "but it is a necessary evil to get trails built properly for everyone to enjoy."

Steve is most proud of the contributions he's made to Fork Run and the Margraff Plantation trails, and chances are you will run into him at Fork Run, his favorite of the two.

With Garrett Trails he hopes to take the Garrett County area to the next level. "I love working on trails, playing in the dirt with tools, and keeping trails open. One of my goals is to make Garrett County a mountain-bike trail mecca." Let's hope he succeeds! If his efforts at Fork Run, along with those of many other volunteers, are any indication, then Garrett County will be the next big thing in mountain biking.

PHOTO COURTESY STEVE GREEN

and completion of the lower Fork Run Loop. In 2014, under the management of Garrett Trails, and still using Maryland Green Jobs grants, the upper loop was completed. In addition, volunteers built the Mighty Bridge that connects the red loop with the green and beige trails.

Fork Run Recreation Area

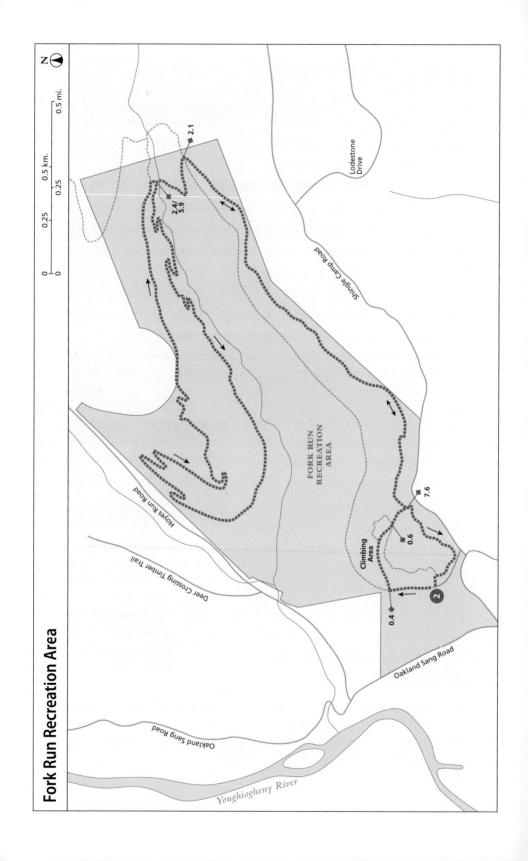

Future development of the system will include a trail that connects the IMBA Trail School loop to the Mighty Bridge, allowing riders an alternate connection point between the loops. That expansion is contingent on Garrett Trails obtaining a Recreational Trails Program (RTP) grant to continue the work. Don't be surprised, however, to see that trail in development by the time you visit.

The overall long-term goal in Fork Run, as it is in many regional trail systems, is to provide connectivity between multiple destinations, thus allowing riders to piece together longer rides. Garrett Trails volunteers would love to see Fork Run connect to the trails at Swallow Falls and ultimately to the trails at Big Bear in West Virginia, another very popular regional destination.

The Fork Run trails are technical and offer advanced riders a challenging playground.

The trails at Fork Run are easy to follow and well marked. My recommendation is that you start at the main Fork Run parking area and take the IMBA School Trail, blazed white, to the red trail. The red trail is an out-and-back that will take you to the green and beige trails. From there, take the green trail to the beige trail in a clockwise direction back to the red trail, and back along the red trail to the starting point. The mile markers below are very general and give you a rough idea of the distance you will cover along the way.

Miles and Directions

0.0 From the parking area, hop on the white-blazed IMBA School Trail. Stay on the white trail past the climbing area to the red trail.

0.4 Cross over the doubletrack to continue on the white trail. (The doubletrack is an alternate return route and basically parallels the red trail.)

0.6 Merge onto the yellow trail for a short distance and then turn left to continue on the red trail. Stay on the red trail for the next 1.6 to 1.7 miles.

2.1 Cross over the doubletrack. (A left turn on the doubletrack will take you back to 0.4. This is an alternate return route. A right turn on the doubletrack will take you toward the Wisp trail system.)

2.4 Cross the Mighty Bridge and reach the intersection of the green and beige trails. Turn left and follow the green trail to the beige trail to ride this loop in a clockwise direction.

5.9 Arrive back at the bridge. Cross the bridge and return back to the white trail along the red trail, or if you prefer, take the doubletrack back to the IMBA School Trail.

7.6 Continue to the right to hop on the white trail, or to the left to finish along the yellow trail.

8.1 Arrive back at the main parking area.

3 Deep Creek Lake State Park

Situated in one of Maryland's most popular vacation spots, the trails at Deep Creek Lake State Park offer a challenging network of rides that is bound to satisfy even the most demanding mountain biker. Expect a well-marked trail system that will take you, among other places, up to the heights of Deep Creek Lake's lookout tower, where breathtaking views of western Maryland's mountainous terrain await. Climbing is not all you'll do, though. Upon reaching the summit and the lookout tower, you'll be treated to some outstanding western Maryland singletrack that takes you downhill all the way back to the car.

Start: Meadow Mountain Trail trailhead
Length: 8.4-mile loop
Ride time: About 1.5–3 hours (depending on ability)
Difficulty: Moderate to difficult due to extended climbs and rutted singletrack
Trail surface: Doubletrack, singletrack, and forest roads
Lay of the land: Wooded and hilly terrain surrounding Deep Creek Lake

Land status: State park
Nearest town: Thayerville, MD
Other trail users: Hikers, cross-country skiers, hunters, paddlers, and snowmobile riders
Trail contacts: Deep Creek Lake State Park, Swanton, MD, (301) 387-4111, www.garrett trails.org
Schedule: May to early October

Getting there: From Cumberland, MD: Take I-68 west to exit 14 and US 219. Follow US 219 south through McHenry toward Thayerville. Before crossing the main bridge over Deep Creek Lake, turn left on Rock Ledge Road. Follow Rock Ledge Road for 2.5 miles, and then turn right on State Park Road. Continue on State Park Road for 2.5 miles, then turn right on Waterfront Avenue. Take an immediate right, traveling parallel to State Park Road, and park at the furthermost end of the last (overflow) parking lot. The trailhead is directly across State Park Road. GPS coordinates: 39.515091, -79.307702

The Ride

If you're interested in traveling to a place with more to offer than just mountain biking, Deep Creek Lake State Park, in the far western panhandle of Maryland's Garrett County, may be just the place.

Not only is Deep Creek Lake State Park one of Maryland's premier mountain-biking destinations, it is also a favorite vacation spot for people of all interests throughout the Mid-Atlantic. Some of the park's more popular activities apart from mountain biking include hiking, cross-country skiing, boating, dining, and an array of other outdoor opportunities.

Deep Creek Lake, Maryland's largest inland body of water, was formed by damming the junction of Deep Creek and the Youghiogheny River in 1925. The park officially opened for public use in July 1959. Today, Deep Creek Lake State Park and Deep Creek

Lake are two of Maryland's most popular destinations for outdoor recreation. This ride is intended to be an introduction to Garrett County trail riding and includes some of the climbs and views associated with western Maryland's scenic mountain ranges.

A short drive from the West Virginia border, Deep Creek Lake State Park is located just 10 miles northeast of Oakland, Maryland. As you enter the park from Rock Ledge Road and State Park Road, pay close attention to your left, keeping your eyes peeled for a sign reading MEADOW MOUNTAIN TRAIL: 50 YARDS. This is where your ride begins. Park in the parking lot to your right, on the other side of the trees directly across from this sign. If you enter the park from Glendale Road, turn left onto State Park Road, and left again onto Waterfront Avenue. An immediate right turn will lead you into the overflow parking area.

Miles and Directions

0.0 Start at the trail sign at the far end of the lot. Cross the street and head up toward the "bear trap" and the Meadow Mountain Trail. After a short climb (50 yards) turn left onto the Meadow Mountain Trail, blazed white.

0.4 Continue straight on the Meadow Mountain Trail (white) past the next two "red trail" intersections. We will make our way back down the red trail a little later.

0.5 The Brant Mine Homestead is in this area. Turn left and follow the red blazes down toward State Park Road.

0.6 Turn right on State Park Road.

1.3 Turn right off State Park Road onto Fire Tower Road and begin the climb toward the Thayerville Lookout Tower, approximately 2.5 miles ahead.

3.4 When you reach the top, and shortly before reaching the fire tower, turn right and then immediately right again to follow the Meadow Mountain Trail. We will descend back down toward the starting point of the ride.

3.6 Continue straight down the Meadow Mountain Trail. (The trail to the left will take you toward a scenic overlook, a short 0.2 mile from the main trail, which offers a panoramic view of the lake. It's best in the fall when the leaves are turning or in the winter when the trees are bare and provide an unobstructed view of the lake below.)

4.0 Continue straight through the intersections. (The fork to the right will take you back toward the gravel road you just climbed, and the one to the left will take you down along the red trail.)

4.4 Reach the point where we veered off at mile marker 0.5. Continue straight along the Meadow Mountain Trail past the next couple of red-trail intersections to the left. (The first and second red forks to the left will take you toward the mine; we'll hit that portion of trail to close out the loop a little later.)

4.8 Continue straight along the Meadow Mountain Trail. (A right turn will take you back to your car.)

5.2 Turn right at the T intersection to continue on the white trail.

5.3 Turn left at the intersection, and then left again to continue on the blue- (Indian Turnip Trail) and white-blazed trail. Begin a climb back up to the top of the mountain. The trail will get technical and challenging now, with lots of rock gardens.

Meadow Mountain Trail has a level, wide stretch that is pleasant and easy. Beware of the bears, though . . .

6.0   Cross a short bridge and continue following the trail to the left. The trail will climb sharply and quickly for 0.25 mile to the top of the mountain. (This intersection marks the point of a new IMBA trail that is slated to bypass the climb ahead. Hopefully, by the time you read this, that trail will be in place. If so, turn right and make the "easier" climb to the top.)

6.4   Reach a T intersection. Continue to the left along the blue/white trails toward the Corduroy Road and the Thayerville Lookout Tower. (The fork to the right will take you toward Savage River State Forest; if you're riding the new IMBA trail, you'll be coming from that direction.)

7.1   Reach the summit and the lookout tower. Continue straight, following the white blazes along the same path we were on earlier. (At this point you have a couple of options. A right will take you down along the gravel road we climbed earlier to State Park Road, a very fast descent. Straight will take you back down toward the Meadow Mountain Trail, where we will double back for a short distance before hitting the red trail.)

7.3   Continue straight past the overlook.

7.7   Once again you have a couple of options. You can continue straight and double back all the way back to the starting point, or turn left and ride the more technical red trail to the bottom. For this ride, opt for the latter and head left.

7.8   Reach the Brant Mine Shack. The red trail splits at this point. The right fork descends quickly back down to the Brant Mine Homestead and the Meadow Mountain Trail, while

Deep Creek Lake State Park

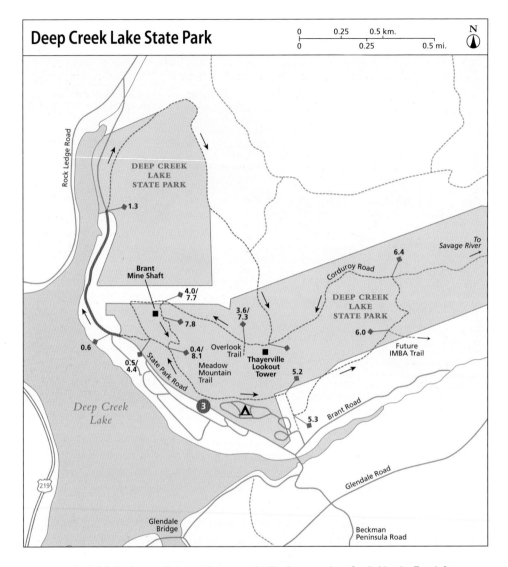

the left fork, above, will descend more gradually along a series of switchbacks. Turn left and climb to the shack and then walk down the steps to continue on the red trail along the more gradual, albeit technical, descent.

8.1 Turn left on the white-blazed Meadow Mountain Trail to make your way back to the starting point of the ride.

8.4 Turn right at the bear trap and head back down toward State Park Road and the beginning of the ride to complete the loop.

4 Rocky Gap State Park

Rocky Gap State Park is the home of the EX2 Adventures Xterra Race. The trails here, and around the man-made Lake Habeeb, offer intermediate to advanced mountain bikers a fun and challenging network of trails. Riders can enjoy great lake vistas and mature hemlock forests thick with rhododendron and mountain laurel.

Start: Between the beach and main bathhouse, by the Lakeside Loop trail marker
Length: 8.0 miles
Ride time: About 1.5–2.5 hours
Difficulty: Intermediate/advanced
Trail surface: Mostly singletrack, some doubletrack, and two short pavement sections
Lay of the land: Hemlock forest with rhododendron and mountain laurel; lake views
Land status: State park

Nearest town: Cumberland, MD
Other trail users: Hikers, campers, and lake users
Trail contacts: Rocky Gap State Park, Flintstone, MD, (301) 722-1480, http://dnr2 .maryland.gov/publiclands/Pages/western/ rockygap.aspx
Schedule & fees: 7 a.m. to sunset; small vehicle fee

Getting there: From Frederick, Maryland, take I-70 West for approximately 51 miles to exit 1A, I-68 W. Continue on I-68 for another 30 miles to exit 50, Pleasant Valley Road, toward Rocky Gap Street. Continue straight into the state park and onto Lake Shore Drive. Park in the main lot by the bathhouse. GPS coordinates: 39.700727, -78.652003.

The Ride

This is one of the newer rides in the book and replaces a couple of the rides included in the previous editions, including the New Germany State Park Ride and the Greenridge State Forest mountain-bike race-course loop.

Rocky Gap has developed into a great vacation destination. The Rocky Gap Casino and Golf Resort, along with the state park, anchors along the 243-acre Lake Habeeb and offer visitors myriad recreational opportunities, including fishing, golf (on a Jack Nicklaus signature course), camping, hiking, and cycling. During the summer months, visitors flock to the lake's beaches looking to beat the heat.

The trails along Rocky Gap offer experienced mountain bikers nearly 10 miles of challenging riding. Rocky Gap is home to various regional race events, including the Rocky Gap Xterra.

Note: At the time of this writing there was considerable construction along the parking areas adjacent to the resort. The trailhead may have shifted location, but the trail directions should remain the same.

Miles and Directions

0.0 The ride starts along the beach in front of the Bath House along a Lakeside Loop trail marker. Begin the ride heading south toward the resort. Follow the markers along the lakeshore and then turn sharply right down a gravel path toward the lodge. When you reach the lodge, either ride along the road or through the parking lot to the far end of the lot, to the access point to the "lower" lodge lot. The trailhead is visible in the wood line.

0.5 Enter the trail and follow it to the right and then left as it parallels the lake. The trail is blazed orange.

0.6 Follow the Lakeside Loop Trail marker. The trail is now blazed orange and purple.

0.7 Follow the trail to the right along the lake's perimeter.

0.9 Turn right along the "paved" trail and continue following the Lakeside Loop Trail markers. The trail is paved for a very short distance.

1.0 Turn right on the paved road to go over the dam.

1.2 Ride over the dam and get ready for a steep "stepped" climb immediately after it.

1.4 Stay to the right at this intersection; continue following the perimeter of the lake. (The trail to the left climbs straight up to a point later on this ride.)

1.8 Stay to the right, continuing on the Lakeside Loop Trail.

1.9 The trail splits and will reconnect a little farther down. Either fork will get you to the same spot. The next section of trail has several "shoots" that wind in and out of the main trail. Stay on the main path.

2.4 Continue following the Lakeside Loop Trail to the right along the perimeter of the lake.

2.6 Stay to the right along the tarmac to continue on the Lakeside Loop Trail. Continue following the trail along the perimeter of the lake.

3.0/ Continue toward the boat rental pavilions and turn left into the parking area. The play-
3.1 ground is to your right as you head in the direction of the stop sign. Turn left at the stop sign along Campers Hill Drive.

3.3 Turn right onto the Hickory "H" loop and stay to the right following the direction of traffic.

3.5 Turn right off the paved road onto Settlers Path.

3.6 Turn left to continue on Settlers Path. (The trail to the right is a connector to the Rocky Trail, which we will be riding a little later.)

4.2 Turn right and get ready for a short but steep climb toward the Evitt's Mountain Homesite Trail. (A left turn will take you down toward the lake and mile marker 1.4.)

4.3 Turn right and follow the signs for the yellow Rocky Trail.

5.5 Continue following the trail down and to the left. (The trail to the right is the Settlers Path connector mentioned in mile marker 3.6.)

5.6 Turn right on the paved Dogwood "D" Loop. The road curves to the left.

5.7 Turn right and follow the trail to the beach.

5.8 Use caution as you go down the steps since you will cross Campers Hill Drive and there may be traffic present. Continue straight past the playground and turn left onto the Lakeside Loop Trail at 5.9. Remain on the clearly marked Lakeside Loop Trail for the remainder of the ride along the perimeter of the lake.

6.3 Turn right onto Campers Hill Drive.

Rocky Gap State Park

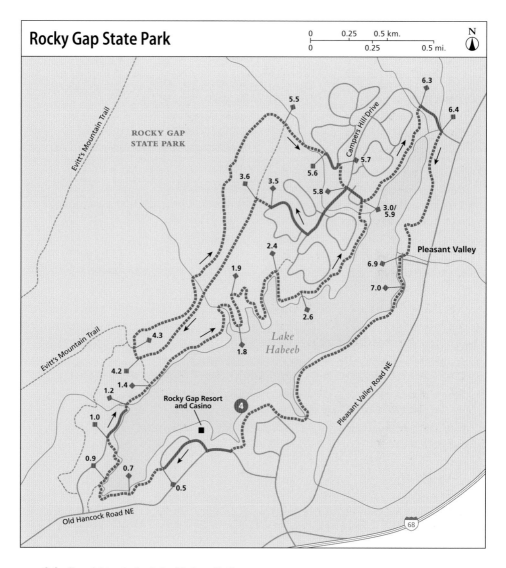

6.4 Turn right onto the Lakeside Loop Trail.

6.9 The trail continues on the far right of the gravel lot and it is clearly marked.

7.0 Turn right on the road to go over the bridge and then immediately right again to hop on the singletrack.

8.0 The loop is complete. Now go for a swim!

Ride Information

Local Information
www.mdmountainside.com

Local Events and Attractions
www.rockygapresort.com

Bike Shops

Cumberland Trail Connection
www.ctcbikes.com
(301) 777-8724

Cycles & Things
www.cyclesandthings.net
(301) 722-5496

Accommodations

Rocky Gap has become an extremely popular regional vacation destination, due largely to the golf course and resort/casino on the property. There are also plenty of camping opportunities within the state park, and more alternatives in nearby Cumberland. Visit www.rockygapresort .com.

Where to Eat

Signatures Bar and Grill
Rocky Gap Resort
(301) 784-8400
www.rockygapresort.com/dining/signatures .php

Stone Age Café
Flintstone, MD
(301) 478-0009

5 Woodmont Natural Resources Management Area (NRMA)

This loop will take you along the short, albeit exciting, trail built within the 1,400 acres co-managed by the Maryland Department of Natural Resources (DNR) and the Izaak Walton League of America. Please respect the posted closures and do not venture into the property between October 1 and March 31, lest you want to become "hunted."

Start: Trailhead parking area along Woodmont Road
Length: 3.0-mile loop
Ride time: About 35 minutes to 1 hour
Difficulty: Easy; one difficult climb
Trail surface: Singletrack and doubletrack
Lay of the land: Rolling, wooded

Land status: Natural Resources Management Area; co-leased with hunting organization
Nearest town: Hancock, MD
Other trail users: Hikers
Trail contacts: Woodmont NRMA c/o Fort Frederick State Park, (301) 842-2155
Schedule: April through September. Closed October through March

Getting there: From Frederick, Maryland, take I-70 West approximately 52 miles to I-68 West. Take exit 77 for US 40 toward MD 144/Woodmont Road and then turn left onto 144 E. Make an immediate right onto Woodmont Road. The parking area and trailhead will be approximately 5 miles on the left. GPS coordinates: 39.649798, -78.294354.

The Ride

The former Woodmont Rod & Gun Club, now Woodmont Natural Resources Management Area, is situated in western Maryland near the town of Hancock. The nearly 3,500-acre parcel was purchased by the Maryland Department of Natural Resources (DNR) in 1995 and is co-managed in partnership with the Woodmont Chapter of the Izaak Walton League of America. The parcel includes a historic lodge with panoramic views of the Potomac River and West Virginia. Erected in 1930 to replace the original small clubhouse, the lodge has been visited by numerous dignitaries, including six US presidents and Babe Ruth, among others.

Built as a sportsman's retreat, the grounds also housed a wild-turkey breeding operation. The location continues to be a hunter's paradise, and from October 1 through March 31 is closed to the general public for the exclusive use of the Woodmont Chapter. Funds generated from the use of the land are in turn used for the conservation and maintenance of the property. The lodge and surrounding buildings, including the turkey breeding operation and the lake houses, are closed to the general public, but each year in September the Woodmont Chapter holds an open house

The trails at Woodmont are clearly marked and easy to follow.

at which park rangers and volunteers speak about the area's rich history. Guests are allowed to tour the hunting lodge and its surroundings.

From April 1 through September 30, DNR manages the public use of the property. The remaining 2,000 acres are open for use by the public year-round. The trail is not very long, but it highlights the potential for new trails in the Woodmont region. I rode the new trails with DNR's trail guru, Dan Hudson, this past summer and later explored the myriad doubletrack trails along Woodmont Road, making our way down to the Potomac River and then back up Woodmont Road to the starting point of the ride.

Miles and Directions

0.0 As you face the trail kiosk, look to your right. Start the ride on the yellow-blazed trail as it heads south and away from the parking area, riding the loop in a counter-clockwise direction. (The trail behind the kiosk will be the end of the ride.) Immediately upon entering the trail, stay to the right past the first intersection. (The fork to the left is the connector trail that bisects the loop into two halves.)

1.5 Continue to the right. (The trail to the left will take you back up to the parking area.)

2.1 Continue following the yellow blazes to the right.

2.2 After a quick downhill the trail veers sharply to the left away from the doubletrack. The trail is blazed yellow.

2.8 The trail veers sharply right; again, continue following the yellow blazes.

3.0 The loop is complete.

Ride Information

Local Information

Maryland DNR: http://dnr2.maryland.gov/public lands/Pages/western/woodmont.aspx

Hancock, Maryland, Chamber of Commerce www.westernmarylandrailtrail.com; www.townof hancock.org.

Local Events and Attractions

Annual open house held at the Woodmont Lodge in September; check the DNR website for details and dates.

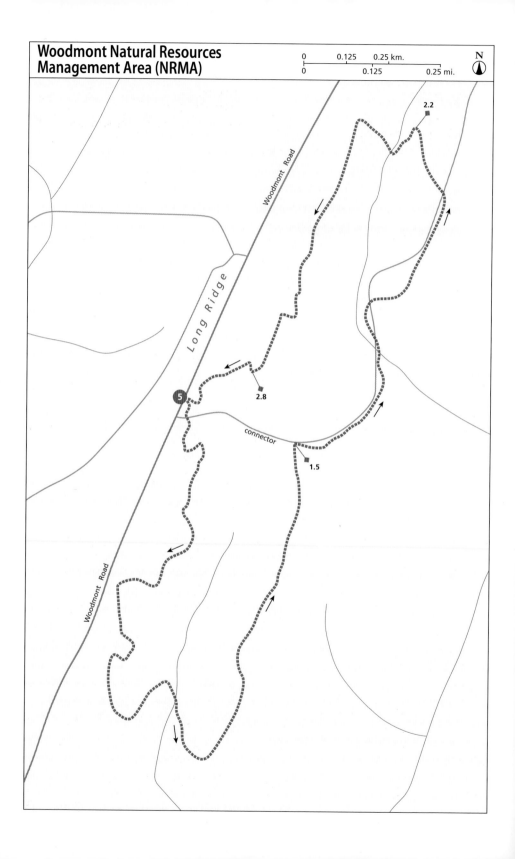

Woodmont Natural Resources
Management Area (NRMA)

N

2.2

Woodmont Road

Long Ridge

5

2.8

connector

1.5

Woodmont Road

Bike Shops

C&O Bicycle
www.candobicycle.com
(301) 678-6665

Accommodations

Check the listings at www.westernmarylandrail
trail.com/lodging.html.

Where to Eat

Weaver's Restaurant and Bakery
Hancock, MD
(301) 678-6346
www.weaversrestaurantandbakery.com

6 Greenbrier State Park

Greenbrier State Park provides many recreational opportunities. Mountain biking is just one of them. Home to a number of mountain-bike races, Greenbrier has become a favorite destination for many Washington, D.C., riders. The challenging trails are great for the intermediate rider who's not quite ready for the arduous trails farther west in Allegany and Garrett Counties. After your ride, take advantage of the beautiful man-made freshwater lake and go for a swim, or simply sit back and lounge on the beach.

Start: Boat launch parking lot, by the dam
Length: 7.2 miles
Ride time: About 1.5–3 hours
Difficulty: Moderate to difficult
Trail surface: Singletrack, doubletrack, and forest roads
Lay of the land: Rocky terrain in mountainous, wooded area
Land status: State park

Nearest town: Hagerstown, MD
Other trail users: Hikers, campers, cross-country skiers, anglers, canoeists, and hunters
Trail contacts: South Mountain Recreation Area, Boonsboro, MD, (301) 791-4767
Schedule & fees: Open year-round; camping quiet hours are from 11 p.m. to 7 a.m.; small vehicle fee

Getting there: From Washington: Take I-270 north to US 40 west. Follow US 40 west for approximately 11 miles. The Greenbrier State Park entrance is on your left. Continue straight, parking at the lake parking lot. GPS coordinates: 39.541279, -77.615457.

The Ride

Greenbrier State Park, 10 miles east of Hagerstown along US 40, is rich in both history and great places to ride.

Nestled in the scenic Appalachian Mountains, one of the world's oldest mountain ranges, Greenbrier was once a popular area for fur trapping, trading, exploration, and farming. Early in its history, farmers settled into the fertile river valleys. Today, the surrounding roads still follow many of the same paths used by those early industrious pioneers. As you ride along the park's many scenic trails, pay close attention to your surroundings—evidence of foundations from old farmhouses, once-thriving iron furnaces, and old log cabins still exist. The singular and distinctive flat circular shapes of hearths where charcoal was made to fuel the old iron furnaces are scattered throughout the area as well.

▶ Greenbrier State Park has become increasingly popular over the years and it is one of only a few Maryland State Parks that will close its gates when capacity is reached. Alternate starting points are marked on the map.

Greenbrier's trails are very popular with riders from the Washington, D.C., area.

Because of its unique history, 1,200 acres of woodlands, 42-acre man-made lake, and miles of mountainous trails, Greenbrier State Park has become one of Maryland's most popular public recreational areas and has most recently begun hosting races for the Maryland Mountain Bike Point Series.

This vast 40,000-acre forest is filled with trails and unimproved dirt roads great for riding. And if you're traveling west already, continue a bit farther to Deep Creek Lake State Park (Ride 3). Southeast a bit from Greenbrier State Park is Gambrill State Park (Ride 7), boasting, unquestionably, some of the East Coast's greatest singletrack, with more than 18 miles of trails, including a section of the famed Catoctin Mountain Trail.

Miles and Directions

0.0 Start from the parking area adjacent to the boat launch ramp and ride over the dam toward the woods at the far end. The lake is to your left.

0.1 Follow the red trail markers into the woods. Begin by following the red trail in a counter-clockwise direction.

0.4 Stay to the right on the red trail. The green (Copperhead) trail is to your left.

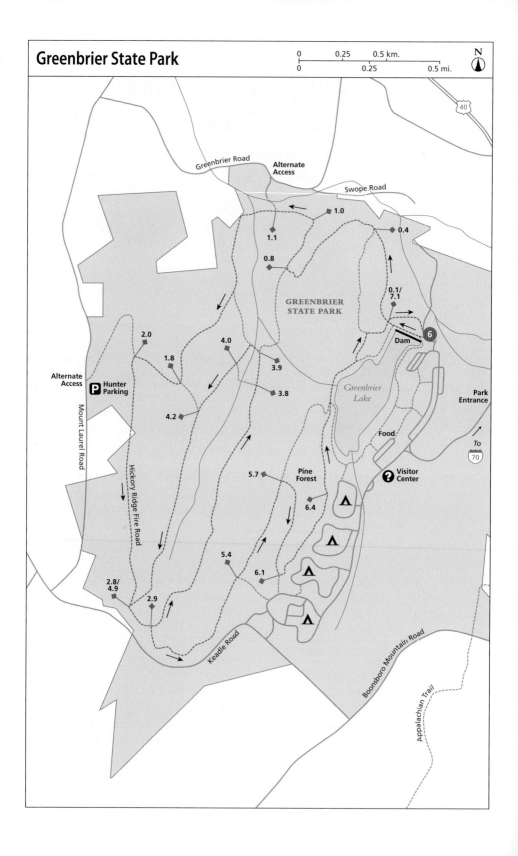

Greenbrier State Park

0   0.25   0.5 km.

0   0.25   0.5 mi.

N

Greenbrier Road

Alternate Access

Swope Road

40

1.0

1.1

0.4

0.8

0.1/ 7.1

GREENBRIER STATE PARK

6

Dam

2.0

1.8

4.0

3.9

Alternate Access

P Hunter Parking

4.2

3.8

Greenbrier Lake

Park Entrance

Food

To

70

Mount Laurel Road

5.7

Pine Forest

Visitor Center

6.4

Hickory Ridge Fire Road

5.4

6.1

2.8/ 4.9

2.9

Keadle Road

Boonsboro Mountain Road

Appalachian Trail

0.8 Stay to the right to continue on the red trail. The trail to the left is the blue Rock Oak Fire Trail.

1.0 Make a sharp left and continue following the red blazes. The trail to the right is closed.

1.1 The trail to the right is an alternate access point. There is a small parking area along Greenbrier Road no more than 0.1 mile away. Continue following the red blazes and get ready to climb!

1.5 Stay on the red trail. The left trail is the silver Snelling Fire Trail.

1.8 Continue following the red trail to the right. The left fork will take you down to the silver Snelling Fire Trail.

2.0 Continue to the red trail to the left. The trail to the right will take you to an alternate parking area along Mountain Laurel Road.

2.8 After a nice descent you will reach the silver Snelling Fire trail. Continue straight; we will soon come down the silver trail to this very point again.

2.9 Continue straight onto the blue trail. After a short climb, begin a fun descent to the silver trail. (This is also a good bail-out point if you want; just continue following the red trail down to the dam.)

3.8 Continue straight on the blue trail. The spur to the left will climb up to the white trail but we want to take the next turn.

3.9 Turn left onto this connector trail and then left again onto the white trail after the creek crossing. The blue trail will continue straight and meet up with the red trail where we first passed it at mile marker 0.8.

4.0 Continue climbing on the white trail to the right. The trail to the left will take you down to the blue trail and marker 3.8.

4.2 Continue to the left along the white trail. The trail to the right will take you back to the red trail and mile marker 1.8.

4.9 Turn left onto the red trail. This time bypass the blue trail and veer right, staying on the red trail to make your way back down to the dam.

5.4 Continue straight on the red trail. The spur to the right will take you down to the Dogwood camping loop.

5.7 Turn right and follow the orange blazes. (You could stay on the red and continue on to the dam, but the range trail is much more fun.)

6.1 Make a sharp left to continue on the orange trail. The spur to the right (straight) will take you to the Dogwood camping loop.

6.4 The trail splits. Either fork will take you toward the dam. The right fork takes an easy route along the east side of the lake while the left fork follows the more challenging route along the west side. For this ride, take the singletrack to the left.

6.7 Continue straight; you are now back on the red trail.

6.9 The trail once again splits. The right fork follows the edge of the lake while the left fork takes a wider route. Stay to the left to avoid the lake crowds. Shortly after, you'll hit the green Copperhead Trail; turn right to continue on the red trail.

7.1 Reach the entrance point to the red trail. Continue straight along the gravel road as it curves to the right. (Or you can turn right and head over the dam back to your car.)

7.2 Hop onto the paved trail and complete the loop.

Ride Information

Local Information

Washington County Visitors Bureau
Hagerstown, MD
(301) 791-3246
www.washco-md.net

Local Events and Attractions

Antietam National Battlefield, Sharpsburg,
Maryland: Bloodiest battle of the Civil War
(301) 432-5124
www.nps.gov/anti

Crystal Grottoes Caverns: Limestone caverns
with stalactite and stalagmite formations.
Guided tours on illuminated walkways
(301) 432-6336
www.crystalgrottoescaverns.com

Bike Shops

The Bicycle Escape
Frederick, MD
www.thebicycleescape.com
(301) 663-0007

Wheel Base
Frederick, MD
(301) 663-9288
www.wheelbasebikes.com

Bike Doctor Frederick
Frederick, MD
(301) 620-8868
www.bikedoctorfrederick.com

Accommodations

Lewrene Farm Bed & Breakfast
Hagerstown, MD
(301) 582-1735

Where to Eat

Dan's Restaurant & Tap House
Boonsboro, MD
(301) 432-5224
www.drnth.com

7 Gambrill State Park: Yellow Trail

Not all singletrack is created equal, and once you complete a loop at Gambrill you'll understand why. The 7 or so miles at Gambrill are not quite the same as the 7 or so miles at Rosaryville (Ride 29). If this is your first time riding the rocky trails of Gambrill make sure you are prepared, both physically and mentally. Once you've tamed this beast you'll be ready for virtually anything in the region. Maintained by Mid-Atlantic Off-Road Enthusiasts (MORE), the yellow trail in Gambrill State Park is one of the most popular mountain-biking destinations in the state of Maryland, attracting riders from as far south as Richmond, Virginia. The yellow trail, at 6.8 miles, is the longest loop in the Gambrill trail system and the perfect trail for up-and-coming mountain bikers looking to test their mettle (and for a beating) on some difficult singletrack. This is not a trail for the novice rider, and will be extremely challenging even to those who are well-versed in rugged terrain.

Start: First trailhead parking area along Gambrill Park Road
Length: 6.8-mile loop
Ride time: About 1–1.5 hours
Difficulty: Difficult due to strenuous climbs and rocky singletrack terrain
Trail surface: Rocky singletrack
Lay of the land: Mostly dense woods over mountainous terrain

Land status: State park
Nearest town: Frederick, MD
Other trail users: Hikers, campers, cross-country skiers, and dogs
Trail contacts: Gambrill State Park, (301) 271-7574; MORE, www.more-mtb.org
Schedule & fees: Open daily from dawn till dusk, year-round; small vehicle fee for picnic shelters, tearoom, and campsites

Getting there: From Frederick, Maryland, take US 40 (Baltimore National Pike) west and turn right on Shookstown Road. Follow Shookstown Road to Gambrill Park Road and turn right. Enter the park, and park in the first parking lot on your right. GPS coordinates: 39.462214, -77.491301.

The Ride

Six miles northwest of Frederick, Maryland, on Catoctin Mountain, is Gambrill State Park—a jewel for mountain bikers. Named for the late James H. Gambrill Jr. of Frederick, the park had its beginnings when spirited conservationists bought the land on the mountain and donated it to the city of Frederick. In September 1934, the park was presented to the state, and since then, it has been a recreational favorite for Washington and Baltimore area residents.

Your ride starts with a brutal climb paralleling Gambrill Park Road. By the time you reach the High Knob Area you'll be cursing me and wishing I'd started you there,

Gambrill State Park is one of the most popular mountain-biking destinations in the state of Maryland.

but don't fret. What's to come will be a phenomenal treat, and the worst (well, sort of) of the climbing will be behind you.

As you ride farther into the park and along the Catoctin Mountain you can begin to appreciate some of the tall stands of chestnut oak, hickory, and black birch that canopy your surroundings. The North Frederick overlook, directly across from mile marker 0.65, will give you a chance to catch your breath and soak in the scenery below, including the tree-covered trails of the Frederick Watershed, another immensely popular riding destination in the region (HM C).

The name Catoctin is believed to have come from a tribe of North Americans called Kittoctons, who lived at the foothills of the mountains along the Potomac. European settlers first arrived in 1732 from Philadelphia, attracted by Lord Baltimore's offer of 200 acres of rent-free land for three years. The land would then cost only one cent per acre per year. Early settlers used the land for logging and supplied charcoal to local iron furnaces. Catoctin's resources, though, were eventually stripped and depleted by extensive clear cutting. Then, in 1935, the federal government purchased more than 10,000 acres of this land to be made into a recreational area. The National Park Service and Maryland Park Service manage the land today, permitting Catoctin to redevelop back into the hardwood forest of pre-European settlement.

Miles and Directions

0.0 The ride starts from the lower main parking area off Gambrill Park Road and immediately heads straight up. Get ready. From the parking area enter the yellow trail as it climbs parallel to Gambrill Park Road. The yellow trail is marked by a sign that reads: THE YELLOW TRAIL IS MAINTAINED BY MORE THE MOUNTAIN BIKE CLUB FOR YOUR ENJOYMENT.

0.3 Reach the top of the hill, cross the street, and turn right on the yellow trail as it parallels the road.

0.6 The North Frederick overlook is to the right across the road. The yellow trail continues across the street and is also blazed black.

1.2 Continue following the yellow blazes to the left. (To the right is the blue Catoctin trail, which leads back toward the parking area.)

1.5 Turn left on the doubletrack and continue following the yellow blazes.

1.6 Turn right to continue following the yellow trail.

1.7 Reach a fire road. The yellow trail continues straight up through a rock outcropping, slightly to the right of the rock formation. (If you've had enough, you can continue to the road, turn left, and head back on the blacktop to the parking area.)

2.2 Continue to the left along the utility right-of-way.

2.3 Arrive at the upper yellow loop. Continue straight to the next intersection to do the upper yellow loop in a clockwise direction. (Turn left to ride back toward the road, or right to do the upper yellow in a counter-clockwise direction.)

2.37 Turn right on the upper yellow loop, staying on the well-blazed yellow trail.

3.1 Continue to the right.

3.9 Arrive back at the utility right-of-way. This is the same intersection we saw at mile marker 2.3. Turn right and follow the doubletrack up the hill to the next intersection.

4.0 Turn left at the intersection. (A right turn allows you to do the upper yellow again.)

4.2 Reach Gambrill Park Road. Continue to follow the yellow trail on the other side. At this point we are making our way back toward High Knob and the beginning of the ride.

4.6 Continue straight and to the right. You are now leaving the upper yellow loop and entering the lower yellow loop. (The trail to the left will take you back over Gambrill Park Road toward marker 2.3/3.9.)

5.6 Get ready for your first real "rock garden." This section is much more difficult in this direction. (If you still have energy, try clearing it in the opposite direction too.) The North Frederick Overlook is up ahead to the left. Continue to the right and continue to follow the yellow blazes down a great technical descent—be ready! (At this point, if you've had enough of the Frederick rocks you can turn left and head back down the way we rode up.)

5.8 Continue following the trail to the left and follow the yellow and black blazes. (The trail to the right is a short hiker-only spur that leads to an overlook. I suggest parking the bikes for a few minutes and taking a look.)

6.1 Arrive at High Knob. Turn right and continue to follow the yellow trail. (High Knob is another bailout point. Turn left and head straight down to the parking area if you want to end the ride.) This next section, I think, is one of the finest in the park.

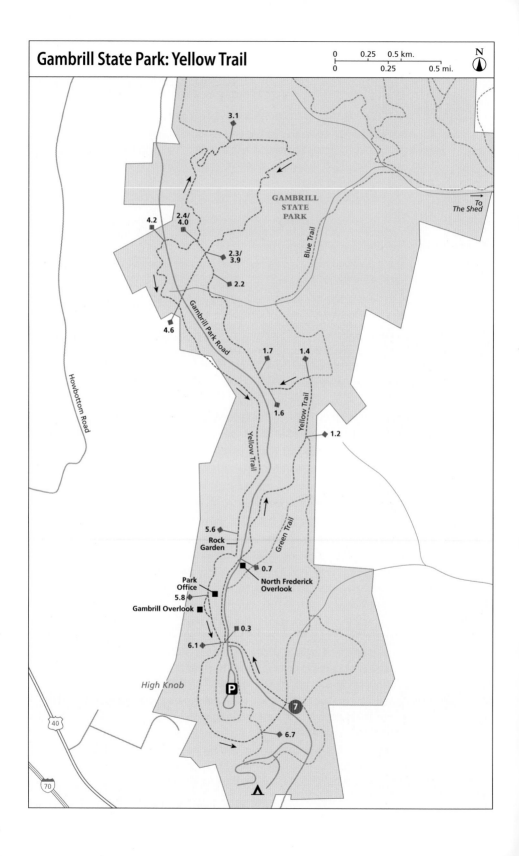

Gambrill State Park: Yellow Trail

0   0.25   0.5 km.
0   0.25   0.5 mi.

N

GAMBRILL
STATE
PARK

To
The Shed

3.1

2.4/
4.0

4.2

2.3/
3.9

2.2

4.6

Gambrill Park Road

1.7

1.4

Blue Trail

1.6

Yellow Trail

Yellow Trail

1.2

Howbottom Road

Green Trail

5.6

Rock
Garden

0.7

Park
Office

North Frederick
Overlook

5.8

Gambrill Overlook

0.3

6.1

High Knob

P

7

6.7

40

70

6.5 Descend quickly before finishing the ride with a very short climb to the parking area. You are now near the epicenter of the park, so you may run into more trail users.

6.7 Continue straight through the intersection toward the road.`

6.8 Cross the road to enter the parking area. The loop is complete.

Ride Information

Local Information

Tourism Council of Frederick County
Frederick, MD
(800) 999-3613

Local Events and Attractions

See Frederick County's online visitors' guide for links about local events and attractions: www .visitfrederick.org.

Bike Shops

The Bicycle Escape
Frederick, MD
www.thebicycleescape.com
(301) 663-0007

Wheel Base
Frederick, MD
(301) 663-9288
www.wheelbasebikes.com

Bike Doctor Frederick
Frederick, MD
(301) 620-8868
www.bikedoctorfrederick.com

Accommodations

There are thirty-four campsites in the Rock Run area.

Nearby Frederick has bed-and-breakfasts, inns, hotels, cottages, and more.

Where to Eat

Sardi's Chicken
Frederick, MD
(301) 620-7717
www.sardischicken.com

8 Emmitsburg–Rainbow Lake

Emmitsburg is slowly, but surely, making an imprint on the off-road cycling map. The new trails at Emmitsburg's Rainbow Lake, coupled with the additional trails extending to the town's community park, offer mountain bikers more than 15 miles of high-quality, professionally built singletrack.

Start: Parking area adjacent to Rainbow Lake

Length: 7.2 miles, with optional 3.3-mile out-and-back (each way).

Ride time: About 1.5-3 hours.

Difficulty: Moderate, difficult climbs

Trail surface: Rocky singletrack with great flow

Lay of the land: Rolling, wooded, some hard climbs

Land status: Public property

Nearest town: Emmitsburg, MD

Other trail users: Hikers, hunters

Trail contacts: Town of Emmitsburg: www .emmitsburgmd.gov

Schedule: Open seven days a week from late spring through August. Trails are open Sundays only, September through February, due to hunting. Check the town's website (www .emmitsburgmd.gov) for additional closures due to hunting

Getting there: From Frederick, Maryland, take Route 15 approximately 29 miles north to Route 140 West (Main Street) toward Emmitsburg. Continue on Main Street for 4.5 miles and turn left onto Frailey Road, and then left again onto Annandale Road. Continue on Annandale for 1 mile and turn left onto Hampton Valley Road. The trailhead will be in approximately 1.5 miles on the right. GPS coordinates: 39.695529, -77.388150.

The Ride

The trails at the historic town of Emmitsburg, Maryland, have been in the planning process for quite some time now, and thanks in part to almost $300,000 in grants, volunteer work, and private donations, nearly 10 miles of trails have been completed, with more to come in the future. Our ride will take us along the completed network of trails on the west side of Hampton Valley Road, with an option to do an out-and-back on the in-progress connector trail that will link riders to the community park in Emmitsburg.

Emmitsburg's ultimate goal is for riders to be able to park at the community park within the town and take the connector trail for approximately 3 miles to the Rainbow Lake network. Along the way, riders will be able to sample additional loops along the connector trail. Facilities at the park will offer cyclists the opportunity to shower, use the community pool in the summer, and enjoy the nearby restaurants within a short walking distance. Coupled with the already existing road riding opportunities in the area, Emmitsburg is poised to become a regional cycling destination. (See *Best Bike Rides Washington, D.C.* for road bike routes.)

Austin Steo, lead builder of the Emmitsburg Rainbow trails, enjoys the fruits of his labor.

As of this writing, the connector trail was partially completed, and can be ridden to add nearly 4 miles to the main loops detailed here. I had the opportunity to ride it with the builders shortly after they completed their work and anxiously look forward to the day it is fully extended to the community park. Like the trails on the west side, the east side connector offers challenging features bound to please the most demanding riders.

The Rainbow Lake trails are set up as a "stacked" system. A 2.4-mile beginner trail offers novice riders an opportunity to experience some of the challenging features they may encounter in the more advanced trails. Dubbed Little Bear by the trail's builder, the trail offers riders flow lines, technical sections, and alternate challenge lines to hone riders' skills. The more advanced Mama Bear and Papa Bear loops present longer climbs, technical rock gardens, and multiple challenge lines.

Miles and Directions

0.0 Start at the dam gate and continue over the dam toward the tree line.

0.1 Immediately after crossing the dam and entering the tree line, head left into the lollipop-shaped beginner loop. We'll ride the "stick" and the "candy" in a counter-clockwise direction.

0.2 Continue to the left.

0.5 Continue to the right; this is the entrance to the "candy." You'll return from the left side.

1.6 You're back at the first intersection again (0.5). Turn right and head back toward the dam to access the intermediate and advanced loops. At this point simply double back to the marker 0.1.

2.0 Turn left to begin the climb up Mama Bear and the beginning of the intermediate loop. We will return from the trail directly ahead before making the turn.

2.1 Continue to the left. (The trail to the right is a connector that would cut your climb short. Skip it.)

2.6 Continue straight. (The trail to the right is the connector mentioned in 2.1. Had enough? Bail right here—but I promise, it gets much better.) What follows is a phenomenal section of trail.

3.0 After a great descent you'll reach an intersection. Continue straight and down through the creek to access Papa Bear. (A right turn at the intersection will take you back to the starting point.) Immediately after crossing the creek the trail is to your right.

3.2 Reach Hampton Valley Road. Turn left on the road and then immediately left again to continue toward Papa Bear.

Option: At this point, if you choose, you can ride the connector trail, which is accessible directly across Hampton Valley Road, to extend your ride by nearly 7 miles. As of this writing the connector reached Annandale Road, approximately 3.3 miles to the east. The connector will eventually take you all the way to the Emmitsburg Community Park. The trail is easy to follow. Find a detailed map at mtbdc.com.

3.3 Cross the fire road and continue on the singletrack.

3.4 Turn left on the gravel road and go over Turkey Creek. Make an immediate right after crossing the culvert and stay along the singletrack. Do not head up the doubletrack to the left.

Emmitsburg—Rainbow Lake

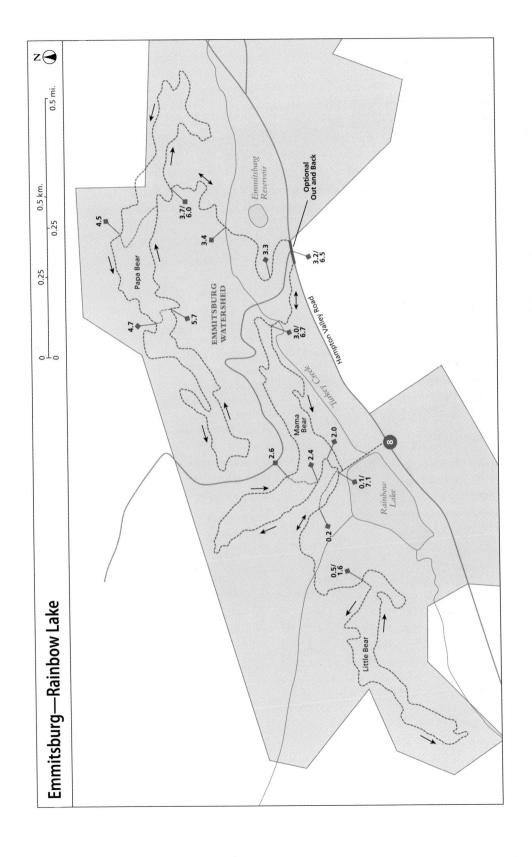

3.7 Reach the entrance to Papa Bear. This spot was marked by an intricate rock pile (cairn) when I documented the ride. Hopefully it's still standing when you read this. If so, contribute to the trail art and build your own. Continue to the right; you will return from the left fork.

4.5 Continue straight. (The left trail is a connector that will take you back toward the rock cairn.)

4.7 Continue straight through the intersection. (The trail to the left is another connector that will send you back down toward the rock cairn and the entrance to Papa Bear. This is a bailout point, but you'll miss the best part of the ride.)

5.7 Continue right at the intersection. (A left turn will take you back up to marker 4.7.)

6.0 You're back at the rock cairn; continue to the right and backtrack to Hampton Valley Road.

6.5 Back at Hampton Valley Road, turn right and right again to backtrack to the creek crossing at mile marker 3.0.

6.7 Arrive back at the creek. Cross and then turn left to finish the Mama Bear loop.

7.1 Arrive back at the three-way intersection and turn left to head over the dam and back to the parking area.

7.2 The loop is complete.

Ride Information

Local Information, Events, and Attractions

Town of Emmitsburg: www.emmitsburgmd.gov.

Gettysburg National Military Park: Less than 15 miles to the north in Pennsylvania; www.nps.gov/gett/index.htm.

Bike Shops

The Bicycle Escape
Frederick, MD
www.thebicycleescape.com
(301) 663-0007

Wheel Base
Frederick, MD
(301) 663-9288
www.wheelbasebikes.com

Bike Doctor Frederick
Frederick, MD
(301) 620-8868
www.bikedoctorfrederick.com

Accommodations

There are limited places to stay in Emmitsburg, but Gettysburg, Pennsylvania, less than 15 miles to the north, has multiple hotels and inns to choose from.

Where to Eat

The Ott House
Emmitsburg, MD
(301) 447-2625

Honorable Mentions

Compiled here is an index of great rides in western Maryland that didn't make the A list this time around but deserve recognition. Check them out and let us know what you think. You may decide that one or more of these rides deserves higher status in future editions, or perhaps you may have a ride of your own that merits some attention. Some of these rides are documented on our website, www.mtbdc.com

A. Margraff Plantation

I'm totally bummed that I did not get to include the Margraff Plantation trails in this edition of the book. Unfortunately, when it came time to document this ride, full logging operations were taking place and many of the existing trails were damaged in the process. By the time you read this, however, the trails at Margraff should have been repaired and you should be able to add it to the list of destinations in the Deep Creek Lake Area. Built and maintained by Garrett Trails, and located within the Savage State Forest, the loop at Margraff offers moderate to technical trails designed specifically for mountain biking. For directions to the trailhead, and additional information on this great destination, visit www.garretttrails.org.

GPS coordinates: 39.630701, -79.290884.

B. Greenridge State Forest

Greenridge State Forest, along Route 68 near Cumberland, Maryland, is a great alternative to some of the other regional destinations. Unfortunately, tough times and dwindling budgets have left the once-promising 12-mile mountain bike loop in a bit of disrepair and with little change since it was first completed in 1998. Still, if you are looking for an adventure, Greenridge is the place to go. The trail is clearly marked and easy to follow. Start your ride from the main parking area along Wallizer Road. Check www.mtbdc.com for a map and more detailed description of the trails.

GPS coordinates: 39.661602, -78.506368

C. The Frederick Watershed

Just north of Frederick, Maryland, adjacent to Gambrill State Park and accessible from the Gambrill State Park yellow trail (Ride 7) is the Frederick Watershed. The "Shed" is a fantastic mountain bike playground extremely popular with Washington, D.C., and Baltimore riders. There are miles of unpaved forest roads and rocky singletrack trails winding all over Catoctin Mountain that will put Gambrill's yellow trail to shame. All of them are perfectly suitable for off-road bikes and provide an incredibly challenging playground for advanced riders. The terrain is very steep and rugged, but if you're heading toward Gambrill anyway, take a small detour and check out the Frederick Watershed.

GPS coordinates: 39.524941, -77.458512

Maryland Piedmont Region

Maryland Piedmont is the area framed by the foothills of the Blue Ridge Mountains and the Chesapeake Bay. By definition, a piedmont is an area formed or lying at the foot of a mountain or mountain range. Its proximity to the Chesapeake Bay and its agricultural richness has made the Piedmont one of the most populated areas in Maryland. Encompassing the counties of Montgomery, Howard, and Baltimore, the Maryland Piedmont area has seen a tremendous amount of development in the last few years.

The terrain in the piedmont plains of Maryland lends itself to some of the best mountain biking in the area. Although not mountainous, the Piedmont offers a tremendous mixture of plains and stream valleys that make mountain biking one of the region's most practiced activities. In addition, the trails in the area are also very popular equestrian and hiking destinations. The tremendous growth in the region has placed an immense demand on the trails in the Piedmont. However, active participation and education by the cycling community and its users has ensured that fat-tire enthusiasts continue to have access and enjoy the Piedmont trails.

Montgomery County (MoCo)

When we set out to write the first editions of this book, mentioning mountain biking in Montgomery County, Maryland, was almost out of the question. But in the mid-1990s a handful of volunteers convinced local government officials to allow the Mid-Atlantic Off-Road Enthusiasts (MORE) to build a dedicated network of trails on the grounds of Schaeffer Farms. Originally the trails were meant to be mountain bike only, much like those at Fountainhead Regional Park in neighboring Virginia (Ride 36), but in 1994 State Senator Brian Frosh helped the Mid-Atlantic Off-Road Enthusiasts (MORE) persuade the Maryland Department of Natural Resources to honor their promise that Schaeffer would remain multiuse.

Over time, the success of the trail network at Schaeffer Farms trickled further, and soon trails at Seneca Creek State Park, Black Hill Regional Park, and Little Bennett

Regional Park were accessible to bikes. Natural resource land managers just couldn't argue with the enthusiasm of MORE's volunteers in helping maintain and improve the available trails, not just for the enjoyment of mountain bikers, but also of other trail users.

MORE has always worked with land managers to ensure that other users also enjoy the trails built by cyclists. The club advocates and practices responsible riding and abides by an unwritten creed to respectfully share the trail with other users. Their efforts in educating riders across the region have been instrumental in fostering lasting relationships with other users. Because of that, what was once an uncommon sight today is the norm: allegiances with equestrian, hiker, and running groups have flourished and additional collaboration has resulted in more trails for bikes, including the creation of the Seneca Ridge Trail, the improvement of the Seneca Bluffs Trail, the building of the Hoyles Mill Connector, and the opening of the Muddy Branch Trail and Blockhouse Point Park along the banks of the C&O Canal.

These additions have allowed mountain bikers to connect several, if not all, of Montgomery County's parks via a network of off-road trails without venturing too far into paved streets and paths. This ultimately resulted in the creation of the MoCo Epic, an annual event that welcomes nearly eight hundred riders to participate in one of several rides, including a 65-mile ride along the natural-surface paths of the county. In this chapter are ten parks and trails that can be ridden individually or in concert to make your own epic.

When you're ready to leave, take a short trip to Germantown and Olde Town Gaithersburg, two of Maryland's most prosperous little cities. Unlike many areas of Maryland, the Germantown/Gaithersburg area doesn't show much evidence of early Indian settlements. However, its proximity to the Potomac and Monocacy Rivers, as well as Seneca Creek, made this area a very popular location for Native American living. It is believed that after the annual spring floods, Indians from the Piscataway, Susquehannock, and Seneca tribes traveled here to hunt roaming herds of bison and other large animals trapped by the swollen waters. Many of the trails by which the Native Americans traveled to reach this hunting ground later became the same routes and roadways that we use today, including Clopper Road and MD 28, MD 118, and MD 355.

In the early to mid-1800s, several German immigrants, most of whom were from German settlements in Pennsylvania, moved down to this area of Maryland and settled along the intersections of Clopper Road and the Darnestown/Neelsville Road (MD 118). This settlement quickly became known as Germantown.

At about the same time, just south of Germantown, many of the younger sons of Maryland's Chesapeake Bay settlers began establishing themselves in the vast, fertile land of Montgomery County. One of the earliest settlements in this area—dating to 1802—was known as Forest Oak, named for the landmark tree still standing near the railroad crossing on Frederick Avenue. Today this area is called Gaithersburg. In 1802, a young settler named Benjamin Gaither built his house on this fertile land, unknowingly giving his name to the town.

With the arrival of the railroad and the invention of the automobile, businesses in Germantown and Gaithersburg began to prosper. Farmers planted and harvested more crops, easily transporting them to other markets throughout the area. Farmers no longer had to make several trips to town. With a newly built steam mill, they could make a single trip to mill their grains, purchase supplies, and market their products all by railroad. The railroad also brought people in from Washington. Soon it became fashionable to escape to the country, and many large estates were built.

Today, Germantown and Gaithersburg are prosperous and growing communities with combined populations reaching nearly one million. In the last couple of decades, both Gaithersburg and Germantown have seen a major boom in development. Its proximity to Washington, D.C., and Frederick, Maryland, has made this part of Montgomery County an attractive business location as well as a residential getaway. Despite all this, however, residents of this prosperous county have learned to cherish the value of natural resources and have chosen to maintain several areas for recreational opportunities; thanks to this there are miles of singletrack trails to enjoy cycling.

Rides 9 to 17 can all be easily and creatively connected to create a mega epic ride. Ride 11, MoCo South, demonstrates this.

Ride Information (Applies to Rides 9 through 17)

Local Information

Montgomery County's website, with information about local events and attractions:
www.montgomerycountymd.gov

Montgomery County Visitors Bureau
Germantown, MD
(301) 428-9702

Local Events and Attractions

Montgomery County's official website with local information:
www.montgomerycountymd.gov

The MoCo Epic
www.moreepics.com

Bike Shops

Germantown Cycles
Germantown, MD
(240) 404-0695
www.germantowncycles.com

Performance Bicycle
Gaithersburg, MD
(301) 590-3000
www.performancebike.com

Accommodations

There are myriad lodging places in the Germantown area. Little Bennett Regional Park is the only park in the county with a campground.

Where to Eat

Picca Chicken
Germantown, MD
(301) 540-6500
www.picca.com

Agrodolce
Germantown, MD
(301) 528-6150
www.agrodolcerestaurant.com

Dogfish Head Ale House
Gaithersburg, MD
(301) 962-4847
www.dogfishalehouse.com

9 Seneca Bluffs Trail (SBT)

Conceived in 2011, the SBT was the result of true cooperation from a coalition of hikers, equestrians, and mountain bikers. MORE volunteers worked tirelessly to get the trail ready for the 2012 MoCo Epic. In 2014, the club received approval to extend the trail an additional 2.5 miles to be ready for the 2014 MoCo Epic. This trail can be ridden as a simple out-and-back, or combined with the Seneca Ridge Trail (SRT; Ride 10) for additional mileage. Both the SRT and SBT are included in the MoCo South loop (Ride 11).

Start: Black Rock Mill Parking Area. The trail can also be accessed from Schaeffer Farms via the Schaeffer SRT Connector.
Length: 7.4 miles one way
Ride time: About 2–3 hours
Difficulty: Easy/moderate
Trail surface: Mostly singletrack, some doubletrack
Lay of the land: Piedmont woods and meadows

Land status: Public land
Nearest town: Germantown, Maryland
Other trail users: Hiking
Trail contacts: Mid-Atlantic Off-Road Enthusiasts (MORE), (703) 502-0359, www.more-mtb.org
Schedule: Open year-round. Trail crosses managed hunting areas. Wear blaze orange in the fall.

Getting there: The trailhead is located on Black Rock Road adjacent to the Black Rock Mill. There is limited parking in and around the mill. An alternate starting point is the Schaeffer Farms parking area. From there you can ride the white trail to the Seneca Ridge Trail (SRT) connector and then pick up the Seneca Bluffs Trail (SBT).

From Route 270 take exit 15 for Route 118 South toward Germantown. Continue on Route 118 for 3.6 miles and turn right onto Black Rock Road. The trailhead will be adjacent to the Black Rock Mill approximately 2 miles to the right. GPS coordinates: 39.127050, -77.314386.

The Ride

The Seneca Bluffs Trail is the result of collaboration between several user groups. Equestrians, hikers, and mountain bikers, represented by the Mid-Atlantic Off-Road Enthusiasts (MORE) worked diligently in 2012 and 2013 to repair, reroute, and build several new sections of the trail that now connects Black Rock Road with River Road in Germantown. The trail has been incorporated into MORE's annual MoCo Epic and continues to be improved and maintained by volunteers from all user groups.

The trail was built as a parallel alternative to the hiking-only Seneca Creek Greenway Trail and runs parallel along it as it makes its away along the forests and meadows of Seneca Creek toward River Road, the C&O Canal, and the Potomac River. To avoid erosion and water damage, the trail has been built far away from and above

The Seneca Bluffs Trail is the result of collaboration between several user groups.

the creek to provide great views of the Germantown waterway. The trail does cross the creek in several locations, including the not-so-dry Dry Seneca Creek.

The trail is a fantastic addition to the network of natural-surface trails that already cross Montgomery County and, in its short existence, has become a regional favorite. For 2014, MORE expanded the trail an additional 2.5 miles to its terminus at Old River Road. Several miles of trail have also been improved, including a section midway through the ride that has been "bench cut" into the side of the hill to provide riders with a more stable and enjoyable experience.

Miles and Directions

0.0 The ride starts from the main Black Rock Mill parking area. As you face the mill the trailhead is directly to the left side of the mill and clearly marked with a sign.

0.6 Cross over a bridge recently retrofitted for cycling. You can clearly see how it was widened to accommodate bikes.

1.1 Reach an alternate parking area adjacent to Route 28. The Seneca Bluffs trail is now blazed orange. The blue trail is hiker only, so please respect that. Hop on Route 28 (be careful) in the same direction you were traveling to cross the bridge over the Great Seneca Creek.

1.5 Turn left to cross Route 28 and to hop back on the SBT. The trail is marked with orange Carsonite markers.

3.9 The trail continues to the left.

4.5 Continue straight through this intersection. (The trail to the right is an old, eroded, unused trail.)

4.9 Cross Dry Seneca Creek. The name does not adequately describe this crossing. You have two options—a stepping-stone bridge, or a gravelly section used by equestrians.

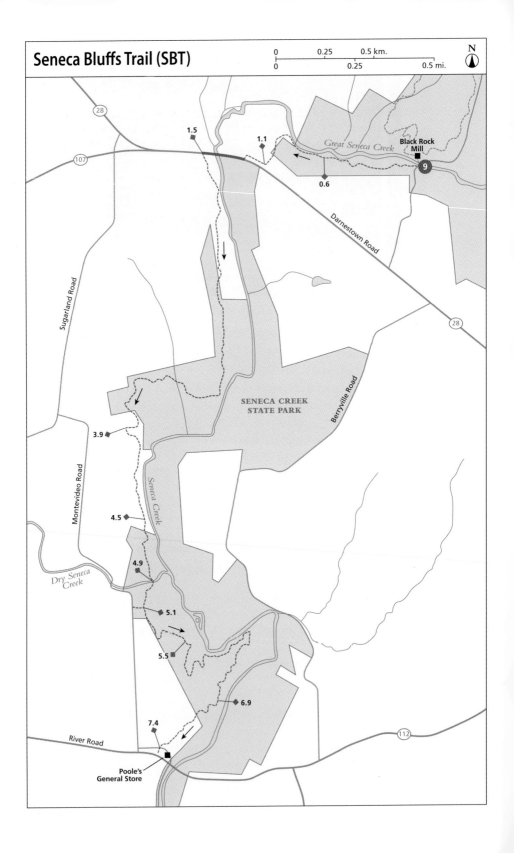

Seneca Bluffs Trail (SBT)

0   0.25   0.5 km.

0   0.25   0.5 mi.

N

28

107

1.5

1.1

0.6

Great Seneca Creek

Black Rock Mill

9

Darnestown Road

28

Sugarland Road

Berryville Road

SENECA CREEK
STATE PARK

3.9

Seneca Creek

4.5

Montevideo Road

4.9

Dry Seneca
Creek

5.1

5.5

6.9

7.4

River Road

112

Poole's
General Store

5.1 Continue straight. To the right is a popular horse-trailer parking area along Montevideo Road.

5.5 Continue following the singletrack to the left.

6.9 Immediately after crossing the bridge, turn left and head up and to the right along the shored-up trail. (The path to the right is a bridle path used mostly by equestrians.) The Great Seneca Creek is down below to your left, along with the foundations of some old buildings.

7.4 Reach the terminus of the SBT on Old River Road. Poole's General Store is down to your left along Old River Road.

10 Seneca Ridge Trail (SRT)

The Seneca Ridge Trail (SRT) is one of the region's new additions to the vast catalog of off-road riding destinations. This trail is pretty special, and bound to become a showpiece for the Maryland Department of Natural Resources. The 7-mile ribbon of singletrack connects Schaeffer's white loop with the Seneca Creek Park System, giving you the chance to ride nearly 20 miles of just singletrack. Add the loops at Schaeffer Farm and you could spin nearly 40 miles in classic East Coast ribbon.

Start: Black Rock Mill parking area. The trail can also be accessed from Schaeffer Farms via the Schaeffer SRT Connector
Length: 5.8 miles each way; 11.6 miles round-trip
Ride time: About 1.5-3 hours
Difficulty: Easy/moderate
Trail surface: Rolling singletrack
Lay of the land: Piedmont forests
Land status: Public land
Nearest town: Germanton, MD
Other trail users: Hiking
Trail contacts: Mid-Atlantic Off-Road Enthusiasts (MORE), (703) 502-0359, www.more-mtb.org
Schedule: Open year-round

Getting there: The trailhead is located on Black Rock Road across the street from the Black Rock Mill. There is limited parking in and around the mill. An alternate starting point is the Schaeffer Farms parking area. From there you can ride the white trail to the Seneca Ridge Trail (SRT) Connector and then pick up the Seneca Ridge Trail (SRT).

From Route 270, take exit 15 for Route 118 South toward Germantown. Continue on Route 118 for 3.6 miles and turn right onto Black Rock Road. The trailhead will be adjacent to the Black Rock Mill in approximately 2 miles on the right. GPS coordinates: 39.127050, -77.314386.

The Ride

Back in the mid-1990s when I was working on my first book, I had the pleasure of heading out with good friend and local advocacy guru David Scull on a flagging mission to Schaeffer Farms, a local tract of land that for the most part lay undeveloped. Much of the wooded land around the farms eventually became the Schaeffer Farms mountain bike trail system (Ride 12). That day we hung tape on what was to become the white loop in the park. Little did we know how far those first steps would take the mountain-bike community and how important that park would become in the development of off-road cycling, not only in Montgomery County, but in the region as a whole.

Fast forward nearly twenty years, and there are more than 18 miles of singletrack trails in that park. And just recently, efforts to add more trails to the system have been successful. Thanks to the efforts of another friend, and also an advocacy and trails guru in our region, Dave Magill, there is a relatively new strip of trail extending from the white loop at Schaeffer Farms to the already established trails at Clopper Lake, the SRT.

The SRT has become a regional favorite for riders of all levels.

The genesis of the SRT harkens to the time when the Schaeffer Farms trails were being first built, but it never materialized. The hiker-only Seneca Greenway trail was also being built at the same time, and unfortunately it was unfeasible to build a second multi-use trail alongside it, simply because the area along the northwest side of Seneca Creek was too narrow and could not support two trails. Furthermore, and despite the fact that there were several neighborhood-maintained trails along the south side of the creek, it was impossible to build a throughway because of the existence of a shotgun skeet-shooting range along the banks of the creek that would have made safe passage via a trail impossible.

That all changed, however, when in 2008 the lease for the shooting range expired and the Maryland Department of Natural Resources (DNR) decided not to renew it. That created the opportunity for the SRT to be built. With the success of Schaeffer Farms behind them, the Mid-Atlantic Off-Road Enthusiasts (MORE) developed a proposal for DNR in which they outlined how to provide all the necessary funds and labor to build the new multi-use trail. DNR and the local area park managers liked what they saw and decided to approach other user groups to get their input, including equestrian and hiker organizations. After a couple of years of environmental studies and reviews, public meetings, and consultations, the SRT and a second trail,

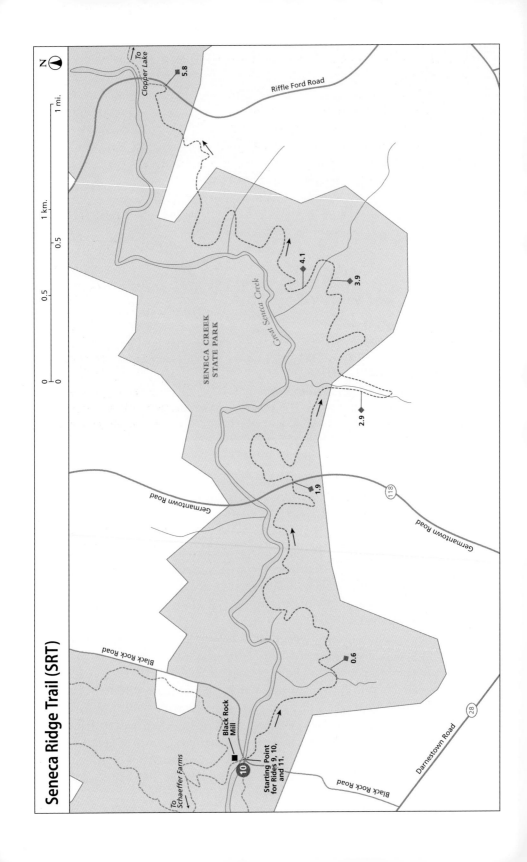

the Seneca Bluffs Trail (Ride 9), were approved, with MORE as the designated lead for their construction.

With the help of hundreds of volunteers from all user groups, MORE began the effort in earnest. By September 2011 the group completed the 6.25 miles of trail that connected the Schaeffer Farms white loop with Seneca Creek State Park, just in time for their annual fall picnic. The second trail, the Seneca Bluffs Trail, was completed in time for the 2012 MoCo Epic and can be combined with this ride to create an epic loop around South Montgomery County (See Ride 11).

The SRT has quickly become one of my favorite singletrack rides in the region. The flow of the trail is fantastic and built with the cross-country rider in mind. It utilizes the contours almost perfectly and it is an absolute joy to ride. If you are a beginner to intermediate rider you'll love it because it caters to your abilities. If you are an advanced rider you'll simply adore it because it will give you an opportunity to find a rhythm you seldom can in other regional trails. You can certainly tell that great thought went into its development.

Miles and Directions

0.0 Start from the trailhead at Black Rock Road. The SRT is immediately across the street from the mill parking area to the left.

0.6 Continue straight through the intersection. This is the first of several neighborhood connectors. As you continue on the SRT you will encounter several more of these branch trails. From trail wear, it is quite obvious which is the SRT and which are simply neighborhood connectors.

1.9 Cross Germantown Road (118). Use caution.

2.9 Continue straight through the intersection.

3.9 Stay to the left at the intersection.

4.1 Stay left past two intersections.

5.8 You've reached the end of the SRT. Turn around and head back along the same path. Alternatively, you can cross Riffle Ford Road and make your way into Seneca Creek State Park; See Rides 11 and 16 for additional information.

11.6 Arrive back at the trailhead.

11 MoCo South

The MoCo South presented here combines two trails already described in detail in previous chapters, the Seneca Bluffs Trail (SBT) and the Seneca Ridge Trail (SRT). In addition, the ride uses two other trails along South Montgomery County recently open to mountain biking, the Muddy Branch Trail and the trails at Blockhouse Point Park in Potomac. The vast majority of the ride is along natural-surface trails, but one section meanders through one of Germantown's newest developments, the Kent-lands. Here you can see the result of the "sprawl and crawl" that has taken place in the D.C. region over the past three decades.

Start: Seneca Bluffs trailhead adjacent to Black Rock Mill
Length: 30.4 miles
Ride time: About 3–5 hours
Difficulty: Moderate/difficult due to distance
Trail surface: Mostly singletrack, C&O towpath, and a short section of paved roads and trails
Lay of the land: Rolling singletrack along southern Montgomery County. Sections through the historic C&O Canal.

Land status: Public lands
Nearest town: Germantown, MD
Other trail users: Hikers, equestrians; walkers on paved surfaces
Trail contacts: MORE, (703) 502-0359, www.more-mtb.org
Schedule: Open year-round

Getting there: The trailhead is located on Black Rock Road adjacent to the Black Rock Mill. There is limited parking in and around the mill. An alternate starting point is the Schaeffer Farms parking area. From there you can ride the white trail to the Seneca Ridge Trail (SRT) Connector and then pick up the Seneca Bluffs Trail (SBT). This will add approximately 10 miles to your ride.

From Route 270 take exit 15 for Route 118 South toward Germantown. Continue on Route 118 for 3.6 miles and turn right onto Black Rock Road. The trailhead will be adjacent to the Black Rock Mill in approximately 2 miles on the right. GPS coordinates: 39.127050, -77.314386.

The Ride

The MoCo South loop is presented to demonstrate how several individual trail systems in Montgomery County can be tied together to build an "epic" ride. Epics are popular these days, and the Mid-Atlantic Off-Road Enthusiasts (MORE) have capitalized on that popularity. Every year the club hosts two Epic events in Maryland. These events showcase the trails the club has built and continues to maintain.

The loop presented here is part of a greater loop highlighted in the MoCo Epic and makes use of two signature area trails, the Seneca Bluffs Trail (SBT, Ride 9) and the Seneca Ridge Trail (SRT, Ride 10), and two little-used parks, Blockhouse Point Park and Muddy Branch Park. Each of the trails featured can be ridden individually as out-and-backs, or combined to form this loop or similar routes.

A portion of this loop utilizes a segment of the popular C&O Canal.

If you really want to go epic, you can add portions of Schaeffer Farms, the Hoyles Mill Connector, Black Hill Regional Park, and other area trails. Riders in the region often piece together rides in excess of 70 miles, usually staying on singletrack most of the time. MORE holds its annual MoCo Epic in the early fall. For additional information and to ride alternate versions of this loop visit www.mocoepics.com.

This ride takes you alongside the ruins of the Seneca stone-cutting mill. The mill was completed in 1868 and provided the red sandstone used in the Potowmack and C&O Canals until it was closed in 1901. Locks 9, 11, 15–27, and 30, along with their corresponding lock houses and hundreds of buildings in the Baltimore and Washington area, used materials from this quarry and mill.

Miles and Directions

0.0 Start on the SBT; follow the markers found on Ride 9.

7.4 Reach the terminus of the SBT on Old River Road. Turn left on Old River Road and head down toward Poole's General Store to the stop sign at River Road. Cross River Road and continue straight along Tschiffley Mill Road.

MoCo South

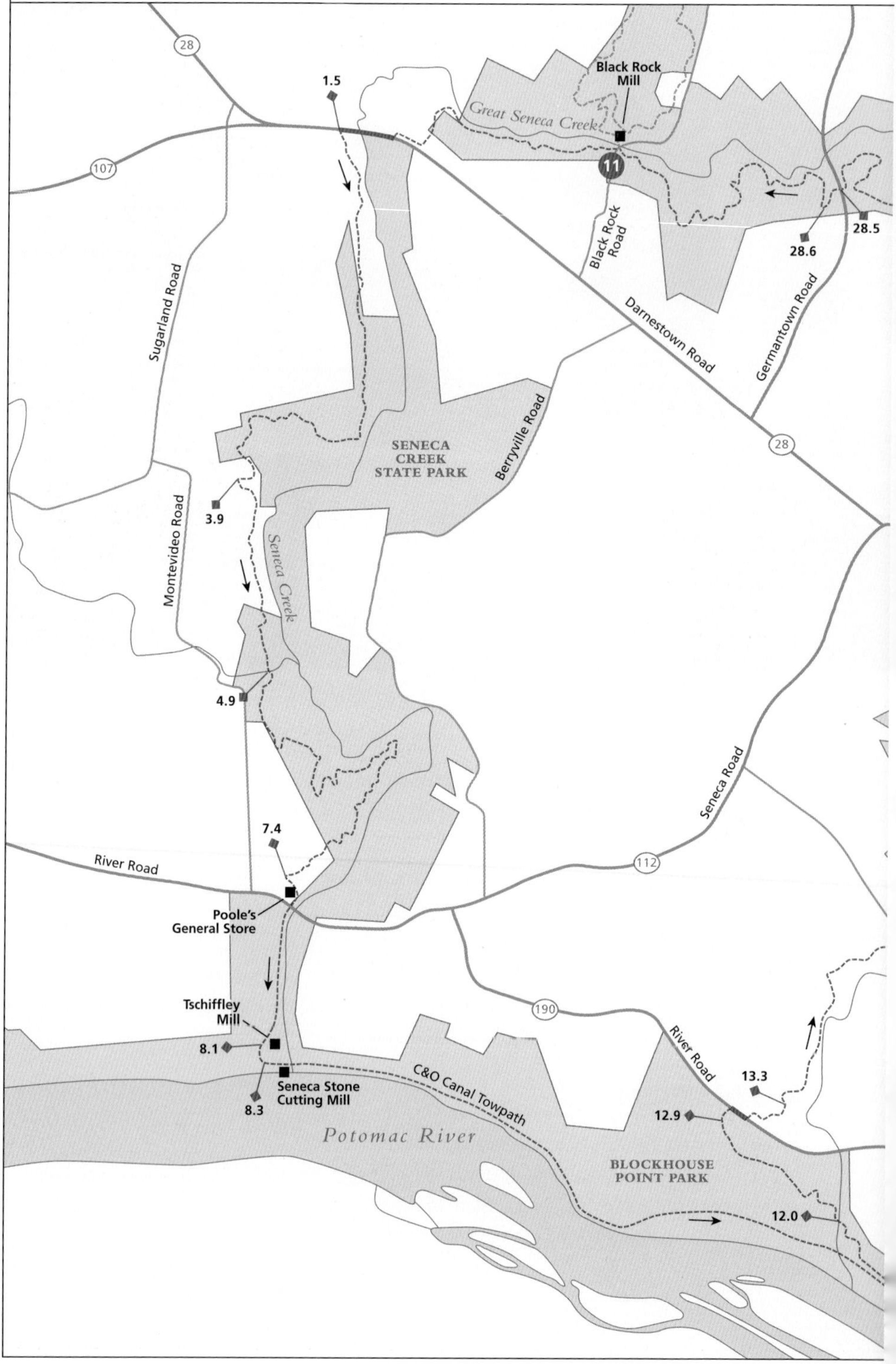

Black Rock Mill

Great Seneca Creek

1.5

(28)

(107)

Darnestown Road

11

Black Rock Road

28.5

28.6

Germantown Road

(28)

Sugarland Road

Berryville Road

SENECA
CREEK
STATE PARK

Seneca Creek

3.9

Montevideo Road

4.9

Seneca Road

7.4

(112)

River Road

Poole's
General Store

(190)

River Road

13.3

Tschiffley
Mill

C&O Canal Towpath

12.9

8.1

Seneca Stone
Cutting Mill

8.3

Potomac River

BLOCKHOUSE
POINT PARK

12.0

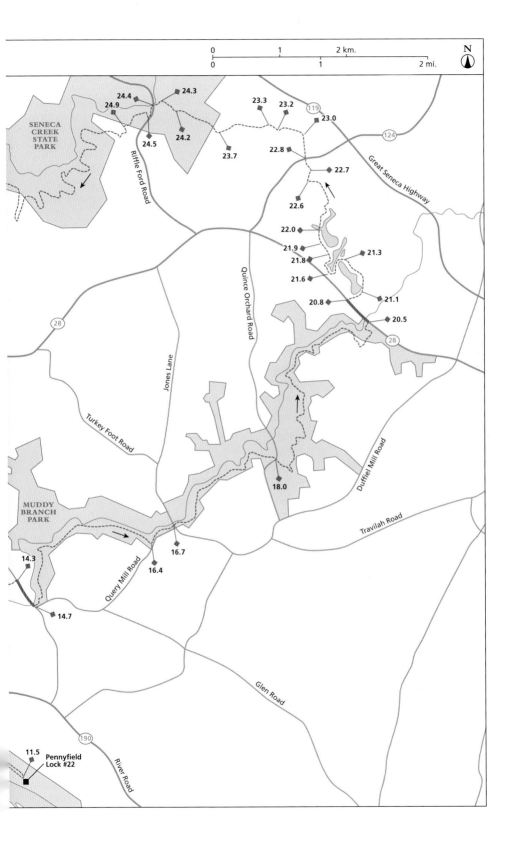

8.1 Tschiffley Mill Road curves left and ends at a gate. The path, however, continues and delivers you to the Chesapeake and Ohio Canal Towpath (See Ride 44). As the road curves left you can see the Seneca stone-cutting mill to the right.

8.3 As you enter the canal, cross over a small bridge that spans the Seneca Creek where it meets the Potomac. (A parking area to the left, the terminus of Riley's Lock Road, is a good alternate starting point for this ride.)

11.5 Turn left and go over the canal along Lock 22, Pennyfield Lock (built with redstone from the Seneca quarry), and then turn immediately left to head back on Pennyfield Lock Road. This is another alternate parking area for the ride.

11.8 Pennyfield Lock Road curves to the right over a one-lane bridge and then curves left.

11.9 Shortly after the bridge, and just before the road curves right again, turn left into the doubletrack.

12.0 Cross a small bridge and turn right onto the field, then immediately left into the light-blue blazed singletrack. You are now in the Blockhouse Point Park trails. Continue following the light-blue blazes. Be mindful that this section of trail is used heavily by equestrians.

12.9 The trail ends at a parking area along River Road, another alternate starting point. This is where you would park to ride the out-and-back Muddy Branch Trail. Go through the parking area and cross River Road. The entrance to the Muddy Branch Trail is slightly to the right on the opposite side. Continue following the blue blazes.

13.3 Continue following the blue blazes to the left.

14.3 The trail climbs sharply and delivers you at Esworthy Road. Turn right on Esworthy for a quick and short road descent.

14.7 The trail continues to the left along Query Mill Road and it is clearly marked. If you pass the intersection of Query Mill Road, you've gone too far. Continue to follow the blue blazes and the general path of the Muddy Branch, which is to your left, for the next 3.5 miles.

16.4 Turn left on Query Mill Road and then left again onto the trail over the guardrail. The trail continues to be blazed blue.

16.7 Reach the intersection of Query Mill Road and Turkey Foot Road. The trail continues on the other side of Turkey Foot and it's clearly visible.

18.0 Cross Quince Orchard Road and continue following the blue blazes on the other side; use caution here. Once you cross Quince Orchard you'll enter an area frequently used by equestrians from the Potomac Horse Center. This section of the ride is the most confusing since there are lots of bisecting trails crossing the main blue trail. Remember to follow the light-blue blazes. The majority of the trails here, however, wind back to the main backbone, the blue trail.

18.1 Turn left and down the wide steps and follow the trail as it switches back on the other side. (If you were to continue straight you'd end up at the Potomac Horse Center.)

18.1 Continue following the blue blazes along the main trail.

20.5 The trail comes out on a closed-off road and veers to the right. Ride under Darnestown Road, Route 28, then immediately turn left and ride along the paved path along 28. This marks the end of the Muddy Branch Trail.

20.8 Turn right onto Edison Park Road. Ride around Lake Placid and the back side of the Montgomery County Police Department.

21.1 Continue following the road to the left toward the police department's building.

YOU MAY RUN INTO: DENIS CHAZELLE

As you ride through the shaded portions of this loop you'll likely chance by Denis, and more than likely he'll just be passing through during one of his epic rides. See, Denis loves long-distance cycling and has completed (actually finished second) in one of the most demanding races on the planet, the Tour Divide. Denis finished the 2,750-mile self-supported mountain-bike race along the Continental Divide, from Antelope Wells, New Mexico, to Banff, Canada, in twenty-three days and nine hours, riding through heat, rain, and snow for nearly sixteen hours a day. It's a grueling race that includes more than 200,000 feet of climbing (imagine riding up Everest seven times) and crosses some inhospitable territory, including deserts with extreme weather changes. "I always liked to be outside and to travel long distance," he told me. "A bike is the best way to accomplish that."

His love for long-distance cycling led him to launch an event that has quickly become one of the most popular in the region, the MoCo Epic (Montgomery County Epic). As Denis rode the Montgomery County trails and dirt roads he realized that he could link them all together to create one epic ride, and he felt the need to share his routes with the rest of us. So, in 2009 he and a group of friends set out to ride what would become the first MoCo Epic.

Today, the annual event draws nearly seven hundred riders who choose from one of four epic rides (25-mile, 35-mile, 50-mile, and 65-mile loops) along some of Montgomery County's best parks and trails.

"It's very easy to forget that you're in the middle of a suburban area with close to a million people," he told me. "I've been cycling all my life, and these are some of my favorite trails."

The ride is supported along the way by several aid stations provided by local businesses and bike shops and volunteers, and all proceeds benefit the local mountain bike club, the Mid-Atlantic Off-Road Enthusiasts (MORE). So, if you're up to it, and want to experience an incredible adventure, join Denis for a short ride through MoCo's trails.

21.3 Follow the road as it curves to the left. You are now on Main Street; there is a paved bike trail on the left side. (A right turn will take you to the Lakelands Park Baseball Fields. There are restrooms and water fountains to replenish your bottles and hydration packs.)

21.6 Turn right to cross Main Street and to continue on the paved trail. The paved trail skirts Nirvana Lake to the right. You will now navigate through the Kentlands.

21.8 Continue following the paved trail to the left.

21.9 Stay to the left on the paved trail.

22.0 Stay left on the paved trail and go over the dam.

22.1 Stay to the left and cross Firehouse Lane. Immediately after crossing the road stay to the left on the paved trail.

22.3 Turn left and cross Midtown Street onto Chestertown Street.

22.6 Turn right onto Tschiffley Square Road.

22.7 Turn left onto Kentlands Boulevard. Stay along the near side and ride along the sidewalk.

22.8 Cross Quince Orchard Road onto Longdraft Road. Stay on the sidewalk.

23.0 Turn left on Sioux Lane.

23.2 Turn right onto the paved path; if you reach Raven Rock Drive you've gone too far.

23.3 Turn left before the bridge onto the unpaved trail. Back on dirt!

23.7 The trail will come out onto an open space and some power lines. Continue following the trail through the stream crossing. After you cross the stream the trail is to your right. You are now entering Seneca Creek State Park.

24.2 Reach the yellow trail. Turn right.

24.3 Turn left to hop on the blue trail and the left again to hop on the doubletrack.

24.4 Reach Riffle Ford Road. Cross the road and turn left.

24.5 The entrance to the Seneca Ridge Trail (SRT, Ride 10) is clearly marked. Turn right and begin the final leg of the loop back to your vehicle. The trail is blazed red all the way back to Black Rock Road.

24.9 Cross the road; the trail continues on the other side. This is the location of the old skeet firing range.

28.5 Cross Germantown Road (Route 118). The SRT is directly on the other side.

28.6 Stay to the right immediately after crossing the small bridge. (The trail to the left is a neighborhood connector.)

30.4 Back at Black Rock Road. The loop is complete!

12 Schaeffer Farms

These trails are a perfect example of mountain bike advocacy at work and the ones that set the tone for the future of mountain biking, not only in Montgomery County, but in many jurisdictions around the region. A group of dedicated mountain bikers approached Maryland's Department of Natural Resources (DNR) in hopes of gaining access to some nearby trails previously off-limits to bikes. The DNR went one step further and offered to build a new system of trails altogether in the Schaeffer Farms area. Today there are nearly 18 miles of accessible singletrack through Schaeffer Farms' rolling fields and forests, with the option of connecting to nearly 50 more miles of singletrack within the same area.

Start: Main Schaeffer Farms parking/staging area
Length: 10 miles
Ride time: About 1.5–3 hours
Difficulty: Easy to moderate
Trail surface: Mostly singletrack
Lay of the land: Rolling singletrack through farm fields and forest

Land status: State park
Nearest town: Germantown, MD
Other trail users: Equestrians and hikers
Trail contacts: MORE, (703) 502-0359, www .more-mtb.org
Schedule: Closed through the winter months. Check www.more-mtb.org for schedule.

Getting there: From the Capital Beltway (I-495): Take I-270 north to Route 117 West (Clopper Road). Go approximately 4.5 miles along Clopper Road. Just past the eighth light at Route 118 (Darnestown-Germantown Road), turn left on Schaeffer Road. Follow Schaeffer Road for 2 miles, then turn left at Black Burn Farm. Follow the Trail Parking sign to the trailhead. GPS coordinates: 39.127050, -77.314386.

The Ride

Schaeffer Farms, near Germantown (northern Montgomery County), is within the boundaries of Seneca Creek State Park. This area is part of a stream valley that extends for approximately 12 miles along Seneca Creek. The trails at Schaeffer are located on a portion of land leased by the county to local farmers, who use it to grow corn and a variety of other vegetables.

For some time, an adjacent tract of land of nearly 2,000 acres lay undeveloped and overgrown. Today, the white-blazed trail (unofficially the Scull loop) and the longer yellow-blazed trail (unofficially the Magill loop) are complete. Several new trails have been added since the main loops were completed, including a connector trail blazed green (unofficially Hurson Heights) that ties both loops together, a red-blazed extension loop, and several orange-blazed bisecting trails in the white and yellow loops. In total there are nearly 18 miles of trails at Schaeffer Farms. Add to that the Seneca

The trails at Schaeffer Farms run right through the middle of working farms.

Ridge Trail, which can be accessed from the white loop, the connecting Hoyles Mill Trail, and the Seneca Bluffs Trail, and you could feasibly ride more than 50 miles of singletrack in one day. It's no surprise that Schaeffer is an integral part of the MoCo Epic, an organized and supported autumn event that takes riders through several Montgomery County Parks and reaches nearly 70 miles in length.

The additions of the green and orange trails were made possible not only by the efforts of volunteers but also by the help of Maryland's leaders in the state's capital. In the early 2000s the chair of the House Environmental Matters Committee, State Congressman John Hurson, invited representatives of the Maryland Department of Natural Resource to his office in Annapolis. Their meeting resulted in the approval of several extensions to the system, including one of the best additions to the park, the green trail that connects the yellow and white loops. Unofficially named Hurson Heights, the trail offers riders additional options previously unavailable. Riders can now take the white loop to the yellow via the green trail and return to the starting point of their ride without riding a trail twice, something that couldn't be done before. The new trails have further improved the quality of Schaeffer Farms and made it a local favorite.

YOU MAY RUN INTO: DAVE MAGILL

Dave Magill is mostly responsible for the majority of the trail you'll be riding here. He's also responsible for several miles of other trail, including the SRT (Ride 10) and sections of Cabin John Regional Park (Ride 18). Now, he'll humble up and tell you otherwise. Truth is he's had help, but really, if it weren't for him, many of the trails mountain bikers enjoy in Montgomery County would not be available today. Dave has lived in Rockville, Maryland, for nearly twenty years, and cycling for as long as he can remember. He rode solo in France for three weeks before taking some time off from cycling to care for his children. He discovered off-road cycling in 1993 when he moved to the D.C. area and loves the freedom cycling offers him. "It gives me a chance to clear my mind," he says, "to feel strong and happy, to enjoy the beauty of the great outdoors; it's what keeps me coming back." He's put that love for cycling to good use. Along with his good friend Dave Scull (who drew on his incomparable contacts from many years of public service in state and county government), they have advocated to build miles of trails in Montgomery County. His first efforts were the loops that cyclists continue to enjoy at Schaeffer Farms. After a short hiatus he came back with a vengeance, and in 2000 led the expansion of Schaeffer and sold regional park managers on a vision that has continued to guide trail development in Montgomery County. Since then things have fallen into place and the Hoyles Mill Connector, the Seneca Ridge Trail, and the Seneca Bluffs Trail have become a reality. The vision for a trail (or trails) to connect Montgomery County's parks is also closer to happening. "I'm not sure what we'll get approved to build in the next few years or so," Magill says, "but I am hoping for more." Let's hope so as well, because judging by his efforts thus far, the results should be highly enjoyable. If you run into Dave on the trail, make sure to say thanks; he certainly deserves it.

The trails at Schaeffer Farms are well marked and blazed. Each intersection is numbered and has a trail map so you can easily locate yourself within the system. I have offered you my personal favorite "guided" route below, but I think you would be best served by exploring the landscape on your own and designing your own favorite loop. There are two main trails at Schaeffer Farms. I have unofficially named each after the men responsible for the creation of this system, Dave Scull and Dave Magill.

The white Scull loop is a 4-mile belt that will give you a good idea of what the rest of the system is like. From the white loop you can access the longer yellow loop (in two places), ride the new orange connector trails, and the green trail, and access the Seneca Ridge Trail (Ride 10). The orange connectors split the white loop in two places allowing you to ride a figure-eight if you choose.

The yellow Magill loop is longer but very much like the shorter white loop. You can access the yellow loop shortly after starting the white loop if you are riding it counter-clockwise or via the green connector trail about 1 mile into the white loop, if you are riding clockwise.

From the yellow loop you can also access another short orange extension, the lightly used red loop, and the blue connector "open field trail," which often serves as a bailout from the yellow loop.

My personal preference, and the ride I detail here, begins with the white loop, then the yellow loop, and returns again to the white loop via the green connector trail. My ride generally skips the two orange bisecting trails in the white loop, unless I still have the legs for them. I encourage you to study the map as you enter the system, or at every intersection and decide along the way what is best for you. Once you familiarize yourself with the system you are bound to find your favorite.

Miles and Directions

(#) denotes the intersection number as marked on the official Schaeffer Farms map and on the trail signs along the trail.

0.0 (1) From the parking area enter the trail system and turn left into the white loop. I personally like heading in a clockwise direction since you get to hit a couple of very nice downhill sections and get to ride most of the white trail before entering the yellow loop.

0.7 (2) Stay left to continue on the white loop and then right over the small bridge. (The orange trail will split the white loop in half.)

0.9 (3) Stay to the left. (The orange connector continues to the right.)

1.8 (5) Stay to the left to continue on the white loop. To the right is the orange connector.

1.9 Continue straight. To the left is the entrance to the Seneca Ridge Trail (SRT).

2.2 (6) Stay to the right after crossing the creek. (We will return from the green trail to the left when finishing the ride and double back along this short section of the white loop.)

2.6 (7) Stay to the left to continue on the white loop. (To the right is the orange connector trail. Taking it would take you to intersection 2, mile marker 0.7.)

2.9 (8) Turn left to enter the yellow loop. (The parking area is 0.5 miles ahead to the right.)

3.8 (9) Stay to the left at this intersection to continue on the yellow trail.

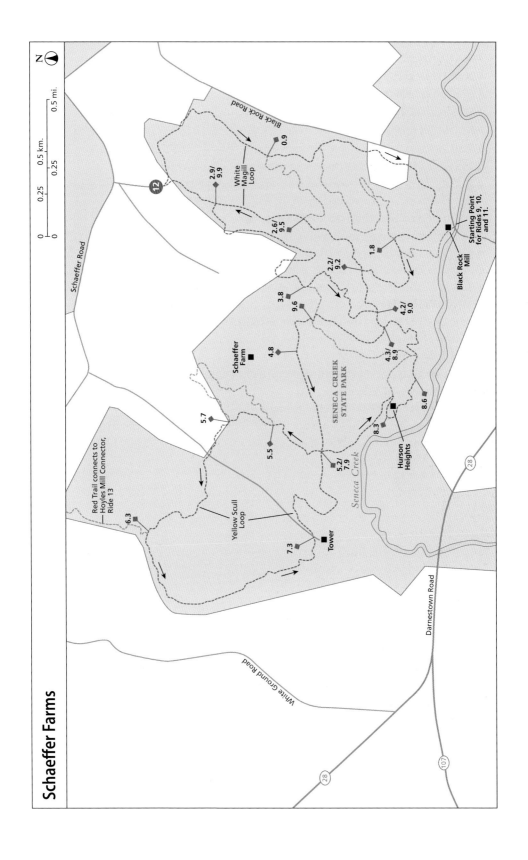

Schaeffer Farms

N

0   0.25   0.5 km.
0   0.25   0.5 mi.

Schaeffer Road

Black Rock Road

White Magill Loop

0.9

2.9/9.9

2.6/9.5

1.8

2.2/9.2

3.8

9.6

4.2/9.0

4.3/8.9

4.8

Schaeffer Farm

5.7

5.5

5.2/7.9

8.3

8.6

Hurson Heights

SENECA CREEK STATE PARK

Seneca Creek

Red Trail connects to Hoyles Mill Connector, Ride 13

6.3

Yellow Scull Loop

7.3

Tower

Black Rock Mill

Starting Point for Rides 9, 10, and 11.

White Ground Road

Darnestown Road

28

28

107

12

4.2 (10) Stay right to continue on the yellow loop. We'll ride the green trail on the way back.

4.3 (11) Stay to the right.

4.6 (12) Continue straight (to the right) to enter the blue open-field trail.

4.8 Stay to the left on the doubletrack.

5.2 (15) Turn right to get back on the yellow trail.

5.5 (16) Stay to the left to stay on the yellow loop.

5.7 (17) Stay to the left to continue on the yellow loop.

6.3 (18) Stay to the left to continue on the yellow loop. To the right is the seldom-used red trail.

7.3 Cross the gravel road. The cell tower is to your right.

7.9 (15) Back at intersection 15, turn right to hop on the yellow trail.

8.3 (14) Turn right and hop on the green trail. Continue following the green Hurson Heights trail all the way down to the white loop.

8.6 Stay to the right at this intersection to continue on the green trail; intersection 13 is about 20 yards to the left.

8.9 (11) Stay to the right; you'll be riding the yellow/green trail. After a short uphill, turn right again to stay on the green trail.

9.0 (10) Stay right on the green trail.

9.2 (6) Turn left on the white trail. (You'll double back along this portion of the white trail on the way back to your vehicle.)

9.5 (7) Continue straight to head back to the parking area, or, if you want to add a little extra mileage to the ride, turn right to ride the orange trail. The available trail maps will show you the way.

9.9 (8) Stay to the right.

10.0 (1) Back at the parking area, the loop is complete.

13 Hoyles Mill Connector (HMC)

The HMC is another trail crafted in Germantown by a coalition of various user groups, led in the effort by the Mid-Atlantic Off-Road Enthusiasts (MORE), to extend riding opportunities in the region. The trail can be ridden as an out-and-back, or combined with loops in Black Hill Regional Park (Ride 14) and Schaeffer Farms (Ride 12) to extend your ride. The HMC is an integral portion of the MoCo Epic series of rides. Our ride will start from the Schaeffer Farms parking area, but the trail can also be accessed along Clarksburg Road and from the South Germantown Park (by the driving range).

Start: The HMC trailhead is along Schaeffer Road directly opposite the entrance to the Schaeffer Farms parking area.
Length: 6.1 miles, one way
Ride time: About 1.5–3 hours
Difficulty: Easy/moderate
Trail surface: Rolling singletrack, one section of pavement along Clarksburg Road

Lay of the land: Rolling singletrack along southern Montgomery County
Land status: Public land
Nearest town: Germantown, MD
Other trail users: Hiking, equestrians
Trail contacts: Mid-Atlantic Off-Road Enthusiasts (MORE), (703) 502-0359, www.more-mtb .org
Schedule: Open year-round, dusk till dawn

Getting there: From the Capital Beltway (I-495): Take I-270 north to Route 117 West (Clopper Road). Go approximately 4.5 miles along Clopper Road. Just past the eighth light at Route 118 (Darnestown-Germantown Road), turn left on Schaeffer Road. Follow Schaeffer Road for 2 miles, then turn left at Black Burn Farm. The trailhead is immediately to the right as you turn left into the Black Burn Farm gravel road. Park along the field to the right and head back over Schaeffer Road to the clearly marked trailhead. GPS coordinates: 39.145249, -77.310819

The Ride

The Hoyles Mill Connector is quite possibly the beginning of what many consider the MoCo North loops. Like the SRT and SBT in the MoCo South loop (Ride 11), the Hoyles Mill Connector provides a vital link between the centralized Schaeffer Farms network of trails with Black Hill Regional Park (Ride 14) and Little Bennett Regional Park (Ride 15) to the north.

The genesis of this ribbon of trails goes back to the year 2000, when the Maryland-National Capital Park and Planning Commission (MNCPPC) purchased a large property on which the trails are located. The sale of the property included a provision (thankfully) that the land be primarily used for conservation and the enjoyment of the equestrian community, that is, riding trails. Unfortunately, the MNCPPC produced a plan that only included equestrian use and glaringly omitted cycling.

A group of MoCo Epic riders makes their way to Black Hill Regional Park along the Hoyles Mill Connector.

Thankfully, however, during a critical meeting in late September of the year 2000, a MORE delegation, including Dave Magill and Austin Steo, met with MNCPPC representatives and presented a coherent and convincing argument to open the trails to cycling use. Magill and Steo pointed out the success of shared-use trails at Schaeffer Farms to the south and Black Hill to the north and drew on the countless hours of volunteer work and effort donated by the organization. Their argument hinged on MNCPPS's "trail connections" initiative and noted that the Hoyles Mill Connector would provide a missing link between two of the area's most popular cycling destinations, where shared use was the norm.

Shortly thereafter MNCPPC saw the value in MORE's vision of shared use and altered their plan to formally include cycling as an accepted activity. And in 2002, construction began on the northern connector. In 2004 the trail was completed and included several improvements to the trails at Black Hill Regional Park (Ride 14), including the first use of machine bench-cutting on a section of trail along the lake. MORE volunteers cleared the path and IMBA's Trail Solutions brought in regional experts to carve the trail.

YOU MAY RUN INTO: JAMES CORBETT

I don't recall specifically the day when I first met James, but I do remember that it was incredibly easy to like him. His southern demeanor (an Alabama native), and his genuine interest in getting to know me has made him a good friend with whom to talk about things other than just biking, such as family or traveling to Peru or other parts of the world.

But it is through mountain biking that I met him, and specifically through his volunteer work both in the MoCo Epic and in making the Hoyles Mill Connector become a reality.

James lives in Montgomery County, so this mecca of trails is his backyard. Early in his thirties he discovered the trails around Seneca Creek State Park on recommendation from a neighbor. "I hit my thirties and found I'd added close to twice my age in extra pounds," he said. "I'd started running and working out to get the weight off. My next-door neighbor suggested I would like mountain biking more than running and, since there were trails that I could ride to from my house, it was about as convenient as suiting up to run. It was love at first ride."

Soon after he discovered riding he began volunteering at local trail workdays and getting to know the people in MORE. During a Rosaryville trail workday he took the plunge and offered to lead the effort to get the build at Hoyles Mill rolling. James organized fourteen workdays and organized more than fifty volunteers to work the trail on Earth Day. He rallied local businesses to donate breakfast for the work parties and helped augment IMBA's Trail Solutions crew with the much-needed labor to make the trail a reality. "Hoyles Mills feel like my baby," he told me. "I do love riding the trails in the Shenandoah Mountains, but there is something very special about this trail."

What's special is that he poured so much effort and energy into it, and like any proud parent, James is extremely proud of what he helped build and continues to maintain. Others have noticed. James is a three-time recipient of MORE's Silver Spoke Award, given to volunteers who go above and beyond the call of duty in support of the club's mission and vision. If you ever run into James you'll understand why. If you've ridden one of the MoCo Epics, chances are he helped get you registered and on your way.

James is not only an outstanding ambassador of our sport, but a great individual and someone you should get to know if given the chance. If you see him riding his rigid single-speed IF on a MoCo trail, say hello, and make sure to thank him for a job well done.

PHOTO COURTESY BRUCE BUCKLEY

Today, like the SRT and the SBT, the HMC is an integral link in MORE's signature event, the MoCo Epic, and is enjoyed by thousands of off-road riders year-round. I encourage you to combine the HMC with the Black Hill and Schaeffer Farms rides to extend your riding enjoyment.

This ride passes by the Black Hill Butterfly Habitat and Meadow Restoration area, a spot monarch butterflies use during their migratory trip to Mexico. Monarchs endure generational trips from the northern US to Mexico in one of nature's most baffling migrations; it takes three generations of monarchs to make the trip south to Mexico. Deep Creek Lake State Park (Ride 3) is also a monarch stopping point.

Miles and Directions

We will start measuring from the trail entrance that is immediately adjacent to Schaeffer Road as you ride out of the Schaeffer Farms parking area. I recommend you park along the edge of the entrance road to the Schaeffer Farms parking area.

0.0 From the gate, head to the right along the grass paralleling Schaeffer Road toward the Germantown Soccer Complex. The entrance is clearly marked and the path is worn into the field. The trail then curves to the left under the power lines and then right along the tree line at the edge of the field.

0.5 Reach the South Germantown Pump Track. The trail curves to the right along a gravel road. This is usually the staging area for the MoCo Epic series of rides.

0.6 Merge onto the paved bike path and continue to the left. The soccer fields are to your right.

0.8 The paved path turns sharply right and then immediately left off the paved path onto the singletrack. The trail is marked.

0.9 Enter the woods. Shortly after the first rock garden (1.0), the trail will curve to the right. The fork to the left will take you to Schaeffer Farms (Ride 12), along the red trail.

1.3 Stay left. (The trail to the right simply connects back to the paved trail along the soccer fields.)

2.0 Turn left on Hoyles Mill Road.

2.1 Enter the Hoyles Mill Conservation Park.

2.2 Go over the bridge.

2.5 Cross over the Little Seneca Creek.

3.1 Go through the gate and continue along Hoyles Mill Road.

3.3 Immediately before you reach the stop sign for White Ground Road, turn right into the clearly marked trail. There is a parking area along White Ground Road to the left that can be used as an alternate starting point.

4.2 Reach Route 117. Cross 117, and go under the railroad tracks and continue straight on Clarksburg Road along the shoulder toward Clopper Lake.

4.5 There is an alternate parking area to your right.

4.8 About 100 yards after crossing the bridge you'll see the trailhead on your right. Turn right. Immediately after entering the trail it will split. Either the right or left fork will do, since both end up in the same place. For this ride, take the longer right fork.

4.87 Continue straight. (The left fork will simply take you back up toward Clarksburg Road.)

Hoyles Mill Connector (HMC)

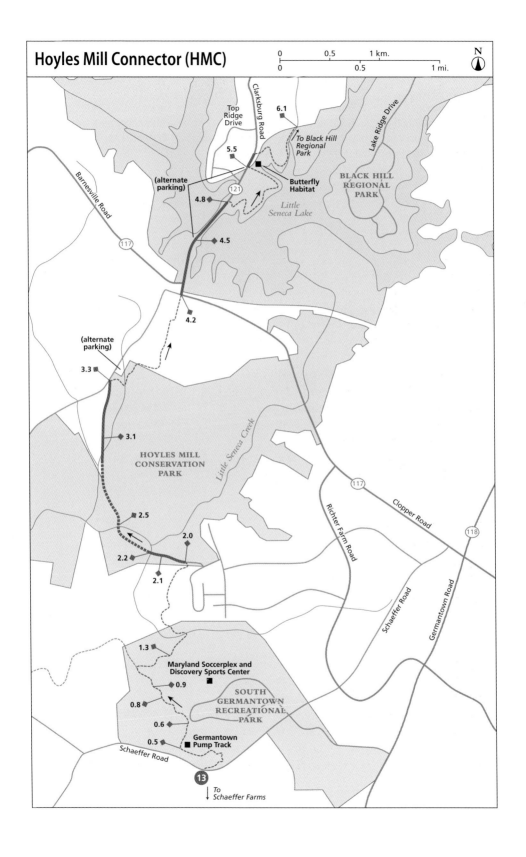

0   0.5   1 km.
0   0.5   1 mi.

N

Top Ridge Drive

Clarksburg Road

6.1

To Black Hill Regional Park

Lake Ridge Drive

5.5

(alternate parking)

Butterfly Habitat

121

4.8

BLACK HILL REGIONAL PARK

Barnesville Road

117

Little Seneca Lake

4.5

4.2

(alternate parking)

3.3

HOYLES MILL CONSERVATION PARK

Little Seneca Creek

3.1

117

Clopper Road

118

Richter Farm Road

2.5

2.0

2.2

2.1

Schaeffer Road

Germantown Road

1.3

Maryland Soccerplex and Discovery Sports Center

0.9

SOUTH GERMANTOWN RECREATIONAL PARK

0.8

0.6

0.5   Germantown Pump Track

Schaeffer Road

13

To Schaeffer Farms

5.5	Another alternate parking spot. As you look to the right you'll see the Black Hill Butterfly Habitat and Meadow Restoration area. The trail will now parallel the road for a short period and then turn right into the woods again.

6.1	Reach the entrance to Black Hill Regional Park (Ride 14). This is the terminus of the Hoyles Mill Connector. At this point simply make a U-turn to make the journey back to the starting point of the ride. The trailhead for the Black Hill Regional Park ride (Ride 14) is approximately 0.5 mile to the right on the left.

14 Black Hill Regional Park

Thanks to the efforts of local mountain bike advocates, the mountain bike community can now enjoy this previously off-limits area. Located in Montgomery County, Black Hill has a great network of singletrack that is bound to put a smile on an off-road cyclist's face. Without serious changes in elevation but with plenty of twists and turns, these trails will delight the casual rider as well as the more advanced mountain bike enthusiast time and time again.

Start: Little Seneca Lake, parking lot 5
Length: 5.5 miles
Ride time: About 1–2 hours
Difficulty: Easy to moderate
Trail surface: Mostly singletrack, rolling dirt trails, and some flat fields
Lay of the land: Typical Maryland piedmont and farmland surrounded by a fast-growing metropolis
Land status: Regional state park

Nearest town: Germantown, MD
Other trail users: Hikers and horseback riders
Trail contacts: Black Hill Regional Park Office, Boyds, MD, (301) 972-9396; MORE, www.more-mtb.org
Schedule: March through October, 6 a.m. to sunset; November through February, 7 a.m. to sunset; park closed Thanksgiving, Christmas, and New Year's Day

Getting there: From the Capital Beltway (I-495): Take I-270 north and exit on Route 118 East. After approximately 0.5 mile on Route 118, turn left on Route 355 North. Follow Route 355 and turn left on West Old Baltimore Road. Follow this road for 1.5 miles to the park entrance and turn left on Lake Ridge Drive. Immediately after entering the park take a right onto Black Hill Road and park on the gravel lot on the right after the dam. The ride starts on the front left corner of the gravel lot and Black Hill Road. The trailhead is marked by a trail marker labeled CABIN BRANCH TRAIL along the grassy area and a NO OUTLET sign along the road. The Hoyles Mill Connector trail (Ride 13) is about 0.5 mile to the left further down the road. GPS coordinates: 39.200986, -77.294473.

The Ride

Black Hill Regional Park, a popular area for all sorts of recreation, is situated in the northern part of Montgomery County, near Gaithersburg and Germantown. Black Hill is home to mountain biking, hiking, horseback riding, boating, fishing, and more.

Upon entering the park, visitors are treated to an outstanding view of Little Seneca Lake. The lake was built through the partnership of the Maryland–National Park and Planning Commission and the Washington Suburban Sanitary Commission. Its design marked it as a dual-purpose lake, providing both recreation and an emergency water supply for the Washington metropolitan area. After a ride, consider having a picnic on the shores overlooking the lake or perhaps renting a boat ($4.75 per hour for a rowboat or canoe; $2.00 per person for pontoon boat rides).

In the summertime, expect the lake to be full of sailboats, canoes, and fishermen. In the fall, if you're here at the right time (early to mid–October), you may be treated to some of the area's most impressive fall colors.

Miles and Directions

0.0 From the trail marker, head up along the grassy hill; you'll notice the trail up ahead. A slightly open field will be to your left.

0.2 Continue straight past this intersection to the left; we'll hit it on the return trip.

0.23 After a short bridge, turn right into the woods and follow the signs for the Cabin John Trail. The trail will be blazed blue.

0.8 Turn right onto the Hamilton trail. The left fork takes you out of the park and onto an AT&T Fiber right-of-way (the initial trail we rode into the park).

1.0 Turn left onto the Cabin John Branch Trail. (Heading straight will take you to Black Hill Road. We will return from that direction.)

1.3 Cross Lake Ridge Drive and continue on the left on the Hard Rock Trail on the other side. (We'll ride the trail to the right on the return trip.)

1.4 Continue following the main trail to the left. (The right branch will connect you to the AT&T right-of-way. You'll encounter several of these along the Hard Rock Trail.)

1.5 Continue straight on the Hard Rock Trail. (The left branch will connect you to the Field Crest Trail and the right branch to the AT&T right-of-way.)

1.7 Turn right to continue on the Hard Rock Trail. (The left branch will take you to the Field Crest Trail.)

2.3 Reach the Field Crest Spur. Turn right at his intersection. Straight ahead across the field is Lakeridge Road.

2.5 Turn left on the AT&T Fiber right-of-way and then left onto Lake Ridge Drive.

2.7 Turn left into the access road for the maintenance yard and then immediately right onto the Field Crest Spur Trail.

2.9 Continue to the right on the Field Crest Spur Trail. (The left branch takes you back to the Hard Rock Trail.)

3.0 Continue to the right on the Field Crest Spur Trail. (The left branch takes you back to the Hard Rock Trail.)

3.2 Continue to the right on the Field Crest Spur Trail. (The left branch takes you back to the Hard Rock Trail.)

3.27 Turn left on Lake Ridge Drive; stay along the grassy area and head back toward the cross-walk we rode over at marker 1.3.

3.40 Reach the crosswalk; turn left and then immediately right on the Hard Rock Trail. (If you turn left you can do the loop again.)

3.5 Continue straight and follow the signs for the Black Hill Trail.

3.6 Reach a T intersection. Turn right at this intersection and head toward Black Hill Road. (The left branch descends to the paved Black Hill Trail.)

3.7 Turn right onto the gravel path and continue toward the intersection of Lake Ridge Drive and Black Hill Road. Cross Lake Ridge and then hop onto Black Hill Road. (The left fork

Black Hill Regional Park

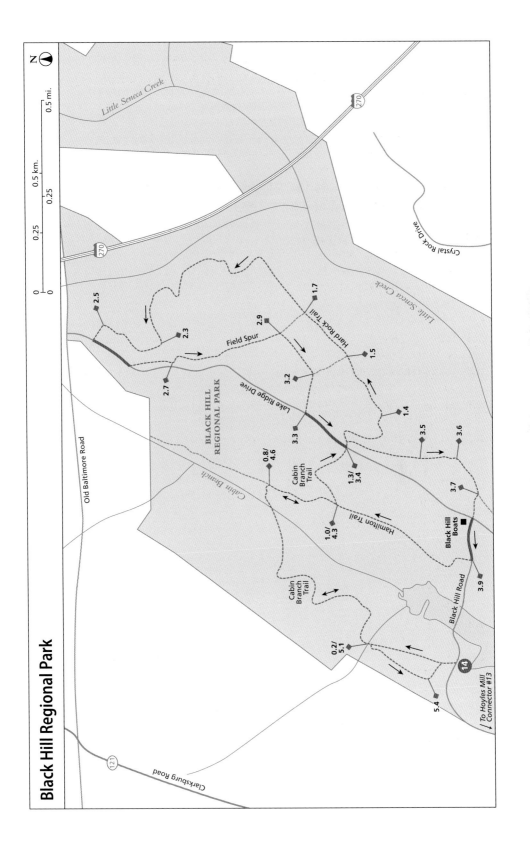

will take you down a steep hill to the paved Black Hill Trail; heading straight will also connect you with the Black Hill Trail.)

3.9 Shortly after getting on Black Hill Road, turn right into a grassy open area marked by a gas-line pylon. Turn right into the Hamilton Trail entrance. (Continuing straight on Black Hill Road will take you back to the gravel parking area and the starting point of the ride.)

4.3 Continue straight. (A right turn will put you back where you were at marker 1.0.) At this point you begin backtracking.

4.6 Turn left.

5.1 Turn left on the AT&T right-of-way. Immediately after crossing the small platform bridge, turn right on the trail you bypassed at 0.2 on the way in.

5.4 The trail will open up onto a slightly open field; continue following the perimeter to the right and the starting point of the ride.

5.5 The loop is complete.

15 Little Bennett Regional Park

At 3,700 acres, Little Bennett is the largest of Montgomery County's regional parks. The park has more than 20 miles of trails, but only half of those, to the north of the Little Bennett Creek, are open to bikes. Our ride will take you past several historical sites, including the Kingsley Schoolhouse, as it meanders through meadows and forests. Little Bennett is also home to the only campground in the Montgomery County system of parks.

Start: Froggy Hollow Trailhead along Clarksburg Road

Length: 12.7 miles

Ride time: About 2-3 hours

Difficulty: Easy/moderate

Trail surface: Singletrack, doubletrack, and open fields

Lay of the land: Rolling piedmont forests

Land status: Public County Park

Nearest town: Germantown, MD

Other trail users: Hiking, equestrians

Trail contacts: Montgomery County Parks, www.montgomeryparks.org, (301) 670-8080; MORE, www.more-mtb.org

Schedule: Open year-round, sunrise to sunset

Getting there: Take I-270 North to exit 18, MD 121 N/Clarksburg Road, toward Clarksburg and make an immediate left onto Gateway Center Drive. At the stop sign take a right onto Clarksburg Road. The Froggy Hollow Trailhead is in approximately 2 miles on the right. GPS coordinates: 39.260930, -77.279571.

The Ride

The story of the addition of the Little Bennett loop of trails into the Montgomery County mountain biking scene in the late 1990s is most interesting. At the time there were very few trails available to off-road riders in the county, or for that matter in the entire state. Only Black Hill Regional Park (Ride 14) and the Schaeffer Farms (Ride 12) network of trails to the south were available to mountain bikers, while the vast majority were open to both hikers and equestrians. Knowing that there were many more opportunities available for riding whetted the appetite of local riders. And their efforts to get park managers to open them went to great lengths.

In an attempt to change those minds and educate park leadership, two of MORE's elders, Dave Scull and Scott Scudamore, reached out to Little Bennett park management and invited then assistant manager Art Nelligan to explore the closed trails by bike. Nelligan agreed, and what ensued was one of the most memorable mountain bike rides in Montgomery County history, and one that would set the tone for other parks in the future.

The ride was more than a simple outing into area trails by a group of friends and a "newbie"; it was an opportunity for MORE's leadership to accurately communicate

The shared-use trails at Little Bennett are incredibly fun to ride.

their vision of shared use, and demonstrate to Art Nelligan that mountain biking and mountain bikers could be a valuable asset to his jurisdiction.

The ride, the first for Nelligan, turned out to be an unforgettable experience. Just shy of the end, and despite a few misgivings on the rideability of the creek crossing, Art was successful and emerged on the opposite bank fist high with an "I love it" declaration. He simply got it.

Shortly after, the wheels were set in motion to formally open most of the park's trails to bikes. In time, several trails were improved both by the park and volunteers. Unofficial trails that crisscrossed many sections were rerouted or replaced and have been reclaimed by the forest. Today, there's very little evidence of their existence. Other trails have been built with mountain biking in mind. And despite early protests from hiker coalitions, shared use thrives along the paths of Little Bennett.

Miles and Directions

0.0 From the parking area, as you face the park kiosk there is a trail marker labeled Froggy Hollow Trail. This is where our ride begins.

0.6 Reach the Froggy Hollow Schoolhouse; go over the bridge to the left and cross Kingsley Road. After crossing the bridge that spans Little Bennett Creek, bear right and climb along Purdum Trail.

0.8 Continue climbing straight along Purdum Trail past this first intersection. You'll take the next one.

0.88 Turn left at this intersection and then right at the next one (Hard Cider Trail, mile 0.96). (Continuing straight would take you right back to Purdum; you'll go that way on the return leg.)

1.9 Reach the Kingsley parking area along Clarksburg Road. Turn right and head up Logger's Trail. Get ready to climb! Little Bennett Creek is to your left, and parallel to it is Kingsley Trail, a gravel road that you can take back to the Froggy Hollow Schoolhouse if you wish. Shortly after the beginning of the climb the trail splits. Either fork will do since both meet up a little farther up the trail. Stay to the left at this and the next intersection.

2.6 Pine Knob Trail is to your left. Continue straight on Logger's Trail until we reach Purdum Trail again.

2.8 Turn left at Purdum. (A right turn will take you back to the schoolhouse.)

2.9 Turn left on Browning Run Trail. Purdum continues straight to the Burnt Hill Parking Area.

3.0 Continue to the left; you're still on Browning Run Trail.

3.1 Continue to the left.

3.6 Continue following Browning Run Trail to the right. (You will hit Pine Knob Trail to the left on your way back.)

3.8 You reach the Browning Run Parking Area along Clarksburg Road. This is the third lot along Clarksburg Road you can use. At this point cross Clarksburg and continue following Browning Run Trail on the other side. Get ready for some great fast and flowy singletrack!

4.4 Cross over Tobacco Barn Trail. We will revisit this section a little later in the ride.

5.0 Turn left at this intersection to hop on the Windy Ridge Trail; there's a bench if you want to hang and take a break. Browning Run Trail continues a little farther to the right and ends on Western Piedmont Trail, a gravel road that parallels the Little Bennett Creek. (If you want to bail take Western Piedmont all the way back to Clarksburg Road and then Kingsley Trail all the way to the schoolhouse.)

5.5 Turn left at this intersection and get ready to climb up Tobacco Barn. (A right turn will take you down to Western Piedmont.)

5.8 Continue left following Tobacco Barn Trail and then through the intersection of Browning Run Trail. It is clearly marked.

6.2 Continue your climb to the right. A little farther to the right you'll see the ruins of the Norwood Tobacco Barn.

6.4 Continue straight onto Timber Ridge Trail. Tobacco Run continues to the right and dead-ends on Prescott Road.

6.5 Stay to the left on Timber Ridge Trail and go over a short bridge. Get ready for a steep, gnarly climb.

6.9 Reach the entrance to the Prescott Road horse-trailer parking area. Continue straight into the parking area to ride a short section of fun new trail along Prescott Road. (Or, if you prefer, just stay left and continue the ride along the Pine Grove Trail.) We'll return to this

Little Bennett Regional Park

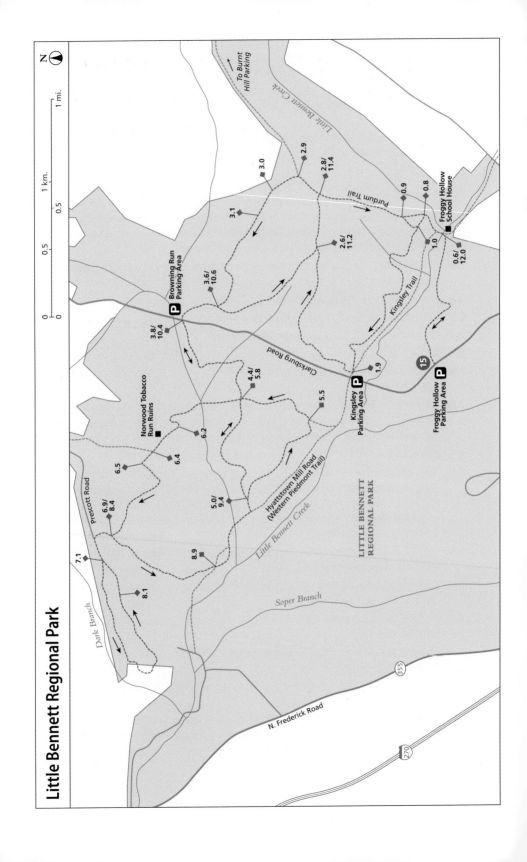

N

1 mi.

To Burnt Hill Parking

Little Bennett Creek

2.9

3.0

2.8/
11.4

3.1

0.9

0.8

Purdum Trail

2.6/
11.2

Browning Run
Parking Area

3.6/
10.6

P

Froggy Hollow
School House

1.0

0.6/
12.0

3.8/
10.4

Kingsley Trail

Clarksburg Road

1.9

Norwood Tobacco
Run Ruins

4.4/
5.8

15

5.5

Kingsley
Parking Area

P

6.2

5.0/
9.4

Hyattstown Mill Road
(Western Piedmont Trail)

Froggy Hollow
Parking Area

P

6.4

6.5

Prescott Road

Little Bennett Creek

6.9/
8.4

8.9

LITTLE BENNETT
REGIONAL PARK

7.1

8.1

Dark Branch

Soper Branch

N. Frederick Road

355

270

1 km.

spot after riding the Dark Branch Trail. As you ride toward the parking area you'll see a trail marker to the right on the opposite side of Prescott Road. Aim for it.

7.1 Cross Prescott Road and enter the Dark Branch Trail loop. The trail will basically loop around and come back along Prescott to the parking area again.

8.1 The trail parallels Prescott Road and heads back toward the parking area. Return to the point where you exited the Timber Ridge Trail.

8.4 Turn right onto the Timber Ridge Trail and then right again to hop onto the Pine Grove Trail.

8.9 Reach Western Piedmont Trail. Turn left.

9.3 Turn left onto Browning Run Trail. (Or, if you want to bail quicker continue straight along Western Piedmont all the way back to Kingsley and the schoolhouse.)

9.4 You're back at the bench. Continue along Browning Run Trail to the left, backtracking a bit now. (Windy Ridge Trail is to the right.)

9.9 Cross over Tobacco Barn and continue straight toward Clarksburg Road.

10.4 Cross Clarksburg Road and continue backtracking along Browning Run Trail.

10.6 Continue to the right on Pine Knob. You initially came from the left along Browning Run.

11.2 Turn left onto Logger's Trail. You'll double back pretty much all the way back to the starting point.

11.4 Turn right on Purdum and head straight back down to the schoolhouse.

12.0 Go over the bridge and turn right on Froggy Hollow Trail and make your way back up to the parking area.

12.7 Arrive back in the parking area. The loop is complete!

16 Seneca Creek State Park

Seneca Creek State Park is located in northern Montgomery County. The trails in this park are challenging and well maintained and are certain to satisfy the most demanding mountain biker. Beautiful vistas of the lake and historical points of interest along the trails will keep you both interested and educated as you pedal along.

Start: Clopper Lake boat center
Length: 4.7-mile loop
Ride time: About 0.75–1 hour
Difficulty: Easy to moderate due to relatively flat terrain with rooty and tight singletrack
Trail surface: Singletrack
Lay of the land: Wooded terrain and open fields surrounding Clopper Lake
Land status: State park
Nearest town: Gaithersburg, MD

Other trail users: Hikers, horseback riders, and anglers
Trail contacts: Maryland Forest, Park, and Wildlife Service, (301) 924-2127; Seneca Creek State Park, (301) 924-2127, http://dnr2.maryland.gov/publiclands/Pages/central/seneca.aspx
Schedule & fees: Open every day April through September, 8 a.m. to dusk; October through March, 10 a.m. to dusk; weekdays are free; small fee May through September on weekends

Getting there: From the Capital Beltway (I-495): Take I-270 north toward Frederick. Just after passing through Gaithersburg on I-270, take the exit for Route 124 (Orchard Road) to Darnesville. Follow Route 124 west 0.5 mile, then turn right on Route 117 (Clopper Road). Go 1.5 miles on Clopper Road to the entrance to Seneca Creek State Park on the left. Follow the entrance road into the park. You may park at any of the lots available, including the visitor center lot, the first stop on the right. You may also park at the boat center. Driving a car through the main gate may cost you an entrance fee of a couple of dollars.

The Ride

Here's a short but challenging ride around Seneca Creek State Park's Clopper Lake, taking you along tricky singletrack trails, through undeveloped natural areas, across open fields, along the lake's shores, and past evidence of times long ago.

You'll begin the ride following the Lake Shore Trail, which crosses old fields and skirts the lake's shoreline. In the spring and summer, these fields are filled with colorful wildflowers that give way in the fall to thick, golden sage grass. Just before the dam, you'll be treated to a spectacular view of the lake from King Fisher Overlook. The trail quickly descends across the park road and follows Long Draught Branch, winding up, down, and around beneath a dense canopy of gray birch before crossing the wooded boardwalk to Mink Hollow Trail. Seneca Creek's longest developed trail, Mink Hollow, travels through pine groves and habitats of local wildlife, including white-tailed deer. Be careful once you begin the challenging ride along the undeveloped trail edging the

The trails at Seneca Creek State Park offer great views of Clopper Lake.

lake. This trail can be tricky and challenging, as exposed roots, steep inclines, occasional flooding, and some quick descents may trip you up if you're not focused.

The lake itself is relatively new, created by damming Long Draught Branch. However, the name Clopper has a rich history in this area, dating back to the early 1800s when Francis C. Clopper, a successful tobacco merchant from Philadelphia, purchased more than 540 acres and an existing mill on Seneca Creek. The mill's most prosperous years were between 1830 and 1880, during which time Francis Clopper farmed the land and raised his family. The land remained in the hands of four generations of Clopper's descendants until 1955, when the state purchased it and added the land to Seneca Creek State Park.

Throughout the park there is evidence of this past: abandoned farms and old meadows now covered by new growth, traces of many of Clopper's old mills, and many of Clopper's old farm lanes. Mill ruins can still be seen from the intersection of Clopper Road and Waring Station Road, just west of the park entrance, and traces of the Clopper home are evident near the visitor center.

Be aware, as always, that many other outdoor enthusiasts share these same trails. Always yield the right-of-way to any other trail users, and ride cautiously, as the trails have many hidden turns and difficult negotiations.

Seneca Creek State Park

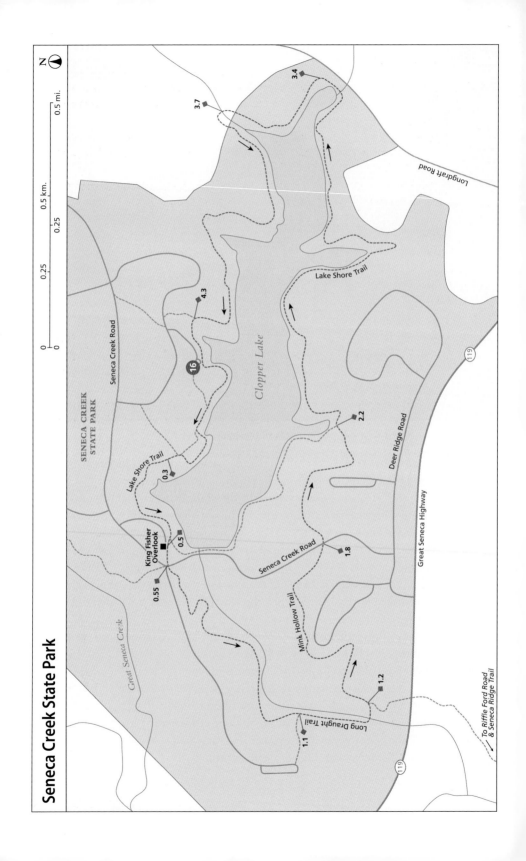

N

SENECA CREEK
STATE PARK

Seneca Creek Road

Great Seneca Creek

King Fisher Overlook

Lake Shore Trail

Clopper Lake

Lake Shore Trail

Seneca Creek Road

Deer Ridge Road

Mint Hollow Trail

Long Draught Trail

Great Seneca Highway

Longdraft Road

To Riffle Ford Road
& Seneca Ridge Trail

0   0.25   0.5 km.

0   0.25   0.5 mi.

3.7
3.4
4.3
16
0.3
2.2
0.5
0.55
1.8
1.1
1.2

119
119

Miles and Directions

0.0 Start at Clopper Lake's boat center (soda machines available). Ride west to the end of the circular drive and go straight into the grass on the other side. Follow Lake Shore Trail (blue) signs.

0.3 Lake Shore Trail (blue) drops you into an open field. On the other side of this field, you will notice the blue trailhead marker. Cross the field and continue on Lake Shore Trail. To the left is the dam.

0.5 Lake Shore Trail (blue) brings you right up to King Fisher Overlook. You can catch a nice view of the lake from here. Follow the remainder of the blue-blazed trail into the woods, at the back of the circular drive. Go down the little hill through the woods and immediately cross the road.

0.55 Long Draught Trail (yellow) begins catty-corner to where the Blue Trail ends.

1.1 Turn left on Mink Hollow Trail (white).

1.2 Bear left, continuing on Mink Hollow Trail (white) over a narrow boardwalk, crossing the creek.

1.8 Cross the park road. Continue straight on the white trail.

2.2 Mink Hollow Trail (white) comes to the lake. Turn right, following the trail around the lake.

3.4 This trail zips up on Longdraft Road. Cross Longdraft Road on the asphalt path. Once you're across the bridge, turn left through the guardrail and back on the trail around the lake.

3.7 This trail drops you down on a flat gravel path. Turn right. A left takes you to a dead end at the lake. Stay on this gravel path only about 20 feet. Then turn left across the creek to hook up with the path that continues to follow the perimeter of the lake.

4.3 Turn left, crossing over a little wooden bridge at the end of the alcove. Continue following the trail.

4.7 Arrive at the boat center and grab a soda from the soda machine. What a ride!

17 Seneca Greenway Trail

Don't mistake this section of the Seneca Greenway Trail, managed by Montgomery County, for the state-managed portion to the south, which runs along the banks of the creek from past Black Rock Mill and on down to the Potomac. The latter is closed to bikes, while the county's is multi-use. The Greenway Trail will take you along the Seneca Creek north of Route 355 toward Damascus through the rolling forests of the Great Seneca Creek Stream Valley Park.

Start: Route 355 Seneca Greenway Trail parking area
Length: 9.7 miles one way
Ride time: About 1.5-3 hours
Difficulty: Easy/moderate
Trail surface: Mostly singletrack
Lay of the land: Rolling trails along the Great Seneca Stream Valley Park

Land status: Public county land
Nearest town: Gaithersburg, MD
Other trail users: Hikers
Trail contacts: Montgomery County Parks, www.montgomeryparks.org, (301) 972-6581
Schedule: Open year-round

Getting there: From Route 270, take exit 11 to route 124 N (Montgomery Village Avenue). Turn left on Route 355 N (N. Frederick Road) and continue for a little over a mile. The parking lot will be immediately to your right after you cross Game Preserve Road. The trailhead is at the far end of the parking lot as you drive in. GPS coordinates: 39.167398, -77.229120.

The Ride

The state Seneca Greenway Trail was conceived shortly before the plan for the Schaeffer Farms trails was put into place. A coalition of MORE representatives was actively involved in the planning process and saw the development of the Greenway Trail (the state's portion) as the perfect chance to expand riding opportunities in the area. Unfortunately, at the time, the view of mountain biking was less than favorable in the eyes of some hikers. Rumor has it that during initial Greenway planning meetings at least one hiker member of the coalition of users said flatly that "I could not enjoy a trail if I knew bikes might ever go on it," and would not budge from his stance against making the trail a multi-use resource. That animosity, fortunately, ended up being a good thing for off-road cyclists. To appease the growing active user group, the Maryland Department of Natural Resources agreed to build (with MORE volunteers) what is now the Schaeffer Farm trails, with MORE's explicit requirement that the trail be multi-use. MORE's message to the hiking and equestrian community was simple: "We'll always share, even if you don't."

MORE clearly saw that the development of the Schaeffer trails was a step in the right direction, even if it meant not having access to the Greenway Trail. Unbeknownst

The Seneca Greenway Trail between Route 355 and Damascus Recreational Park is perfect for the beginner to advanced rider.

to all user groups, however, the county went ahead and began construction of a trail on the north side of 355 toward Damascus along the Great Seneca Stream Valley Park. And, when that trail was completed, the county announced it would be open to all, even though the state's section was hiker only. Despite vehement protests from the hiking community, county managers held their ground and kept the trail as a multi-use resource for everyone to enjoy.

Fast forward nearly two decades and the state portion of the Greenway Trail remains closed to bikes. But two new multi-use trails have been built in its general vicinity, the Seneca Ridge Trail (Ride 10) and the Seneca Bluffs Trail (Ride 9). Cyclists can now enjoy far more riding opportunities in the region, and hikers, despite their continued opposition to keep cyclists off "their" trails, no longer have to resort to just an out-and-back along the southern portion of the Greenway Trail. Instead, they can head out along the hiker-only portion and return along the multi-use portion, a win-win situation for almost everyone.

There are plans to extend the Greenway Trail from its current terminus into Damascus Recreation Park. Check www.montgomeryparks.org for additional information.

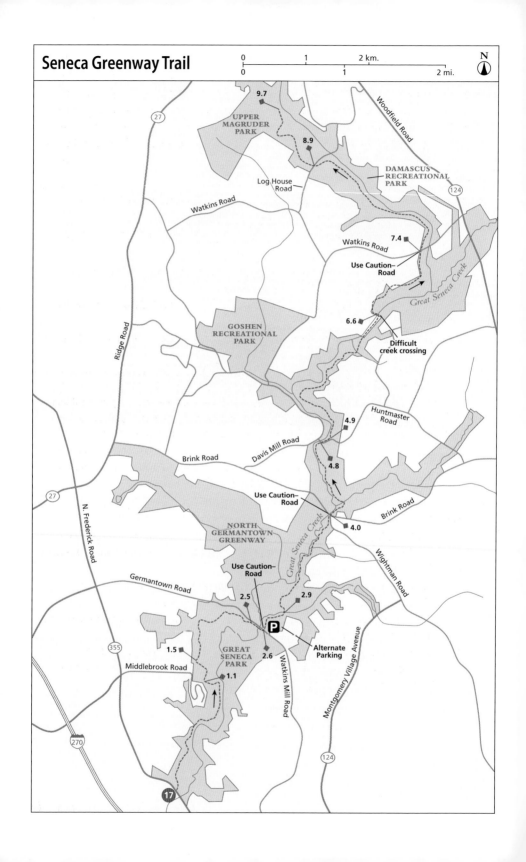

Seneca Greenway Trail

0   1   2 km.
0   1   2 mi.

N

27

UPPER
MAGRUDER
PARK

9.7

8.9

Woodfield Road

124

DAMASCUS
RECREATIONAL
PARK

Log House
Road

Watkins Road

7.4

Watkins Road

Use Caution–
Road

Great Seneca Creek

Ridge Road

GOSHEN
RECREATIONAL
PARK

6.6

Difficult
creek crossing

Huntmaster
Road

4.9

Davis Mill Road

4.8

Brink Road

27

Brink Road

Use Caution–
Road

4.0

N. Frederick Road

NORTH-
GERMANTOWN
GREENWAY

Great Seneca Creek

Wightman Road

Use Caution–
Road

Germantown Road

2.5

2.9

355

P

Alternate
Parking

Montgomery Village Avenue

1.5

GREAT
SENECA
PARK

2.6

Watkins Mill Road

Middlebrook Road

1.1

270

124

17

The trail is clearly marked and blazed blue. Stick to the blue blazes and you will be fine. The ride includes several road crossings and at least one difficult creek crossing (6.6) where you will undoubtedly get wet. Be prepared, especially if the temperatures are low. The markers below are reference points for those intersections, and for the creek crossing. Other than one trail that veers to the left to an alternate parking area on Midcounty Highway the trail is easy to follow and requires very little guidance.

Miles and Directions

0.0 Begin the ride at the trail marker behind the lot kiosk. Enter the trail and stay to the left and follow the clearly marked blue blazes.

0.7 Continue to the right. (The left fork will take you to the Midcounty Highway parking area.)

1.1 Overlook to the right.

1.5 Stay to the right at this intersection. (The trail to the left will take you to Middlebrook Road and Midcounty Highway.)

2.5 Reach Watkins Mill Road. Turn right to go over the Great Seneca Creek and continue for about 0.1 mile.

2.6 Turn left to continue on the Seneca Greenway Trail; the trailhead is clearly marked. There is a small parking area here.

2.9 Continue to the left at this intersection and continue to follow the blue blazes. The trail straight ahead will simply climb straight up, while the path to the left will circle around to make the ascent more gradual. This area of the Seneca Greenway is crisscrossed with several trails. You could feasibly spend some time exploring the many paths that turn in and out of the main Greenway Trail. Only the Greenway is blazed blue, however.

4.0 Reach the intersections of Brink Road and Wightman Road. Use caution on this crossing. The trail will continue on the opposite side along Brink Road and it is clearly marked: 1 MILE TO HUNTMASTER RD. The trail continues to be blazed blue.

4.8 The trail veers sharply right; you are now riding parallel to Huntmaster Road.

4.9 Cross Huntmaster Road. Use caution here. The trail is clearly marked: TO WATKINS ROAD.

6.6 Reach a difficult creek crossing of the Great Seneca Creek. You can continue and complete the remaining 2.1 miles, or simply turn around and head back; no shame, especially if it's a cold day.

7.4 Reach Watkins Road. Turn right and then left to get back on the trail, which is clearly marked: TO LOG HOUSE RD.

8.9 Reach Log House Road. Continue across the street. (The trail to the left will take you to the Log House Road parking area.)

9.7 Reach the paved path at Damascus Recreational Park and the terminus of the Seneca Greenway Trail. There's a conveniently placed bench for a quick break before you make your way back to your vehicle.

18 Cabin John Regional Park

Located in Montgomery County, Maryland, Cabin John Regional Park is a great destination for any local mountain biker who can't get away to more remote locations. It's also great for the visitor looking for a quick ride close to the urban landscape. Cabin John offers a variety of rolling trails that descend and run parallel to Cabin John Creek and within the vicinity of I-270 and the Capital Beltway. Its proximity to the Beltway; Rockville, Maryland; and the conveniences of Montgomery Mall makes it the ideal urban getaway.

Start: Pauline Addie Betz Tennis Center
Length: 7.1 miles
Ride time: About 1–2 hours
Difficulty: Easy/moderate
Trail surface: Mostly singletrack
Lay of the land: Rolling wooded trails
Land status: Public county park

Nearest town: Potomac, MD
Other trail users: Hikers
Trail contacts: Cabin John Regional Park Manager's office, (301) 299-0024
Schedule: Sunrise to sunset year round. Operational hours of other facilities vary; call park manager's office directly for information

Getting there: From the Capital Beltway (I-495) take the 270 Spur North. Take exit 1 onto Democracy Boulevard and turn left. The Pauline Addie Betz Tennis Center will be on your right approximately 0.5 miles after the exit. If you reach Seven Locks Road you've gone too far. GPS coordinates: 39.033119, -77.149901.

The Ride

Say the phrase "Captain John" several times. Continue saying it long enough, and you'll begin to notice that *captain* slurs into *cabin*. At least that's what local folklore suggests. Rumor has it that the area was named after the famed British explorer Captain John Smith, although there is no evidence to back this up.

Folklore also suggests that the area was named for either one of two hermits that lived along the banks of the creek or after a pirate who buried his treasures along the creek.

The first hermit kept to himself and hunted along the valley, where he lived in a cabin. Others in the area referred to him as "John of the Cabin." Eventually, when the area was developed, the name evolved into Cabin John.

The second was a commoner, an English settler named John who came to the colonies with his fiancée to escape the wrath of her nobleman father. On the trip to the colonies his fiancée fell ill and ultimately died in Alexandria shortly after their arrival. Out of fear that her father would make the journey to claim her body for interment at the family plot in England, John had her buried in an unmarked grave in Alexandria where he could visit and grieve for her. John followed the river valley and

Cabin John is a popular urban destination.

ultimately settled in a cabin in the area that is now Cabin John. Again, locals referred to him as "John of the Cabin."

The last legend suggests that a pirate captain named John sailed upriver to Little Falls and then traveled inland to the area near the creek. There he buried his treasures to hide his riches from his enemies, killing the men who helped him, so that they would never speak of the location or return to rob him.

I personally prefer the legend of Captain John Smith the explorer, who certainly spent lots of time exploring the area, and whose adventures helped shape the colonies. After settling in Jamestown, Virginia, in the winter of 1607, Captain Smith survived an ambush by Native Americans. He was captured and taken as prisoner to the chief of the tribal confederacy, Chief Powhatan. Impressed by Smith's confidence and determination, Powhatan interviewed his captive to learn more about his travels and allowed Smith to participate in a ritual, a test to determine his worth and courage.

YOU MAY RUN INTO: DAVID SCULL

I first met David Scull during a local county meeting where I spoke on behalf of mountain bikers seeking access to a trail in Montgomery County in about 1993. Dave introduced himself as a cycling advocate and together we spent some time talking about the issues that concerned cyclists in the region. Later, Dave, a DNR representative, and I walked the woods in what is now Schaeffer Farms and flagged some of the initial trails that would eventually be built there. We've ridden together on countless occasions, and I've had the pleasure of taking him back home to Peru to ride the trails of my original neck of the woods.

Dave is a gentleman and an articulate diplomat. He's built trails with the rest of us, and wielded a McLeod on more occasions than many can count, but it's his off-the-trail efforts that have set him aside. He's spent countless hours reaching out to local park managers and politicians, educating them on the merits and benefits of off-road cycling. He's even taken a few on rides around area trails, including here at Cabin John, his neighborhood loop. Through his efforts, the off-road cycling community has created and maintained relationships with area politicians. While intangible, these have been critical in getting access to, and permission to build, miles of trails in the region.

You'll often find Dave and his wife Nancy riding Cabin John and other trails in the Montgomery county region. He'll be easy to spot, since he's the self-proclaimed "oldest mountain biker alive." If you ever have the pleasure to meet him, give him a pat on the back for all the efforts he's made to ensure we all have off-road places to ride.

Painfully unaware of his fate, Smith endured and passed all of the challenges placed upon him. With the help of Pocahontas, Powhatan's eleven-year-old daughter, Smith survived and was made a subordinate chief of the tribe. After four weeks of captivity, Smith left the tribe in friendship and returned to Jamestown.

As a result of unrest, lack of supplies, and dissent within the colony Smith left Jamestown again to explore and map the lands of the Chesapeake Bay Region. Because of his efforts and mapping endeavors, the early colonists were able to more easily expand their settlements and survive in the new lands. References to "Captain

John's Run" (or Creek) that date back as far as the early 1700s would suggest that he traveled through here and perhaps that is how the area near the creek was named Captain John, and eventually slurred into Cabin John. However uncertain, this is the most romantic legend that suggests how the area got its name, and one that many residents in the area subscribe to.

This ride starts at the Pauline Addie Betz Tennis Center off Democracy Boulevard. If you are facing the tennis center, the trailhead will be on the left side of the parking area and is marked by a 6x6 timber post. Restrooms are available in the tennis center if you ask nicely. In this ride I detail a little-known loop through the park. The more common ride will take you along the Cabin John Trail as it parallels the creek from the main park to River Road. If you prefer to do the out-and-back, simply follow the blue blazes to the trail's terminus shortly after crossing River Road.

Miles and Directions

0.0 Enter the trail from the Pauline Addie Betz Tennis Center parking area.

0.1 Turn right as you reach Cabin John Creek.

0.3 Turn left at this intersection.

0.5 Stay to the left at this intersection.

0.6 Go over the small wood bridge and then immediately bear left to head up on the trail. The trail is blazed blue.

0.7 Stay left and continue following the trail as it parallels the creek.

1.0 Turn right and follow the trail as it climbs away from the creek.

1.1 Turn left to ride on Diamond Circle.

1.2 Stay to the right and then follow the trail to the left. (The trail to the right will simply take you up to the athletic field.) Continue following the blue blazes. Come out into a clearing and stay to the right to continue on the Cabin John Trail and then immediately bear to the left.

1.4 Stay to the left again and cross under the power lines.

1.5 Immediately after crossing the power lines stay to the left.

1.8 Continue right at this intersection; continue following the trail as it parallels the creek.

1.9 Bear left to reach Tuckerman Lane. (We'll take the right fork on the way back.) Use caution when crossing Tuckerman Lane. Turn left to head in the direction of the scout gate and access point to the campground. Continue riding northwest on Tuckerman past the gate.

2.0 The trailhead to the north section of the Cabin John Trail is to the right and marked with a 6x6 post similar to the one we encountered at the beginning of the ride.

2.4 After crossing the bridge stay to the right. The majority of branches from the main trail are short access points.

2.6 Continue following the trail to the right as it parallels Cabin John Creek.

3.0 After going over a short wood bridge, turn right at this intersection. (The left fork will take you to the North Terminus of the Cabin John Trail at Goya Drive.)

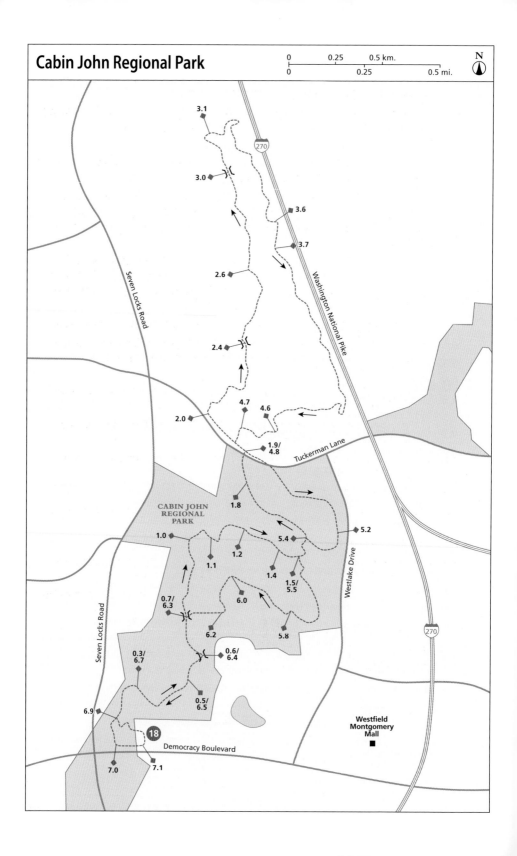

Cabin John Regional Park

0   0.25   0.5 km.
0   0.25   0.5 mi.

N

3.1
3.0
3.6
3.7
2.6
2.4
2.0
4.7
4.6
1.9/
4.8

Seven Locks Road
Washington National Pike
Tuckerman Lane

CABIN JOHN
REGIONAL
PARK

1.8
1.0
1.1
1.2
5.4
5.2
1.4
1.5/
5.5
0.7/
6.3
6.0
6.2
5.8
0.3/
6.7
0.6/
6.4
0.5/
6.5
6.9
18
7.0   7.1

Seven Locks Road
Westlake Drive
270

Democracy Boulevard

Westfield
Montgomery
Mall

3.1 Cross Cabin John Creek. At the immediate T intersection turn left and follow the trail as it climbs toward I-270. The trail will then turn right and south as it parallels the highway. You can hear it but can barely see it through the trees.

3.6 Turn left at this intersection and again left at the subsequent fork in the trail. (The right fork will head down a steep hill while the left will follow a more forgiving path.)

3.7 Stay to the left again.

4.6 Stay to the right and then left at the next fork. (The left fork follows the low side while the right fork will climb up and then descend a steep section of technical rocks.)

4.7 Stay to the left once again to come out on the Camp Ground Road. To the left is Tuckerman Lane and the access gate mentioned at 1.9. Head left to it, cross Tuckerman Lane, and turn left again to head back to the trail on the opposite side from which we popped out on 1.9.

4.8 Turn right into the Cabin John Trail and then immediately left to climb up on the Cabin John Trail as it parallels Tuckerman Lane for a short distance until you exit into the Cabin John Train Station parking area. Follow the road toward the left as it passes Cabin John Station and then bear right through a second parking area (5.1).

5.2 When the parking area ends you'll see the trailhead marked by a large 6x6 timber. Enter it.

5.4 Turn left at this intersection. You will double back on some of the initial trails you rode in. This is the intersection you first saw at 1.5. Cross under the power lines and then turn left into the trail on the opposite side.

5.5 Come out into the parking area for the Shirley Povich Field and turn left to head toward the Cabin John Ice Rink. (Restrooms are available here.)

5.7 Turn right and follow the signs toward fields 5, 6, and 7 and then bear right to continue following the restricted-access paved road.

5.8 Directly across from the tennis courts turn left into the gravel path and then immediately right to enter the singletrack.

6.0 Turn left and then left to join the Goose Neck Loop.

6.2 Turn left at this intersection and then, after a quick downhill, right. Continue to follow the blue blazes.

6.3 Turn left and go over the small wood bridge and then bear to the left.

6.5 Turn right and then quickly left to go over the small bridge. Shortly after, continue to the right. Do not ride on the Tulip Tree Trail; bikes are not permitted there.

6.7 After crossing the field, turn right. (If you continue straight, you'll reach the back of the Tennis Center.)

6.9 Stay to the right, continuing to follow the creek trail.

7.0 Turn left on the sidewalk that parallels Democracy Boulevard.

7.1 Turn left into the tennis center parking lot to complete the loop.

Ride Information

Local Information

City of Rockville
www.rockvillemd.gov

Bike Shops

Revolution Cycles
Rockville, MD
(301) 424-0990
www.revolutioncycles.com

Big Wheel Bikes
Potomac, MD
(301) 299-1660
www.bigwheelbikes.com

Fresh Bikes
Bethesda, MD
(301) 312-6159
www.freshbikescycling.com

Performance Bikes
Rockville, MD
(301) 468-0808
www.performancebike.com

Local Events and Attractions

Cabin John Mall: 11325 Seven Locks Road. Free children's entertainment, crafts, and more on the first and third Friday each month at 10:30 a.m. in the Cabin John Mall Atrium.

Rockville Farmers' Markets: Check www.rockvillemd.gov/farmers for seasonal schedules.

Accommodations

Chevy Chase B&B
Chevy Chase, MD
(301) 656-5867

19 Fairland Regional Park

Nestled along the border of Montgomery County and Prince George's County is this little gem of a park. Over the years, and thanks to the efforts of dedicated volunteers, the trails at Fairland have become a regional destination.

Start: The Fairland Regional Park main parking area by the playground and restrooms
Length: 8.3 miles
Ride time: About 1.5–2 hours
Difficulty: Easy/moderate
Trail surface: Mostly singletrack trails
Lay of the land: Rolling wooded trails
Land status: Public County Park

Nearest town: Burtonsville, MD
Other trail users: Hikers
Trail contacts: Montgomery County Parks, www.montgomeryparks.org, (301) 670-8080; Prince George's Parks, www.pgparks.com; MORE, www.more-mtb.org
Schedule: Open year-round, sunrise to sunset

Getting there: From the Capital Beltway (I-495) take I-95 north to exit 33B to merge onto MD 198 W toward Burtonsville. Continue for 1.4 miles and turn left onto Old Gunpowder Road. After 2 miles turn right on Greencastle Road and then right again onto Chelsea Park Lane. Continue straight to the stop sign and turn left. The main parking area will be in front of you. GPS coordinates: 39.082006, -76.929515.

The Ride

It's hard to believe how far Fairland has come since I first laid knobby wheels on it in the mid-1990s. My wife and I were fresh out of the army and had just bought a home in Burtonsville, MD. I generally packed the gear and bike and headed north to Patapsco Valley State Park (Rides 20 to 23) for my regular mountain-bike dosages, but more often than not time kept me from making the trip. So, one day I ventured out of the house in search of suburban trail opportunities. A quick glance at an area map showed that Fairland Regional Park was just around the corner, so I headed out to explore.

Back then there was a network of trails that crossed the park—nothing to write home about, but at least there were trails. For the most part, they followed the grade and were often in pretty bad shape. That said, the park was so close to the house, and the trailhead was literally just a stone's throw away, so I didn't complain. Plus, bikes were allowed, which was a luxury back in those days.

Roughly at the same time that I moved to Burtonsville, I was introduced to Austin Steo. Austin lived opposite me on the other side of Fairland, and we would often meet somewhere in the middle to spin our bikes through the woods. Back then I had just finished the third edition of this book and was heavily involved with the Mid-Atlantic Off-Road Enthusiasts (MORE), a local mountain bike social and advocacy

Fairland sights.

group that has grown to become a force in our region, as well as one of the most successful IMBA-affiliated clubs in the states. It was during those rides that Austin and I (well, mostly Austin) talked about the potential that Fairland offered, and how the trails could be rerouted and rebuilt to make them much more fun. On several occasions we left the bikes at home and simply walked through the woods envisioning what the place could become.

Austin acted on all those brainstorming sessions and reconnaissance outings, and as I phased out from MORE, he phased in and became the club's Maryland advocacy director. That's when he began working with the Fairland Park managers on a plan to improve the trails and overall riding experience within the park. Slowly but surely he cut and built the ribbon that now exists in the park. With the help of Austin's volunteer army—and the backing of MORE—the trails at Fairland were transformed from just a few unplanned miles to a fun and twisty network consisting of nearly 8 miles of trails. His job hasn't ended there, though. Today there are additional plans to add even more singletrack to the system, and chances are that by the time you read this chapter there will be a few additional miles of freshly cut ribbon at Fairland.

YOU MAY RUN INTO: AUSTIN STEO

I first met Austin back in the mid-1990s. Our good friend Dan Hudson (now with the Maryland Department of Natural Resources [DNR]) thought it would be a good idea for us to meet, especially since the trails at Fairland Regional Park were in need of some help. I remember riding with Austin through Fairland and him always envisioning how the trail would work best. "This section should be routed over there," he used to say. Or, "This creek crossing would be better if . . ." Austin was (and still is) always envisioning a better way for the trail to flow. That vision, and all of his hard work, eventually led to him leading the effort to create the network of trails highlighted on this ride. To this day Austin continues to be involved with Fairland in some capacity, but now has his hand in other projects as well. "While driving to Cedarville State Park to meet some friends for a ride I noticed a gated, underused park," he once told me. "I later explored it and saw a huge potential for trails. At that time I had just joined the MORE board and went down the long path of initiating a new trail system. Now when I see a full parking lot at Rosaryville State Park (Ride 29), it brings a smile to my face."

His love for mountain biking has even taken him further, and now Austin is the executive director of the Trail Conservancy (www.trailconservancy.org), a nonprofit organization whose mission is to provide assistance in developing, building, and maintaining natural-surface trails using sustainable design principles. He's still hard at work and involved in several other trail-building projects in the region, including the Emmitsburg, Maryland, project (Ride 8), as well as other trails in Montgomery County. If you do run into Austin, say hi, and ask him how he would have built that particular section of trail up ahead. He'll be happy to share his "trail vision."

Miles and Directions

0.0 Start from the main parking area closest to the restrooms. Continue to the right along the paved trail. The playground will be on your left. The trail entrance is clearly marked.

0.1 Immediately upon entering the dirt trail, follow the trail to the left and toward the Holly Trail.

0.15 Continue following the Holly Trail straight.

0.4 The trail continues to the right. (The left fork is a short neighborhood connector.)

0.57 The trail curves sharply to the right and then curves left as it crosses the creek.

0.7 Reach the entrance of the Holly Trail loop. You can choose to go in either direction at this point. My preference is to do it in a clockwise direction, so follow the left fork.

0.73 Reach the entrance to the Silverwood Trail. Turn left onto this short out-and-back that includes some fun sections of singletrack. (Or you can choose to avoid it and continue right on the Holly Trail.). Additional trails are planned at the far end of the Silverwood Trail in the future.

1.3 Reach the terminus of the Silverwood loop, turn around, and head back. This can be an alternate entry point, although there is no parking available in the neighborhood beyond.

1.6 Back at the Holly Trail, turn left on Holly to continue the loop.

2.1 Continue to the right; the trail is clearly blazed blue.

2.4 Log ride and jump line.

2.7 Reach the starting point of the Holly Trail loop. Turn left and backtrack to the starting point of the ride.

3.2 Arrive back at the starting point of the ride; turn left to follow the Crow's Foot trail. The trail will be blazed blue.

3.8 Immediately after crossing a short bridge you'll reach an intersection. Continue to the right to stay on the Crow's Foot trail. (The left branch will connect you to the paved Paint Branch Trail. I document the paved loop in my other book, *Best Bike Rides, D.C.*

3.96 Turn left to continue on Crow's Foot and then cross the paved Paint Branch Trail. (You can bail to the right on either the dirt or paved trail if you want and reach the starting point of the ride in approximately 0.25 miles.)

4.4 Continue following the trail to the left. You're pretty much riding parallel to the paved Paint Branch Trail.

4.8 The baseball fields are to the right; continue following the trail as it curves to the left.

4.9 A future skills area will be built along the right side shortly after crossing the boardwalk. It may very well be there by the time you read this. Continue following the trail to the left toward Greencastle Road. The trail will dead-end at Greencastle Road, so be careful.

5.1 Turn left on Greencastle Road and then immediately left again to get back into the woods.

5.25 Cross the paved Paint Branch Trail and follow the signs for the Viper Trail. You'll immediately reach the utility right-of-way, turn left, and then immediately right to follow the Viper Trail in a clockwise direction. We will return to this spot shortly.

5.3 Continue following the Viper Trail to the right. The gravel road to the left will take you toward the Ice House complex, an alternate starting point for this ride.

5.87 You're back at the utility right-of-way. Turn right and then left, go over the paved Paint Branch Trail, and follow the Viper Trail in the other direction.

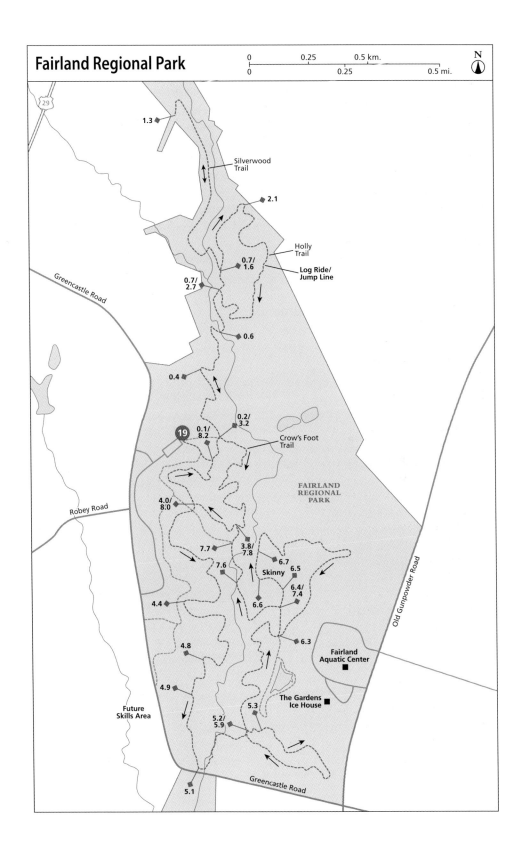

Fairland Regional Park

0   0.25   0.5 km.

0   0.25   0.5 mi.

N

29

1.3

Silverwood
Trail

2.1

Holly
Trail

0.7/
1.6

Log Ride/
Jump Line

0.7/
2.7

0.6

0.4

Greencastle Road

0.2/
3.2

0.1/
8.2

19

Crow's Foot
Trail

FAIRLAND
REGIONAL
PARK

4.0/
8.0

Robey Road

7.7

3.8/
7.8

6.7

7.6

6.5

Skinny

6.4/
7.4

4.4

6.6

6.3

4.8

Fairland
Aquatic Center

Old Gunpowder Road

4.9

The Gardens
Ice House

Future
Skills Area

5.3

5.2/
5.9

5.1

Greencastle Road

6.1 Continue following the Viper Trail to the right. A new trail that will extend the Viper loop will be built at this intersection, and chances are it is there when you read this. Look closely to the right and you'll notice an old family cemetery and the foundations of an old home.

6.2 Continue following the trail to the right at this and the very next intersection. This is the intended intersection for the new Viper Trail extension mentioned in the previous marker.

6.3 Reach the utility right-of-way. The Viper Trail and Roller Coaster continue straight, but we want to hit it in the opposite—down—direction. Turn left and follow it toward the Pine Trail loop. (Note: there are future plans for a parallel trail along the right-of-way that will take you up to the same spot we're headed now.)

6.4 Continue straight. We'll head left after the roller-coaster ride.

6.5 Turn left along the trail features. You can spend a little time playing on the skinnies and log rides here.

6.6 Continue following the Viper Trail to the right; you'll cross the Paint Branch Trail once again.

6.7 Cross the Paint Branch Trail again. This is the beginning of the Roller Coaster section, one of my favorite parts of the ride.

7.3 Back at the utility right-of-way. Turn right to head back down toward the creek.

7.4 Immediately after crossing the creek, turn left. The trail is very well marked.

7.5 Turn right at this intersection. Up to the left is the section of the Viper Trail we rode a few minutes ago.

7.6 Turn right when you reach the creek, and when you reach the paved Paint Branch Trail turn left to go over the bridge.

7.74 Immediately after crossing the bridge turn right into the singletrack. The trail is clearly marked.

7.78 You're back at Crow's Foot Trail. You can turn right and head back toward the beginning of the ride, but we'll head to the left to make sure we hit all of the trails in the park.

7.95 At the top of Crow's Foot turn left to continue following the trail back toward the starting point of the ride. There will be several short spurs to the left that can get you on the paved Paint Branch Trail if you prefer.

8.2 You're pretty much done. Turn left and then right on the paved Paint Branch Trail to the starting point of the ride.

8.3 The loop is complete.

Ride Information

Local Information
www.cityoflaurel.org

Bike Shops
Laurel Bicycle Center
Laurel, MD
(301) 490-7744
www.bicyclefun.com

REI
College Park, MD
(301) 982-9681
rei.com

Local Events and Attractions
Briggs Chaney-Greencastle Farmers' and Artisans' Market
www.bcgmarket.org

Dutch Country Farmers' Market
www.burtonsvilledutchmarket.com

Where to Eat

Pasta Plus
Laurel, MD
(301) 498-5100
www.pastaplusrestaurant.com

Howard County

T he Howard County area is rich in history and was once the hunting and farming grounds for various Native American tribes. By the 1600s, Captain John Smith had sailed up the Patapsco River, and Adam Shippley, the first known settler of Howard County, had arrived. At that time, a Native American settlement existed along the banks of the Patapsco River in what is today Elkridge. Shipley's home, granted to him by Lord Baltimore, was located along the banks of the Patapsco. It is here that the roots of the county's rich agricultural heritage began.

In the 1700s, the family of Charles Carroll, one of the original signers of the Declaration of Independence, acquired more than 10,000 acres of forests and farming grounds. They built an elaborate masonry home west of Ellicott City and called it Doughoregan. Today, heirs to the Carroll family still occupy the home, yet only about 3,000 acres of the original estate remain.

In 1772, John, Andrew, and Joseph Ellicott, Quakers from Bucks County, Pennsylvania, chose the picturesque wilderness area upriver of Elkridge to establish a flour mill. With the help of Charles Carroll, the Ellicotts revolutionized farming in the area. Wheat was chosen over tobacco, and fertilizer was first used to revitalize the county's soil. Soon, wheat, oats, and rye crops filled the rolling hills. Evidence of this rich agricultural heritage is proudly displayed in the county's flag, which incorporates a golden sheaf of wheat.

Howard County has not been immune to the sprawl and crawl that has affected the entire Washington, D.C., and Baltimore regions over the past three decades. Despite that, however, Howard County has managed to retain some of the rural flavor of its past. You'll see that firsthand as you ride through the trails of Patapsco Valley State Park. Along the way, serene forested surroundings isolate you from the daily grind and hectic world of the Washington–Baltimore area, transporting you deep into a peaceful wilderness, echoing the county's early beginnings.

Ride Information (Applies to Rides 20 to 22)

Local Information

Columbia Association, www.columbiaassocia
tion.com
Howard County Tourism Council
Howard County, MD, www.visithowardcounty
.com

Local Events and Attractions

For a complete and updated calendar of events
for Howard County, MD, go to www.co.ho.md.us.

Accommodations

Oak & Apple Bed & Breakfast of Distinction
Oakland, MD
(301) 334-9265

Deer Park Inn
Oakland, MD
(301) 334-2308

Red Run Inn
Oakland, MD
(301) 387-6606

The Wayside Inn Bed & Breakfast
Ellicott City, MD
(410) 461-4636

Hayland Farm
Ellicott City, MD
(410) 531-5593

There are several other hotels and motels in
Columbia and Ellicott City, MD.

Patapsco Valley State Park

Howard County contains perhaps one of the best riding destinations in the Washington, D.C./Baltimore regions, Patapsco Valley State Park. The park extends for over 30 miles along the Patapsco River from the Orange Grove area along Landing Road to the south, and the McKeldin Area to the northwest. Along the way the park contains nearly 70 miles of maintained trails, and most are open to bikes. Patapsco includes eight developed recreational areas, including the Avalon/Glen Artney/Orange Grove areas (Ride 22); the Hollofield, Hilton, Pickall, and Daniels areas (Ride 21); and McKeldin area (Ride 20). The park is rich in history, and as you ride its trails you'll see glimpses of the past hidden within the forests.

I've selected three rides within Patapsco that I think will introduce you to what this park has to offer. Each can be ridden independently or connected with each other to give you an epic adventure. You can easily connect the McKeldin, Woodstock, Daniels, and Pickall areas without leaving the park to craft an epic loop. Unfortunately, the Hilton and Avalon/Glen Artney/Orange Grove areas are segmented from the park by Historic Ellicott City. Still, a short section of road would allow you to tie these areas together for a ride that can extend more than 50 miles. MORE held its inaugural Patapsco Epic in 2014 offering riders the opportunity to ride either a 25-, 35-, or 50-mile loop. And an annual race, the Patapsco 100, pits riders against each other while they make their way around the park on a grueling 33-mile loop with more than 4,000 feet of climbing. Patapsco is not for the weary. The trails in the park are challenging, but incredibly rewarding; it's no surprise this 16,000-acre park has become a regional favorite for mountain biking.

20 McKeldin Area

Located in the southeastern corner of Carroll County, on the border with Howard and Baltimore County, and at the confluence of the Patapsco River's north and south branches, the McKeldin area of Patapsco Valley State Park is best known for its rolling, wooded terrain, smooth singletrack, log piles, river crossings, and great riding. McKeldin is a perfect place for beginning to intermediate riders looking to hone their skills on hilly singletrack or to pedal peacefully along the scenic Patapsco River. Advanced riders will also enjoy the nearly 7 miles of singletrack within the park and will be thrilled to explore dozens of trails on the other side of the river along the Woodstock area of Patapsco (HM F).

McKeldin is a unique stop in Patapsco Valley State Park. It's nudged into the southeast corner of Carroll County, where the north and south branches of the Patapsco River converge. Scenic Liberty Lake, one of Baltimore's primary water supplies, fills the valley just north of McKeldin. Damming in the north branch created Liberty Lake, less than 1 mile from the Switchback Trail. During late fall and winter, cyclists can enjoy a picturesque view of the lake at Liberty Dam Overlook, located at the northern end of Switchback Trail.

Switchback Trail is open to hikers, bikers, and equestrians alike and is quite popular throughout the year.

Start: Switchback Trail trailhead
Length: 3.7 miles
Ride time: About 0.75–1.5 hours
Difficulty: Easy to moderate
Trail surface: Smooth singletrack and doubletrack
Lay of the land: Rolling, wooded terrain in the Patapsco River Valley

Land status: State park
Nearest town: Ellicott City, MD
Other trail users: Equestrians and hikers
Trail contacts: Patapsco Valley State Park headquarters, (410) 461-5005
Schedule: Open from 9 a.m. to sunset; small vehicle fee

Getting there: From the Baltimore Beltway (I-695): Take I-70 west. Follow I-70 west for 8.5 miles to exit 83 (Marriottsville Road North). Follow Marriottsville Road North for 4 miles, passing through Marriottsville. The McKeldin area entrance road is on the right. Turn right on the entrance road and follow it uphill to the parking area. As you enter the park and just before the ranger station, look to your right. You'll see the trailhead. Park in the first lot immediately to the left as you drive in. GPS coordinates: 39.359358, -76.888906.

Miles and Directions

0.0 Start at the Switchback trailhead adjacent to the park entrance. The trail will be blazed white.

The Switchback trailhead is very easy to locate.

0.3 Continue following the trail as it curves to the left. Marriottsville Road is to the right, along with alternate parking areas.

0.5 Continue following the white blazes to the right. The Tall Poplar Trail is to your left.

0.7 Continue following the doubletrack to the left; the trail will now be blazed purple. (You will return from the fork to the right.)

0.8 Continue following the trail to the left.

1.0 Reach a shelter and trail kiosk. Continue following the trail to the right. (To the left is the Tall Poplar Trail, which will climb back up toward the starting point of the ride.) When you come out of the woods you'll see a sign for the Plantation Trail. Continue straight along the gravel road toward it past the basketball courts on the right.

1.2 Take the left fork at this intersection and then immediately right onto the red trail. The right fork will also descend to relatively the same location, but the ride along the left side is much better.

1.7 Reach the intersection of the Plantation Trail and the Switchback Trail. Continue to the right. The left side is open to foot traffic only.

1.8 Continue to the left to continue on the Switchback Trail. The trail to the right is the other fork of the Plantation Trail. (A right turn will take you back to the top and mile marker 1.2.)

2.0 Continue straight at this intersection. (You'll come back to this point to take the Switchback Trail to the right. You're simply going to do a quick out-and-back to extend the ride

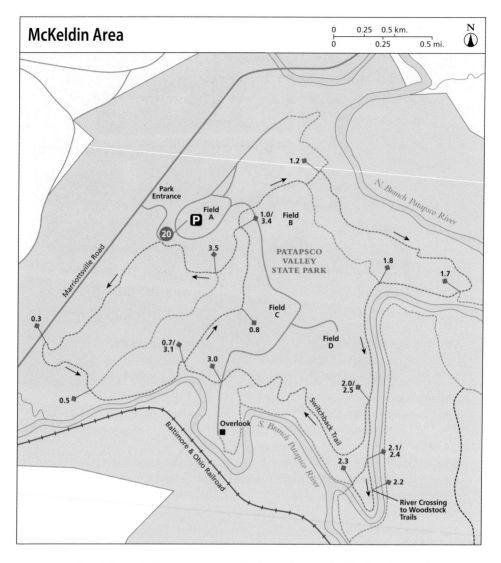

and mark the spot where you can cross the river and access the Woodstock area of Patapsco Valley State Park.)

2.1 The trail splits here; you can go in either direction. For now, continue along the river to the left/straight.

2.2 Pay attention to the left; this is the general area where you can shoot left and cross the river to explore the Woodstock trails on the other bank. We will continue straight.

2.3 Reach the entrance to the Rapids Trail. Make two successive right turns to return back toward the intersection of the Switchback Trail.

2.4 Continue to the left, backtracking along the river.

2.5 Make a sharp left onto the Switchback Trail and get ready for a quick climb up some great singletrack. Follow the white blazes.

MARYLAND'S RIVERS

Formed by the junction of the north and south branches west of Baltimore, the Patapsco River flows southeast for 65 miles to the Chesapeake Bay.

Maryland's longest river is the Potomac, flowing east along the state's southern border. The primary eastward-flowing rivers north of the Potomac are the Patuxent, Severn, Patapsco, and Susquehanna. Each of these rivers, and most of those on the eastern shore, enter the Chesapeake Bay.

The Potomac River has its origins in northeast West Virginia, flowing nearly 285 miles along the Virginia-Maryland border into the Chesapeake Bay. It is navigable for large ships as far as Washington, D.C.

Patapsco State Park's McKeldin area is situated at the junction of Carroll County, Howard County, and Baltimore County, on the edge of Maryland's Coastal Plain and its Piedmont Plateau. The Piedmont is a rolling upland, about 40 miles in width, and includes the Frederick Valley, which is drained by the Monocacy River.

3.0 Continue straight. A right turn will take you back to the park entrance along the road.

3.1 Reach the intersection with the Tall Poplar and Switchback Trails. Turn right to reride this section of trail back to the shelter and kiosk mentioned in mile marker 1.0.

3.4 Turn left onto the Tall Poplar Trail to begin the final climb to the end point.

3.5 Continue following the trail to the right. The left fork will shoot down to the Switchback Trail and mile marker 0.5.

3.7 Arrive back at the starting point. The loop is complete.

21 Daniels Area

Roughly between the McKeldin and Avalon areas of Patapsco Valley State Park is the largely undeveloped Daniels area. Extremely popular with paddlers, anglers, hikers, and mountain bikers, the Daniels area is an all-year playground rich in history.

Riders will see few glimpses of a once-thriving mill community as they make their way along the park's trails on either side of the Patapsco River. In 1886, communities along the banks of the Patapsco were devastated by a great flood and very little evidence of their existence remains. Today, the area is marked by the presence of the Daniels Dam. The dam once served as a primary source of energy for a denim and canvas mill that produced, among other items, tents for the Union Army. The mill remained operational until 1968 and in 1972 it, along with the town surrounding it, was destroyed by the power of the river fueled by tropical storm Agnes.

Today, the river is popular both above and below the dam. Fishermen flock to it year-round to catch smallmouth bass. Don't be surprised if on a cold winter day you spot a lonely fisherman along the banks of the frigid waters waiting for a bite.

For that reason, this ride is a warm-weather venture. A deep river crossing along the north side of the ride will force you to forge the river's waters, undoubtedly soaking you in the process. But don't fret; on a warm or hot day, the timely dip will be a refreshing respite during a challenging ride through the area's rugged terrain.

Start: Daniels area, shortly before reaching the dam
Length: 8.4 miles
Ride time: About 1.5-3 hours
Difficulty: Intermediate/difficult; one deep river crossing
Trail surface: Mostly singletrack
Lay of the land: Hilly, rugged singletrack along both banks of the Patapsco River; one short section of road

Land status: State park
Nearest town: Ellicott City, MD
Other trail users: Hikers, fishermen and anglers, paddlers
Trail contacts: Patapsco Valley State Park headquarters, (410) 461-5005
Schedule: Open daily, sunrise to sunset

Getting there: From I-70, take exit 87 to US 29 North. Continue for less than a mile and at the dead end turn right on MD 99 (Rogers Road). Stay on 99 for approximately 0.75 mile until you reach a traffic circle. Take the third turn to exit onto Old Frederick Road, then in 0.5 mile turn left onto Daniels Road. The parking area is in 1 mile on your left slightly before you reach the dam. Pay attention as you drive in; about 0.75 mile in you'll see a gate to your left, which is where you'll enter into the trails. GPS coordinates: 39.313746, -76.815634.

The loop at Daniels takes you very near an active railroad. Use caution!

Miles and Directions

0.0 From the first parking area after the gate, head back along Daniels Road in the direction you drove in.

0.1 Turn right and go through the gate to hop on the doubletrack. Stay right, away from the white blazed trail. Cross the stream and continue to the left.

0.2 Continue following the trail to the right. You'll begin a gradual climb. You are now on the lower side of the Switchplate Trail Loop.

0.27 Make a sharp right to begin a much more arduous climb. This trail leads to a very technical rocky section and delivers you to a sweet singletrack downhill. The trail is blazed with white metal markers on the trees.

0.6 You've completed the hardest part of the ride—really. There are a few more climbs to deal with, but none quite like this one. Continue following the trail to the right to the backside of Daniels. (The trail to the left will take you back down toward marker 0.2.)

1.1 You've descended down to the Patapsco River. Turn left onto the Old Main Line trail and ride parallel to the Patapsco River.

2.1 Bear left at this intersection. If you continue to the right you will reach the railroad tracks. Both trails meet up a little farther down the path, but the track to the left is both safer and nicer.

2.2 Continue to the left at this intersection. (The right fork will take you back toward the railroad tracks and marker 2.1. Had you stayed right at the previous intersection this is where you would have ended up.)

2.3 Stay to the right through the series of three close intersections and cross the stream. After crossing the stream stay right again and begin a nice gradual climb.

2.5 At the T intersection turn right onto the Ballard Trail. Begin your descent toward the Patapsco River.

2.7 Stay to the right as you head down to the river. If you continue straight you'll basically be following the fall line. The trail to the right switches back down to the river and is much more pleasant.

2.8 After a series of switchbacks you'll reach the Old Main Line trail again. Make a right, and then a quick left to get to the river. The trail continues directly on the opposite bank. Time to get wet! Once you cross, turn right onto the Thru Trail on the other side. The left fork will take you toward the Woodstock area of Patapsco Valley State Park (HM F).

3.0 The trail veers away from the river and begins to climb. It's another difficult one, but still not quite like the first.

3.1 You'll come out in the open under the power lines. Turn right and continue to climb. After clearing the first two towers, turn left onto the doubletrack and then take an immediate right into the singletrack. The trail is pretty easy to spot.

3.3 Continue following the path to the left; follow the orange markers.

3.4 Continue following the trail to the left.

3.5 The trail veers to the right.

3.7 Descend toward the railroad tracks below, continuing to follow the trail to the left as it parallels the tracks. You are now on the Thru Trail.

4.1 Shortly after you see the DANGER ACTIVE RAILROAD sign, the trail will turn left; Continue following it for about 100 yards and then cross the creek to the right and turn right again to go under the railroad tracks to get back on the Thru Trail.

4.5 Depending on the river level you should be able to hear the water going over the Daniels Dam. If you were to cross the river you'd be back at your car. Continue following the Thru Trail to the left as it parallels the river.

4.7 Go under the railroad tracks again. There will be some ruins to your left. Continue riding the trail that parallels the river. This is generally a crowded area of the park, so you'll spot people enjoying the river or even doing some rock climbing along the left side.

5.7 Go through the gate and hop onto Alberton Road. You are still paralleling the river.

5.8 Reach a small parking area at the end of Alberton Road and Dogwood Road. Continue straight and make a right on Dogwood Road and then a quick right onto Hollofield Road. Use caution along this next section; there is vehicle traffic and this is a narrow road. (Or you could turn right before the gate and cross the creek and then turn right onto Hollofield Road if you want.)

6.2 Immediately after crossing the bridge and railroad tracks, turn right into the small parking area to the right. The trailhead is immediately to your right along this spot. (There is a larger parking area to the left before you cross the railroad tracks that you can use as an alternate starting point to this ride, or to access the Pickall Trails of Patapsco.)

7.2 The trail climbs along the power line and turns left immediately after you pass the electric tower. Continue along the open field toward the single pole ahead. The trailhead turns into the woods to the right shortly after the electric pole. Heed the private-property signs all around you and don't stray from the trail.

Daniels Area

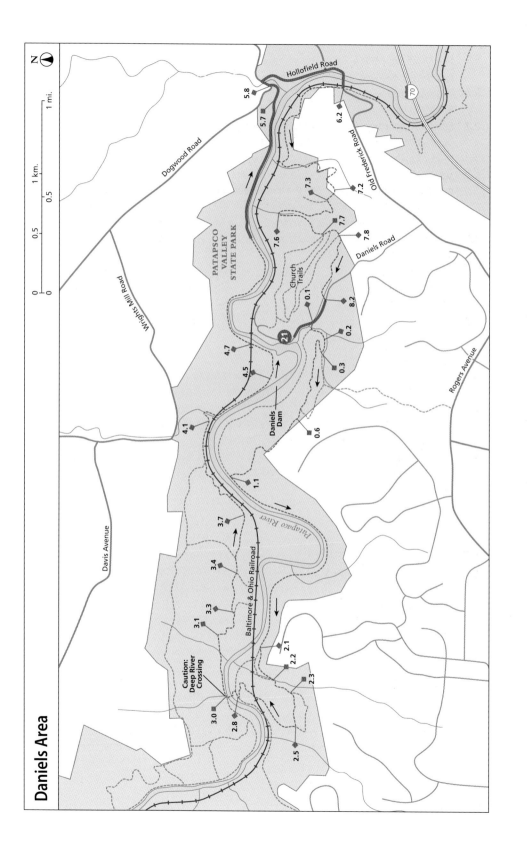

N

0   0.5   1 km.
0   0.5   1 mi.

Dogwood Road

Wrights Mill Road

Davis Avenue

PATAPSCO VALLEY STATE PARK

Hollofield Road

70

Old Frederick Road

Daniels Road

Church Trails

Rogers Avenue

Daniels Dam

Patapsco River

Baltimore & Ohio Railroad

Caution: Deep River Crossing

21

5.8
5.7
6.2
7.3
7.2
7.6
7.7
7.8
0.1
8.2
0.2
0.3
0.6
4.7
4.5
4.1
1.1
3.7
3.4
3.3
3.1
2.1
2.2
2.3
3.0
2.8
2.5

7.3 Turn left into the singletrack shortly after entering the tree line. (The doubletrack to the right will just take you back out to the power lines.) Shortly before the dip and creek crossing, make a sharp right into another section of buff singletrack. You are basically at the tail end of the ride and entering the Church Loops of the Daniels Area.

7.6 Make a sharp left onto the doubletrack. (A right turn will simply take you back out to the power lines.)

7.7– Go through the next four intersections to the right. These are the Church Loop trails. If you
7.8 still have something in you, give them a shot. These are four trails that run perpendicular to the trail you are on and parallel to each other up to the Methodist church. (The only intersection to the left will take you back to marker 7.3.)

8.0 Turn right into the Daniels Road Trail, clearly marked with a TRAIL sign. If you continue straight you'll reach a gate and private property.

8.2 Reach Daniels Road. Turn right.

8.4 The loop is complete.

22 Glen Artney/Avalon/Orange Grove/Hilton Areas

In Celtic mythology, the word Avalon refers to an island paradise. The Avalon area of Patapsco Valley State Park might also be thought of as a sort of singletrack paradise in the middle of two huge metropolitan areas. Known simply as the Avalon area by most cyclists, this small corner of the Patapsco Valley State Park is quite possibly one of Washington, D.C./Baltimore's most popular mountain-biking playgrounds. Avalon's terrain is oftentimes severe and nearly always challenging, but for serious off-roaders, these conditions represent nothing less than prime mountain-biking real estate.

It's worth noting that there are countless routes within Patapsco Valley State Park. Given this area's proximity to Baltimore, it's easy to understand why this ideal section of parkland is so popular with off-road cyclists. The area's popularity does, however, raise some concerns regarding overuse and trail damage. Hundreds of cyclists, hikers, and equestrians may crowd this trail system on any given weekend, making trail maintenance a very serious issue, not to mention a serious challenge. To maintain access to this priceless off-road habitat, make sure you get involved with local clubs, organizations, park officials, and other trail users to help preserve the trails and the integrity of the area.

Start: Rockburn Branch Regional Park
Length: 20+ miles
Ride time: About 3–5 hours
Difficulty: Difficult, due to tight singletrack over steep climbs, fast descents, and rugged terrain
Trail surface: Mostly rugged, hilly singletrack with some pavement
Lay of the land: Wooded and hilly terrain in a deep river valley

Land status: State park
Nearest towns: Ellicott City, Columbia, and Elkridge, MD
Other trail users: Hikers and equestrians
Trail contacts: Patapsco Valley State Park headquarters, (410) 461-5005
Schedule & fees: Open daily sunrise to sunset; small vehicle fee

Getting there: From Washington: Take I-95 north to exit 43B and merge onto route 100 W toward Ellicott City. Take exit 4 for MD 103 East; turn right at the traffic circle to continue on 103/Meadowbridge Road. Continue for approximately 1.5 miles and turn right onto Ilchester Road. Turn right onto Landing Road. The park entrance will be in approximately 1.3 miles on your right. Once you enter the park simply follow the road until it ends at a small traffic circle beyond field #3. Park here. You can also park along Landing Road (the lot beyond the park's entrance), although parking is very limited there. GPS coordinates: 39.220432, -76.761111.

The Ride

With more than 20 miles of singletrack and a seemingly endless network of trails winding up and down the river valley, this section of Patapsco Valley State Park is a do-it-yourselfer's paradise. However, I'm including one of my favorite loops for you

The creek crossings at Patapsco's Avalon area are a summer favorite.

to enjoy as well. My loop starts at neighboring Rockburn Branch Park (Ride 23), but you can also start either from the Glen Artney area's parking lot, or one of the Landing Road parking areas. Get a good look at the map of the trail system before you start. There's also a very handy and fairly detailed map available for $5 at Patapsco's ranger station. We highly recommend you get one before disappearing on such an extensive trail network. Plenty of people have gotten lost in this forest and have had to feel their way out in the dark. With a good park map indicating all the newest trails in the area, you won't get lost.

I also highly recommend you sign up for MORE's annual Patapsco Epic (www .moreepics.com). Like the MoCo Epic, MORE takes the hard part out of navigating the trails in the park by providing 25-, 35-, and 50-mile routes. They'll also provide you with a great map you can use as reference on future rides. Whatever route you end up choosing, I do highly recommend you incorporate the Avalon's Valley View Trail into the mix. This trail is not included in my loop—when I documented it it was still closed to bikes!. That ribbon of trail is by far my favorite trail out of every single segment detailed in this book. Closed for a considerable amount of time to bikes, the Valley View Trail is now open again thanks to the efforts of Patapsco's trail liaisons and army of volunteers. Check www.mtbdc.com, where I detail a couple of other loops in Patapsco that you can download and follow if you choose to.

For even more miles of riding, consider pedaling through the Orange Grove area or the trails at Rockburn Branch Regional Park, the starting point of our outing. Rockburn Branch Regional Park has an additional 6 miles of singletrack, just across the road (see Ride 23). You can also connect the Avalon area with other trails in Patapsco's vast network and feasibly ride all the way to McKeldin (Ride 20) and back for a truly epic adventure. Our ride starts from the parking area beyond Field #3 of Rockburn Branch Park (Ride 23).

Miles and Directions

0.0 From the far parking lot, ride down to the small traffic circle. Use the trailhead to your left adjacent to the paved path that leads toward the athletic fields. As soon as you enter the trail turn to the left.

0.1 As you come down the short hill and cross the small creek, turn right. Follow the fence line as it curves to the left.

0.2 Continue following the fence line to the left.

0.3 Stay to the left and follow the trail as it continues under the power lines.

0.5 Cross Landing Road and enter the Morning Choice Trail of Patapsco Valley State Park. Shortly after entering the trail, turn right.

0.6 Turn left into the singletrack trail. If you reach an open field you've gone too far. This trail is a narrow and twisty path that will circumvent an often muddy and troublesome area in the park. This trail has several log obstacles along the way.

1.5 Continue to the left at this T intersection.

1.6 Stay to the left again.

1.7 Cross the private road and continue straight on the trail in the opposite side.

1.8 Turn left on the main trail and prepare for a nice downhill. Use caution since this is a two-way trail.

2.0 The trail curves to the right.

2.4 Continue following the trail to the right and then as it curves up and to the left. Your first climb starts here.

2.5 Turn left and follow the purple blazes. (The trail to the right is a shortcut to the intersection at mile marker 2.9.)

2.6 Stay to the right after crossing the small ground-level bridge. The climb will get a little steeper here.

2.8 Turn right at this intersection.

2.9 Turn left on the yellow-blazed Morning Choice Trail. The trail will climb for a short time and then come out to the perimeter of the field. At dusk there are often multiple deer on the fields.

3.4 The trail turns back into the woods. As soon as you enter the tree cover you'll turn right to follow the connector trail to the orange-blazed Ridge Trail. (To the left the yellow trail continues back toward the intersection for mile marker 11.0; you can cut the ride considerably here if you choose.)

3.5 Turn left at this intersection; you'll now be on the orange loop as it descends (mostly) to the Patapsco River.

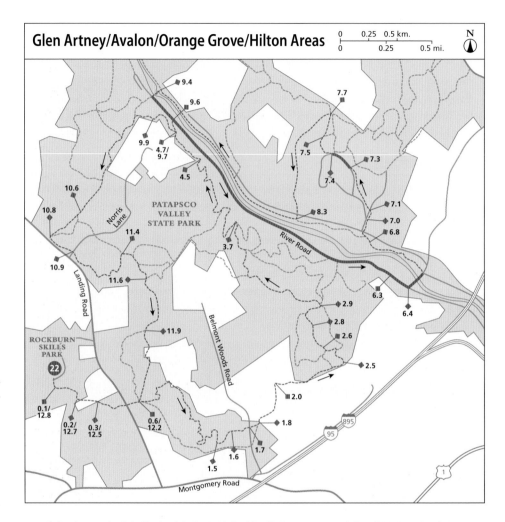

3.7 Stay to the left. (To the right is the Valley View Trail, now open to bikes. Ride it and make your way back to this spot.)

4.5 Stay to the left to continue on the orange trail.

4.7 Stay to the right and continue down the doubletrack to the road. (Our return trip will take us up the path to the left. This is another bailout point if you choose to head back.) When you reach the road, turn right.

6.3 The Avalon area is to the left. Restrooms and water are available here.

6.4 Turn left on Gun Road to go over the bridge that spans the Patapsco River. Immediately after crossing the bridge turn left into the singletrack trail that parallels the river.

6.8 Come out of the trail and head through the parking area and go under the tunnel that crosses the railroad tracks toward the upper and lower Glen Artney areas.

7.0 At this point you have three options. You can climb up on the road to the left, continue straight and turn left to climb up on the trail adjacent to the restrooms, or take the Soapstone Trail, slightly ahead to the left as you ride on the right fork. For this ride, take the right

YOU MAY RUN INTO: ERIC CRAWFORD OR ED DIXON

Back in the early days of the Mid-Atlantic Off-Road Enthusiasts (MORE), the club began a trail liaison program. The program basically designated one or two people who would be MORE's voice in a park or regional jurisdiction when it came to any issues related to mountain biking. I was lucky to serve as Patapsco's first liaison for a short period of time (a long time ago). By virtue of that, I'm incredibly fortunate to be included in the same company as two of our region's most successful liaisons and mountain bike ambassadors, Eric Crawford and Ed Dixon, MORE's current representatives in Patapsco.

Eric and Ed have been instrumental in fostering a relationship with Patapsco's managers and in helping develop "connectivity" in the park's vast trail network. Their efforts have yielded phenomenal results. In 2013 the inaugural Patapsco 100 took place, largely due to Ed's efforts in the northwest portion of the park along the Hollofield, Daniels, and Woodstock Areas. And, in 2014, MORE held the inaugural Patapsco Epic. The ability to do so hinged on their efforts, leadership, and a small army of volunteers.

Both Eric and Ed will be quick to pass the praise to every volunteer who helped achieve their vision. Rightly so; they should all be thanked. But without the drive, determination, and leadership of both Eric and Ed, Patapsco would continue to be a segmented system of trails.

Both Ed and Eric have lived in the vicinity of the park for nearly two decades. They both know the trails and have focused their energy on making them better for everyone. Their proudest achievements continue to be the way people have responded to their calls for help and the hours they have amassed maintaining and building new trails for all of us to enjoy.

I'm grateful that their efforts have led to the reopening of the Valley View Trail in the Avalon area of the park, quite possibly one of the best ribbons of singletrack in our region. When I was Patapsco's liaison we were forced to compromise on access to that trail to keep other sections of the park open to bikes, a decision that weighed heavy on me for many years. The joy that reopening that trail brought to me is immeasurable, and when you ride it, you'll understand why.

So, if you come upon Eric or Ed in the park—chances are they'll be working a trail so we can ride it—stop and lend them a hand. And thank them for all the work they continue to do to make the trails at Patapsco the most popular destination in our region.

Ed Dixon (left) and Eric Crawford. Patapasco's champions.

fork to the Soapstone Trail to the top. Either option will be a grueling cat-4 climb to the top, but it's worth it, trust me . . .

7.1   Continue straight through this intersection and then follow the trail to the left to join the road, one final push on this climb. The trail to the right is one of the options I outlined at 7.0.

7.3   Turn right on the pavement; had you taken the road climb, this is where you would have ended up.

7.4   Continue on the road to the split and follow it to the right through the small parking area. Go through the gate and continue on the doubletrack as it climbs slightly to the left. The trail is blazed red.

7.5   Continue straight on the path following the red blazes. The trail to the left is hiking only.

7.7   Turn left into the Vineyard Trail and enjoy one of the best singletrack descents in the region.

8.3   Turn right on the paved path.

9.4   Turn left and walk over the hanging bridge. As soon as you cross the bridge turn left on the road.

9.6   Turn right into the dirt path as it climbs into the tree cover. This is the same point where we exited on marker 4.7.

9.7   Make a sharp right and continue on the orange trail.

9.9   Stay left at this intersection and follow the blue blazes.

10.6   Continue to the right at this intersection.

10.8   Turn left at the trail sign shortly before you reach Landing Road. Follow the trail as it slightly climbs and rides parallel to Landing Road.

10.9   Cross the road and continue on the trail straight across.

11.0   Continue straight.

11.4   Turn right at this intersection. You are now on the yellow loop. Stay right again to follow the red blazes.

11.6   Stay to the right again and continue following the yellow blazes.

11.9   Stay to the left. The fork to the right will ultimately take you to the same place but it is a longer route.

12.2   Continue to the right. At this point you are doubling back along the trail you came in on and heading back to Rockburn Branch Park.

12.3   Cross Landing Road and enter Rockburn Branch Park.

12.5   Turn left into the second turn that enters the tree cover.

12.7   Continue following the trail and fence line to the right and then swing left to cross the creek.

12.8   Follow the trail to the right and out into the parking area.

12.9   Complete the loop.

23 Rockburn Branch Regional Park

The Rockburn Branch Park area is an excellent place to introduce people to mountain biking. Its rolling trails give the novice to intermediate cyclist a chance to focus on developing skills rather than trying to make it up the next climb. Don't let this situation fool you, though. Rockburn is also a great place for the advanced cyclist to enjoy Howard County's great outdoors. And its proximity to Patapsco Valley State Park makes it a great addition to any ride. If you want to pack on the miles, you should definitely combine Rockburn's picturesque trails with the paths of the Avalon area.

Rockburn is also home to the award-winning Rockburn Branch Skills Park. The park is a compact cycling playground that includes a pump track, three jump lines, and various other skill-building obstacles where you can hone your riding skills. It is quite feasible to spend a few hours in this little gem without leaving its cozy confines.

Start: The Rockburn trails can be accessed from various locations; I recommend parking in the parking area beyond field #3. From there you can easily access the dirt road that leads up to the Skills Park, or the trailhead that will lead you into the majority of the natural surface trails on the south side of the park.

Length: Varies, depending on trails ridden. There are 6.6 miles of natural surface trails at Rockburn.

Ride time: Varies, depending on trails ridden and skill level

Difficulty: Easy, with mostly doubletrack trails and very few elevation changes

Trail surface: Mostly doubletrack, some singletrack, and several sections of asphalt, mostly on the park's north and west sides.

Lay of the land: Criss-crossing trails connecting various sports fields and the Rockburn Skills Park. Option to connect to Patapsco Valley State Park's Avalon area.

Land status: Howard County Regional Park

Nearest town: Columbia, MD

Other trail users: Hikers, equestrians

Trail contacts: Howard County Department of Recreation and Parks, (410) 313-4700, TTY (410) 313-4665; Rockburn Branch Park Manager, (410) 313-4955

Schedule: 7 a.m. to dusk (or as posted)

Getting there: Take I-95 north to exit 43B and merge onto Route 100 West toward Ellicott City. Take exit 4 for MD 103 East. Turn right at the traffic circle to continue on 103/Meadowbridge Road. Continue for approximately 1.5 miles and turn right onto Ilchester Road. Turn right onto Landing Road. The park entrance will be approximately 1.3 miles on your right. Once you enter the park simply follow the road until it ends at a small traffic circle beyond field #3. Shortly before you reach the traffic circle you will notice a dirt road to the right. This is the access point to the Rockburn Branch Skills Park. GPS coordinates: 39.220432, -76.761111.

One of the most popular riding destinations in the Washington, D.C./Baltimore area is Patapsco Valley State Park. But not many people know that adjacent to Patapsco Valley State Park is Rockburn Branch Regional Park, part of Howard County's 7,000-acre scenic park system. This vibrant parcel of parkland is managed by Howard County and has more than 6 miles of dirt trails on which to ride and a brand new skills park (www.rockburnskillspark.com), including an extremely popular jump line and pump track.

Although not nearly as technical or hilly as the trails in Patapsco, Rockburn Branch offers a series of well-marked trails that will delight any mountain-bike lover. The park, located in northern Howard County, is not only a trail playground but is also a popular destination for many sports enthusiasts. There are more than eight softball and baseball fields, numerous basketball courts, several soccer and football fields, four tennis courts, and several children's play areas. In addition, during the spring and summer months, the park has a snack and concession stand offering freshly cooked burgers and hot dogs. Rockburn is also a popular picnic destination for those less interested in adrenaline and more in pleasing the palate.

Rockburn is minutes away from the heart of Columbia, Maryland, one of this country's youngest planned communities. Designed to encourage interaction among its citizens, the thirty-two-year-old city of Columbia has 2,900 acres of open space,

The Rockburn Skills Park has become a favorite addition to our regional stock of riding destinations.

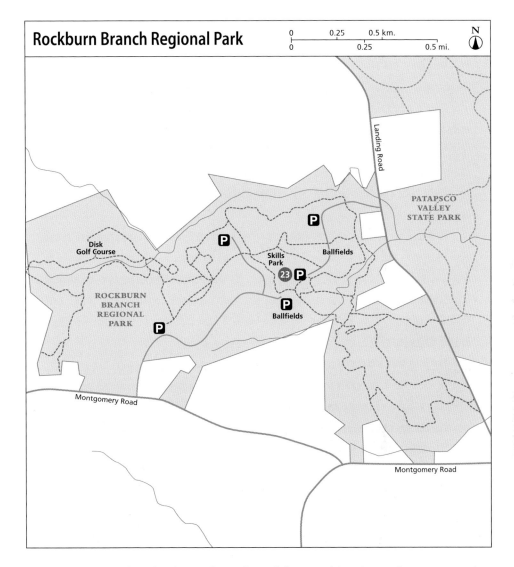

Rockburn Branch Regional Park

0   0.25   0.5 km.
0   0.25   0.5 mi.

N

Landing Road

PATAPSCO
VALLEY
STATE PARK

Disk
Golf Course

Skills
Park

Ballfields

P

P

P

23 **P**

ROCKBURN
BRANCH
REGIONAL
PARK

P

Ballfields

P

Montgomery Road

Montgomery Road

more than 78 miles of pathways for walking, biking, and jogging, and a vast network of plazas and public areas. The streets and neighborhoods are named after historical figures as well as historic locations from Maryland's past. Its layout partially follows the original land grants made by five of the six members of the Calvert family, founders and proprietors of the royal colony of Maryland.

Miles and Directions

Rockburn Branch is compact and the trails are well marked and easy to follow. For that reason, I'm only providing you with a starting point and general guidance on where to head. Park at the far end of the parking area beyond field #3 and just past

YOU MAY RUN INTO: MELANIE NYSTROM

Rockburn was just another nice park in Howard County until Melanie Nystrom walked into the picture.

During a family visit to the Baltimore area in the mid-1990s, Melanie ventured into the trails at Patapsco. Four hours later, Melanie had found her passion. "After that ride I simply couldn't get enough," she told me. "I felt rejuvenated; riding in the woods helps me have clarity in my life. It helps me forget about the distractions of life for a while. The minute I get off the bike, I want to be back on it. Biking makes me a better person, a better parent, I just love it!"

That love for cycling, and becoming a parent, led Melanie to look for chances to spend more time with her kids and enjoy the sport she loves so much. Shortly after she moved to Ellicott City in 2006, a perfect opportunity arose. Melanie volunteered to become Rockburn's MORE trail liaison to lead the collaborative effort with Howard County, IMBA, MORE, and several area businesses, including REI, Diamondback, and CLIF Bar, to build the Rockburn Branch Skills Park.

The idea was simple: Many kids want to ride on natural-surface trails, but generally, their parents don't. The skills park, which is in a relatively confined space, allows parents to mindfully watch over their children as they practice on their bikes. Some parents have even joined in the fun and graduated to become accomplished mountain bikers themselves.

The skills park has several mountain bike lines that test a rider's ability on what they may encounter on a regular regional trail. Each line progressively gets harder, culminating in a technical uphill rock garden that will test the most experienced cyclist. In between these skills sections are two jump lines and a compact but extremely fun pump track. Like the mountain bike lines, the jump lines offer easier and advanced alternatives. Novice riders can practice their handling skills along bermed turns whlle more advanced riders hone their piloting maneuvers over the multiple tabletop jumps.

"The skills park is very special to me," said Melanie. "We forged a very successful partnership with Howard County, MORE, and several regional businesses to build and maintain a park that both kids and adults in the area can enjoy." That effort has paid off. Rockburn recently won IMBA's Community

Bike Park Award, which recognizes "well-designed bike parks that accommodate a variety of skill levels, with progressive features and flow-based designs that encourage cyclists of all abilities, on all kinds of bikes, to ride together and learn from one another in the same space, at the same time."

Melanie is primarily responsible for making sure the park is in tip-top shape, and it always is; she loves the attention the skills park receives. All who know her and her passion for riding clearly know that she is a driving force at Rockburn and the reason for its success. If you happen to see her, say hi, and thank her for a job well done.

the dirt road that leads up to the skills park (you can also park by the skills park along the dirt road). From there you can access both the skills park (up along the dirt road to the left) or the trailhead that will give you access to the park's natural-surface trails (along the small traffic circle). This spot is also the starting point for Ride 22, Patapsco Valley State Park, Avalon.

Additional Riding: If you are yearning for more riding, follow the yellow trail under the power lines toward Landing Road and the trailhead (Morning Choice Trail) into Patapsco Valley State Park (see Ride 22). There are more than 20 miles of great riding in this portion of Patapsco, with access to nearly 50 more.

Ride Information

Local Information

Columbia Association
Columbia, MD
(410) 715-3000
www.columbiaassociation.com

Local Events and Attractions

Howard County
www.visithowardcounty.com

Accommodations

There are several hotels and motels in Columbia and Ellicott City, MD

24 Northern Central Rail-Trail

This converted rail-trail leads its visitors across Maryland's beautiful fields and meadows, past forests and rural farmland, and along the rushing waters of Little Falls and Gunpowder Falls. As you pedal along, you'll pass through the many historic little towns whose whole history is based upon the corridor's connection between Baltimore and Harrisburg. Celebrate the thousands of volunteers who helped make this 20-mile stretch of uninterrupted rail-trail possible by taking time to enjoy this converted and historic old rail line. Continue an additional 20.5 miles along the trail's latest extension, the York Heritage County Rail-Trail, all the way to York, Pennsylvania.

Start: Ashland parking lot
Length: 19.7 miles one way to the Pennsylvania state border. Continue an additional 20.5 miles along the York Heritage County Rail-Trail to York.
Ride time: About 2–3 hours one way
Difficulty: Moderate, due to length
Trail surface: Flat, hard-packed dirt trail
Lay of the land: A rail-trail ride through Maryland's scenic Piedmont region

Land status: Public right-of-way
Nearest town: Baltimore, MD
Other trail users: Hikers, equestrians, and dogs
Trail contacts: Gunpowder Falls State Park, (301) 592-2897; Rails-to-Trails Conservancy, (202) 797-5400
Schedule: Open daily, from dawn till dusk

Getting there: From the Baltimore Beltway (I-695): Take I-83 north 5.5 miles to exit 20 (Shawan Road). Go east on Shawan Road less than 1 mile, then turn right on MD 45 (York Road). Go 1 mile and turn left on Ashland Road. Follow Ashland Road 1.5 miles, passing Hunt Valley Shopping Center on your left. Stay right on Ashland Road (do not bear left on Paper Mill Road) to the parking lot for the southernmost starting point on the Northern Central Rail-Trail.

Public transportation: From downtown Baltimore, take the Central Light Rail Line north to Hunt Valley Station. Cross MD 45 to Ashland Road and follow the driving directions to the starting point. Total distance from the station is approximately 1.8 miles. GPS coordinates: 39.495282, -76.638301.

The Ride

Back when rails were king, the Northern Central Railroad was among the few rail lines dominating the Mid-Atlantic, carrying everything from milk, coal, and US mail to presidents of the United States. For nearly 134 years, the Northern Central Railroad was the locomotive link that carved its way through Maryland's hilly Piedmont region and Pennsylvania's rolling farmlands. It connected Baltimore with Gettysburg, York, and Harrisburg, Pennsylvania.

Scores of small towns sprang up along the line, prospering from Northern Central's service to the large cities. Such towns as Freeland, Bentley Springs, Parkton,

IN ADDITION: RAILS-TO-TRAILS

The mission of the Rails-to-Trails Conservancy is to "enhance America's communities and countryside by converting thousands of miles of abandoned rail corridors and connecting open spaces into a nationwide network of public trails."

Every large city and small town in America, by the early twentieth century, was connected by steel and railroad ties. By 1916, the United States had laid nearly 300,000 miles of track across the country, giving it the world's largest rail system. Since then, other forms of transportation, such as cars, trucks, and airplanes, have diminished the importance of the railroad, and that impressive network of rail lines has shrunk to less than 150,000 miles. Railroad companies abandon more than 2,000 miles of track each year, leaving unused rail corridors overgrown and idle.

It wasn't until the mid-1960s that the idea to refurbish these abandoned rail corridors into usable footpaths and trails was introduced. In 1963, work began in Chicago and its suburbs on a 55-mile stretch of abandoned right-of-way to create the Illinois Prairie Path.

In 1986, the Rails-to-Trails Conservancy was founded, its mission specifically to help communities realize their dreams of having a usable rail corridor for recreation and nonmotorized travel. At the time the conservancy began operations, only 100 open rail-trails existed. Today, nearly 2,000 trails are open to the public, totaling more than 22,000 miles of converted pathways. The Rails-to-Trails Conservancy is currently working on more than 700 additional rails-to-trails projects with a potential of an additional 8,200 miles of potential trails.

Ultimately, its goal is to see a completely interconnected system of trails throughout the United States. If you're interested in learning more about rails-to-trails and wish to support the conservancy, please contact:

Rails-to-Trails Conservancy
1100 17th Street, NW
Washington, D.C. 20036
(202) 331-9696
www.railtrails.org
railtrails@transact.org

Whitehall, Monkton, Corbett, Phoenix, and Ashland all sent their flour, milk, paper, coal, textiles, and other goods to Baltimore markets.

The Northern Central also served in the Civil War, carrying wounded soldiers from the bloody battlefields of Gettysburg south to Baltimore hospitals. Abraham

Lincoln rode the rail line north to Gettysburg to deliver his famous Gettysburg Address. It later carried his casket through Gettysburg on its way to Harrisburg, as it made its way to his burial site in Springfield, Illinois, following his assassination in April 1865 at Ford's Theatre in Washington, D.C.

The rail's rich history began to recede with the advent of trucks and automobiles, and in 1959 the Northern Central had to give up its local passenger service. But it was Agnes, the powerful hurricane of 1972, that dealt the final blow to the faltering rail line. Agnes washed out and destroyed many of the railroad's bridges, ultimately knocking out remaining mainline passenger services and the line's important freight transportation. Northern Central Railroad's commercial success ended, but its new identity and prosperity were just beginning.

The rail line south of Cockeysville was purchased by the state of Maryland for freight service. This left the remaining line from Cockeysville north to the Pennsylvania border open for a unique and wonderful opportunity. The residents of Baltimore County realized this opportunity in 1980 when they purchased the 20-mile corridor from Penn Central and began the backbreaking process of converting the rails to trails. After nine long, hard years of work and thousands of volunteers later, the Northern Central Rail-Trail from Ashland to the Pennsylvania border was finished.

Now, more than 180,000 people visit and enjoy the trail each year. The Northern Central Rail-Trail leads its visitors across Maryland's beautiful fields and meadows, past old forests and rural farmland, along the rushing waters of Little Falls and Gunpowder Falls, and through many historic little towns.

Be warned that this once quiet treasure is gaining tremendous popularity, and parking is very limited during the prime outdoor months. Take this into account when you travel the rail-trail. Get there early.

Miles and Directions

0.0 Start from the NCRR Trail parking lot in Ashland and travel north on the Northern Central Rail-Trail.

2.0 Pass through the town of Phoenix, site of the Phoenix textile mill, razed for Loch Raven Reservoir. The reservoir, when built in 1922, never reached the mill. The mill ruins survive, still above the waterline.

4.0 Pass through the town of Sparks.

6.0 Pass through the historic Victorian village of Corbett, listed on the National Registry of Historic Places.

7.5 Pass through Monkton, showcasing the renovated Monkton train station, now a museum and park office. Monkton is also listed on the National Register of Historic Places. Restrooms, telephones, and food available. Monkton Bikes rental and repair shop just off the main path.

10.8 Pass through the village of White Hall. Telephones and parking on the left. White Hall is a former paper-mill town that used the rail to export its paper to Baltimore.

12.9 Pass through Parkton. Parkton was the railroad's hub for exporting dairy products south to Baltimore.

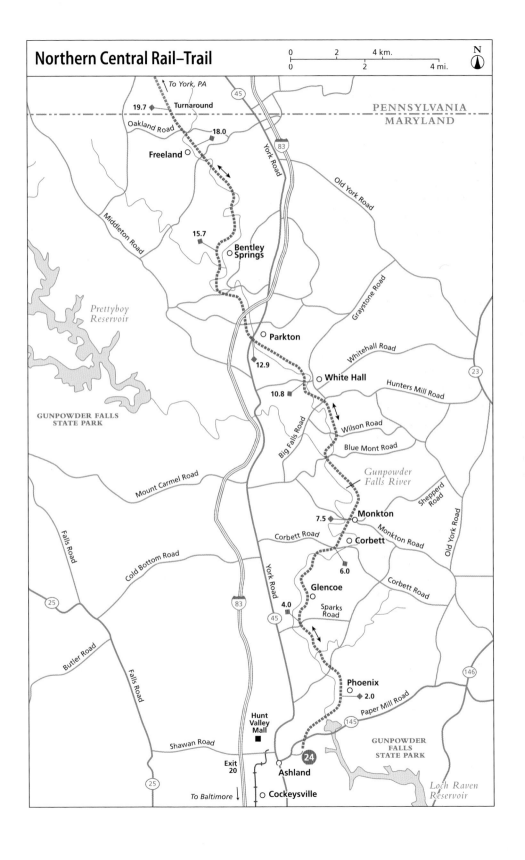

Northern Central Rail–Trail

0 2 4 km.

0 2 4 mi.

N

To York, PA

45

PENNSYLVANIA
MARYLAND

19.7 Turnaround

Oakland Road

18.0

83

Freeland

York Road

Old York Road

Middleton Road

15.7

Bentley
Springs

Prettyboy
Reservoir

Graystone Road

Parkton

Whitehall Road

12.9

23

White Hall

Hunters Mill Road

10.8

Big Falls Road

Wilson Road

GUNPOWDER FALLS
STATE PARK

Blue Mont Road

Gunpowder
Falls River

Mount Carmel Road

Sheppard
Road

7.5 Monkton

Old York Road

Corbett Road

Corbett

Monkton Road

Falls Road

Cold Bottom Road

6.0

Corbett Road

25

Glencoe

York Road

4.0

83

Sparks
Road

45

146

Butler Road

Phoenix

2.0

Falls Road

Paper Mill Road

Hunt
Valley
Mall

145

Shawan Road

GUNPOWDER
FALLS
STATE PARK

24

Exit
20

Loch Raven
Reservoir

25

To Baltimore

Ashland

Cockeysville

15.7 Reach the historic resort town of Bentley Springs. Portable toilet available.

18.0 Pass through the town of Freeland. Restrooms and parking available.

19.7 Reach the Maryland/Pennsylvania state border. From here, you either must have arranged a car shuttle back to the Ashland parking lot or you must ride back.

(Note: The NCRR Trail continues as the York County Heritage Rail-Trail all the way north to York, Pennsylvania. This adds an additional 20.5 miles one way to your trip. The York County Heritage Rail-Trail was completed in the summer of 1999.)

Ride Information

Local Information

www.baltimore.org

www.visitmaryland.org

25 Gunpowder Falls State Park: Sweet Air

The Sweet Air area of Gunpowder Falls State Park offers perfect intermediate trails. Located in northern Baltimore County, Sweet Air has 1,250 acres of trails. The variety of trails, from steep rocky climbs and descents to fields and flat twisty riverside trails, gives the intermediate rider the perfect stage to hone her or his skills.

Start: From the Gunpowder Falls State Park–Sweet Air trail parking area
Length: 5.25-mile loop
Ride time: About 1.5 hours
Difficulty: Moderate to difficult due to elevation changes and technical trail sections. This is the perfect trail for the novice who wants to increase her or his abilities.
Trail surface: Doubletrack and singletrack loop through rolling fields and riverside trails
Lay of the land: Rolling hills and river valley

Land status: State park
Nearest town: Fallston, MD
Other trail users: Hikers, equestrians, and pets (on leashes)
Trail contacts: Gunpowder Falls State Park, Kingsville, MD, (410) 592-2897
Schedule & fees: Gunpowder Falls State Park is a day-use park. No fees in this area, but other areas of the park have fees and require permits. Call the park directly for specific information.

Getting there: From Baltimore, Maryland: Take I-95 north to exit 74. Turn left onto MD 152 (Mountain Road) and head toward Fallston, Maryland. Continue on MD 152 for approximately 11 miles and turn left onto MD 165 (Baldwin Mill Road). Turn right at the second intersection onto Green Road. Continue on Green Road and turn right onto Moores Road. Take your first left onto Dalton-Bevard Road—the sign is hard to see. Continue on the gravel road until you reach a gate and a sign for Gunpowder Falls State Park–Sweet Air. Turn right and park at the top of the hill near the large trail sign. GPS coordinates: 39.536071, -76.505058.

The Ride

Although not readily apparent when you start your ride, the Gunpowder Falls State Park area is part of the Chesapeake Bay watershed and its delicate ecosystem. The watershed covers 64,000 square miles and spans sections of several states, including Maryland, Virginia, West Virginia, Pennsylvania, Delaware, and New York. About 20,000 years ago, the sea level was more than 300 feet below what it is today. At that time, the Great Gunpowder and Little Gunpowder Falls Rivers—along with many major tributaries, such as the great Susquehanna River—emptied directly into the Atlantic Ocean. As the northern polar ice caps melted—which they still are doing, by the way—the sea level rose. Over the next thousands of years, the fertile Susquehanna River Valley filled with water, flooding to form the Chesapeake Bay.

Today the bay is one of North America's most bountiful estuaries—an estuary being a body of water where freshwater from rivers mixes with the ocean. The bay

The Sweet Air area is very popular with equestrians. Use caution and be courteous.

is also the richest source of seafood in the United States. Its relative shallowness and hundreds of undisturbed inlets and bays create an ideal place for aquatic life.

Native Americans lived and flourished from the bounties of the Chesapeake as far back as 10,000 B.C. In Maryland, it was the Susquehannocks who dominated the area and survived mainly on what they could draw from the water. It is unclear who was the first European to reach this specific part of the coast. Legend has it that a Spaniard, Captain Vicente Gonzales, was the first explorer to sail the head of the Chesapeake. However, in 1608, Captain John Smith sailed the Chesapeake and mapped it, thus becoming the first known settler to reach its banks.

Later, settlers came to the Chesapeake Bay area and flourished from the wealth of resources at hand. Settlers used the bay's resources for themselves and traded them with people from other regions.

Unlike the early Native Americans who believed that natural resources belonged to all, European settlers began aggressively laying claim to the lands along the bay. The settlers armed themselves with the belief that anyone could claim and own private property. Large parcels of land were cleared to make room for farms and other businesses. Unfortunately, to the detriment of the natural beauty and survival of the bay, many forests were cleared. Several animals, such as wild turkeys, bison, and various fish, became extinct, and the unintended effects have taken a serious and quite visible toll.

Rapid development in the area, including new housing, shopping malls, and the necessary infrastructure to support them has increasingly strained the balanced ecosystem of the bay region. Today, government institutions and several citizen organizations are taking steps to ensure that future generations of Americans can continue to enjoy the resources of the Chesapeake Bay.

Miles and Directions

(**Note:** Take a moment before you begin your ride to study the trail map in the parking area. As you can see, there are several options and available loops. The following loop is by no means the only route—it's only a sampling.)

0.0 Start at the trailhead adjacent to a gate and a large birdhouse that is directly opposite the large trail map sign in the parking area. The trail is blazed blue. This is the Boundary Trail. As its name suggests, it travels along the perimeter of the Sweet Air area.

0.3 Turn left at this intersection and continue following the yellow blazes. You are now on the Pine Loop Trail.

0.9 Stay to the left to continue on the yellow. The right fork will meet up with the yellow again but will take a much steeper route.

1.1 Continue left at this intersection. A right turn at this intersection will take you back to the previous intersection.

1.3 Stay left at this intersection. You are back on the Boundary Trail, marked by blue blazes. A right turn will take you back to the parking area.

1.4 Continue to the left at this intersection and head toward the brown fence and the blue blazes on the left. The yellow trail continues to the right.

1.5 Continue following the blue blazes straight into the woods.

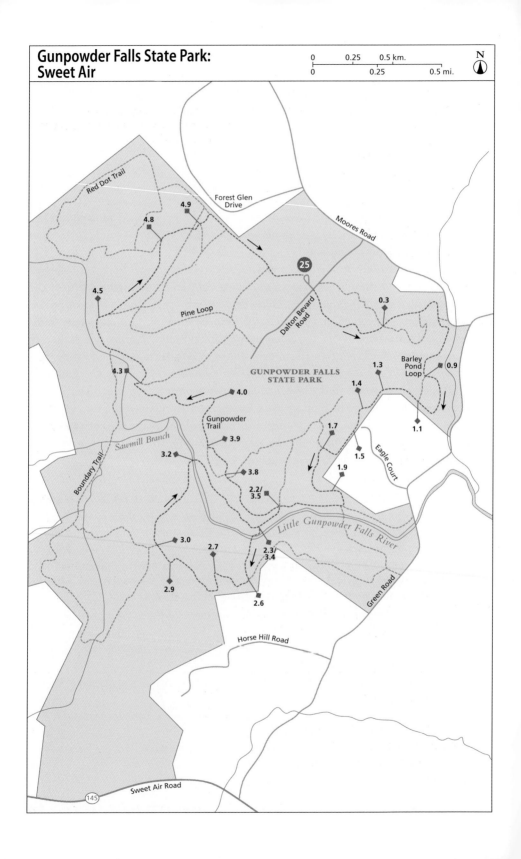

0   0.25   0.5 km.

0   0.25   0.5 mi.

N

Red Dot Trail

4.9

4.8

Forest Glen Drive

Moores Road

25

4.5

Pine Loop

0.3

Dalton Bevard Road

4.3

GUNPOWDER FALLS STATE PARK

1.3

Barley Pond Loop

0.9

1.4

4.0

1.1

Gunpowder Trail

1.7

Sawmill Branch

3.9

1.5

Eagle Court

Boundary Trail

3.2

3.8

1.9

2.2/ 3.5

Little Gunpowder Falls River

3.0

2.7

2.3/ 3.4

2.9

2.6

Green Road

Horse Hill Road

Sweet Air Road

145

1.7 After a short descent along the field, turn left into the Little Gunpowder Trail, blazed white.

1.9 The trail will split. Follow the hiker path to the right. The horse path to the left is usually an absolute mess. Continue following the white blazes.

2.2 Reach the intersection of the white and blue trails. Continue following the trail to the left. You are back on blue. (Note: If you do not want to cross the river you can continue straight and bypass the next section of the ride, 2.3–3.5. We will come back to this intersection after we cross the river.)

2.3 Turn left and cross the river. (The middle trail continues straight along the river. You will come back in that direction once you cross the river on the return leg.) The trailhead is clearly marked on the opposite bank of the river with a bright orange arrow painted on one of the river rocks. After crossing the river, continue to the left following the blue blazes. The red-blazed trail to the right tends to be very muddy.

2.6 Continue to the right along the blue. (The trail to the left, blazed red, will take you up toward the Black Forest and High Rock Overlook.)

2.7 The trail spills out onto an open field. Continue following to the right as it parallels the tree line.

2.9 Continue following the trail as it curves to the right.

3.0 Turn right and head back down toward the river along the orange-blazed trail. (The blue perimeter trail continues to the left.)

3.2 Cross the river and turn right. You are now headed back toward the spot where you crossed the river first.

3.4 Continue to the left at this intersection. (You crossed the river to the right at 2.3.)

3.5 Turn left at this intersection to get back on the white trail.

3.8 Turn right at the second orange trail marker. This will allow you to bypass a section of the white trail that has been damaged by equestrian use.

3.9 Continue to the right to hop back on the white trail.

4.0–4.3 Stay on the white trail.

4.5 Turn right then bear left and follow the blue blazes. (The white trail, which used to continue straight ahead, is now closed to the public.)

4.8 Turn right on the white trail.

4.9 After crossing the right-of-way you'll reach the intersection with a connector to the Barley Pond Loop to the right. Continue straight on the Little Gunpowder Trail and then make a right at the T intersection and head back to the starting point. (If you want to add a little extra distance to your ride, turn right at the Barley Pond Loop connector and follow the yellow trail around and back to the white trail.)

5.25 The parking area is to your right. The loop is complete.

Ride Information

Local Information

www.havredegracemd.com

Accommodations

Spencer Silver Mansion
Havre de Grace, MD
(800) 780-1485

Currier House Bed & Breakfast
Havre de Grace, MD
(800) 827-2889

26 Susquehanna River Ride

This challenging ride meanders through the varying topography of the Susquehanna River Valley, taking you through such diversity as heavy forest cover and open fields. Apart from its natural diversity, Susquehanna State Park offers a unique glimpse into the past, with several historic landmarks located within its boundaries, including the only working gristmill in Harford and Cecil Counties. Home to several mountain-bike races, the trails in this park do not make for an easy ride. So bring your best pair of legs and all the bike-handling skills you can muster, and be ready to have some fun.

Start: Deer Creek Picnic Area
Length: 8 miles
Ride time: About 1-2 hours
Difficulty: Moderate to difficult due to winding singletrack through dense woodlands
Trail surface: Singletrack, doubletrack; one very short section of pavement

Lay of the land: Dense forest and open fields along the Susquehanna River
Land status: State park
Nearest town: Bel Air, MD
Other trail users: Hikers and equestrians
Trail contacts: Susquehanna State Park, (410) 557-7994
Schedule: Day-use only, dawn to dusk

Getting there: From Baltimore: Take I-95 north to exit 89 (MD 155 West) toward Bel Air. Turn right on MD 161 (Rock Run Road) and follow the brown signs to the Rock Run Gristmill Historic Area. Turn left at Stafford Road toward the Deer Creek Picnic Area. As you drive into the picnic area, drive directly to the far right corner of the lot. The trail begins here. GPS coordinates: 39.619778, -76.159110.

The Ride

The setting for this ride is Susquehanna State Park, 30 miles north of Baltimore near the Pennsylvania state line. First inhabited by the Susquehannock Indians, this area later became a center for the Maryland and Pennsylvania Railroad. Today, all that remains of the railroad are abandoned structures from a past when the rail line helped farms and quarries of northern Harford County prosper. Also present is a network of trails and recreation areas for folks to enjoy year-round.

This ride takes you along five of Susquehanna State Park's many different trails. Cyclists will ride through the river valley, beneath heavy forest cover to huge rock outcroppings, and across wide-open fields. The ride also passes by Harford and Cecil Counties' only working gristmill, one of the many historic points of interest on this ride.

As you enter the park, you will clearly see evidence of the past. Make time for a walking tour of the gristmill area or explore the park's several buildings, all of which were built between 1794 and 1815. They include the Rock Run Gristmill, a springhouse, a carriage barn, and a tollhouse. Each of these unique and historic buildings offers a glimpse into the lifestyle of the 1800s. In operation until recently, the Rock Run Gristmill features a twelve-ton, eighty-four-bucket wheel that was powered by water running down Mill Race, a man-made stream draining from a small-dammed pond on higher ground.

The power from the gristmill wheel's rotation operates a complex set of pulleys, belts, and gears that can be quickly adjusted by the miller to determine the grain's consistency. As you walk inside the mill, pay close attention to the flood level markers, especially the one from 1889. It's hard to imagine that nearly the entire first floor of this structure was at one point completely submerged. Pictures of past floods, storms, and ice flows that greatly affected and shaped this area are also on display.

If your thirst for information on the area's history has not been quenched, you might consider visiting Havre de Grace and the Susquehanna Museum of Havre de Grace at the Lock House (thelockhousemuseum.org). The museum is a historic home along the banks of the Susquehanna River that tells the rich story of those who lived and worked in the house. There are four other museums, numerous shops, and fine restaurants along the promenade and waterfront, as well as several historic homes, some of which have been converted into wonderful bed-and-breakfasts.

Miles and Directions

0.0 Start at the picnic area from the intersection of the red and green trails. A WALK ZONE sign marks the entrance. Turn right and follow the green blazes.

0.8 Stay to the left. The trail to the right will meet up with the green trail a little farther up. Once it does, stay left again.

1.0 The American Beech Tree is to your right; continue straight along the green trail.

1.6 The intersection marked WHITE OAK to the left will take you to a small opening where you can admire Maryland's state tree. This particular white oak grew from a small acorn at the time of the Revolutionary War. This is a perfect spot for a water break or picnic.

1.7 Continue straight through this intersection to continue onto the blue-blazed Farm Road Trail. (A right turn will take you to the campgrounds, or a left turn will take you back to the beginning of the ride along the green trail.)

1.9 Cross the creek and follow the blue trail to the right. A left turn will take you back down to the parking area along the creek.

2.5 Continue following the trail to the right through an open field. (The trail to the left is a connector that will take you to the Susquehanna Ridge Trail, which you will hit on the way back.)

2.7 Follow the perimeter of the field and then turn right where the blue trail turns left into the woods. You are now on the Orange Ivy Branch Trail. The trail will continue to follow the tree line.

3.2 Pass the park office and maintenance complex. Continue straight. This area also serves as the equestrian parking lot. The gravel road curves right toward the camping area, but you want to stay left.

3.3 Turn left into the woods to stay on the orange trail.

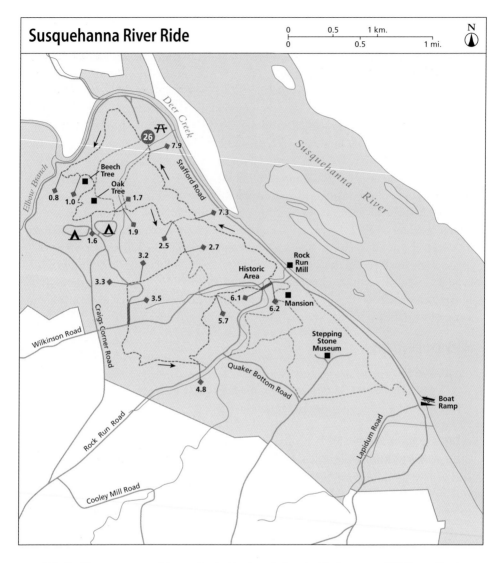

Susquehanna River Ride

0   0.5   1 km.
0   0.5   1 mi.

N

3.5 You'll come out on a driveway lined with pines. Follow the blacktop toward Wilkinson Road. Cross the road. The orange trail picks up directly on the other side. After a short ascent, you will be treated to some of the best singletrack in the park. Continue following the orange blazes.

4.8 Continue following the orange blazes to the left. The fork to the right is a short connector down to Rock Run Road below.

5.7 Reach an intersection with the blue trail. Continue following the orange blazes to the right and then again to the left at the next intersection (also blue). Ahead of you is a short, exciting, twisty, and highly technical descent.

6.1 Reach Wilkinson Road again. Turn right on Wilkinson Road, then immediately left on Rock Run Road. Head toward the historic area.

6.2 Turn left at the connection with the red trail. Follow the red blazes across the creek and get ready to climb. It will be worth it . . .

7.3 Continue on the red trail to the right. (The connector to the left takes you to the Farm Road Trail at marker 2.5.)

7.9 Continue straight through this intersection. (A left turn will take you on the blue trail back up to marker 1.9.)

8.0 Immediately after crossing the small wooden bridge, bear right and follow the PETS PROHIBITED IN THIS AREA sign to come out into the parking lot and finish the loop.

Ride Information

Local Information

Havre de Grace Chamber of Commerce/ Tourism Board
(410) 939-3303

Harford County's website, with information about local events and attractions: www.har fordmd.com

Accommodations

Camping is available in Susquehanna State Park from March through October. Specific dates and fees can be found on the Maryland Department of Natural Resources website at www.dnr2.maryland.gov.

The Everything and More Inn
Delta, PA
(717) 456-7263

27 Fair Hill Natural Resource Management Area

Known primarily for its rich equestrian heritage, the Fair Hill area does not conjure up images of mountain biking. However, this northern Maryland natural resource management area has some of the most enjoyable singletrack in the state. Similar to the trails in Patapsco Valley State Park, the Fair Hill area offers a superb network of trails sure to satisfy the most demanding riders.

Start: From the Fair Hill Natural Resources Management Area parking lot adjacent to the covered bridge on Tawes Road

Length: 5.2-mile loop

Ride time: About 0.75–1.5 hours

Difficulty: Twisty, technical singletrack with elevation changes makes this a moderate to difficult trail.

Trail surface: Singletrack, doubletrack, and gravel roads

Lay of the land: Singletrack trails that run through rolling fields and forests

Land status: Natural resource management area—Department of Natural Resources

Nearest town: Elkton, MD

Other trail users: Hikers, equestrians, and anglers

Trail contacts: DNR Office, Fair Hill, MD, (410) 398-1246; Delaware Trail Spinners, Bear, DE, www.trailspinners.org

Schedule: Varies. Call park manager's office directly for information, (410) 398-1246

Getting there: From Baltimore: Take I-95 north to exit 109A. Get on MD 279 south to Elkton. Continue on MD 279 to the intersection with MD 213. Turn right onto MD 213. Follow it for approximately 6 miles and turn right at the Fair Hill Inn, immediately before the intersection of MD 213 and MD 273. Take an immediate right onto Ranger Skinner Drive. The DNR office will be to your immediate right. Follow Ranger Skinner Drive through the traffic circle and parking lots and continue to the left. Ranger Skinner Drive will run parallel to MD 273 on your left and the Fair Hill Race Track on your right. Continue on Ranger Skinner Drive for approximately 0.75 mile and turn left on Training Center Road. Continue for 0.5 mile and turn right onto Tawes Drive. Follow Tawes Drive for about 1 mile to the parking area immediately before the covered bridge. The ride begins here. GPS coordinates: 39.710091, -75.838115.

The Ride

The earliest known settlers of the Fair Hill area were the Susquehannock Indians. They belonged to the Iroquois Confederacy. Looking for a peaceful home, the Susquehannocks left the Seneca Nation and settled in this area because of the natural abundance the northern Chesapeake River and the Susquehanna River had to offer. In the early 1600s, Captain John Smith traveled these areas, bartering with the Native Americans and exploring the region. The charter of Maryland to Lord Cecil Calvert by King Charles I of England, in 1632, marked the beginning of European exploration and settlement in the area.

In 1926, William du Pont Jr. bought his first of many parcels of land in the area. After acquiring the land, du Pont brought his hounds from Montpelier, Virginia, and hired a huntsman to establish his kennels. An avid hunter and equestrian, he hunted three times a week, usually before breakfast. Despite du Pont's passion for horses and racing, he did not build the Fair Hill Racetrack until the 1930s. The racetrack was fashioned after the Ainsley Track in England, and it firmly established Fair Hill's equestrian tradition.

William du Pont's 5,700-acre estate would become one of the largest holdings in the east. Soon after his death in 1965, his heirs sold the property to Maryland's Department of Natural Resources. Since then, the Department of Natural Resources has managed and maintained the land, continuing the rich equestrian tradition that William du Pont Jr. began.

Fair Hill is nothing short of breathtaking, and this ride scratches the surface of the beauty of the area. As you ride in and out of the woods and through the open fields, you'll soon forget about the rest of the world and begin to see why the Susquehannocks chose this area as their home. You will also see why William du Pont Jr. chose Fair Hill as his home and hunting site. The natural splendor, beauty, and quality and quantity of trails in the area make it a great place to mountain bike.

Note: The loop I detail here is the tip of the iceberg, but it gives you a good sampling of what is available at Fair Hill. There are miles and miles of trails available to mountain biking at the Fair Hill Natural Resources Management Area, so many that it may literally take you an entire season to explore and ride them all. I highly recommend that you stop by the park office and pick up one of their detailed maps ($4) so that you can explore all of the available options on your own. Or, better yet, sign up for the annual Fair Hill Classic Race and Mountain Bike Festival, held and organized by the Delaware Trail Spinners (www.trailspinners.org) every summer. The classic offers riders of all abilities the chance to ride the best trails at Fair Hill without having to worry about getting lost.

Miles and Directions

0.0 From the parking lot cross Tawes Drive and hop onto the orange trail. The covered bridge is to your left. Ride between the pond and the Fair Hill Nature Center (green barn to the right).

0.1 The trail veers left into the woods. The green barn is now behind you to the right. Follow the orange blazes.

0.6 Make a sharp right to stay on the orange trail.

1.0 The trail splits. Keep following the orange blazes.

1.3 Follow the singletrack as it curves left onto the open field. You'll enter back into the woods shortly to the right.

1.4 Continue following the trail as it curves to the right.

1.8 Continue to the right at this split.

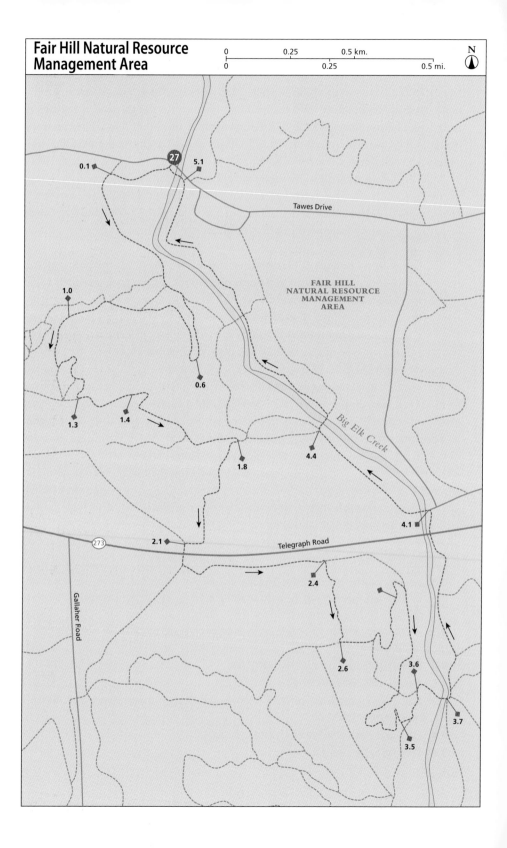

Fair Hill Natural Resource Management Area

0   0.25   0.5 km.

0   0.25   0.5 mi.

N

27

5.1

0.1

Tawes Drive

FAIR HILL
NATURAL RESOURCE
MANAGEMENT
AREA

1.0

0.6

Big Elk Creek

1.3   1.4

1.8

4.4

4.1

273   2.1   Telegraph Road

Gallaher Road

2.4

2.6   3.6

3.7

3.5

2.1 Come out onto another open field. Turn left to go over Telegraph Road (273) and then immediately left again to follow the trail along the tree line that parallels Telegraph Road.

2.4 Make a sharp right turn into the woods. A NO HORSES sign marks the entrance to this trail. A challenging yet rewarding singletrack climb follows.

2.6 Turn left as you reach the top of the climb. Fun awaits!

2.9 Continue straight through this intersection. (A left turn will take you back toward 2.4 should you choose to ride this section again.) Continue straight through the next two doubletrack intersections.

3.5 Reach the yellow trail; turn left to head down and cross the Big Elk Creek to the right. (You can easily extend your ride here by making a right and following the yellow blazes to the south. The area enclosed by Appleton Road to the east, Gallaher Road to the west, Telegraph Road to the north, and Scott's Mill to the south has a lot of great trails worth exploring. An alternate parking area along Appleton Road to the south of 273 provides easy access to these trails.)

3.6 Make a sharp right to continue on the yellow trail. You can see the bridge that spans the creek from this point.

3.7 Go over the bridge and immediately turn left to ride north along the creek.

4.1 Turn left onto the old 273 bridge to cross over the Big Elk Creek and then immediately right along the doubletrack.

4.4 Veer right at the fork in the trail to cross over the Big Elk Creek again. Immediately after crossing the creek turn left and follow the trail that parallels the creek. Stay along the creek virtually all the way back to the covered bridge.

5.1 Turn left on Old Union Road (Tawes Drive) and go through the covered bridge.

5.2 The loop is complete.

Ride Information

Local Information

Cecil County's official tourism website: www .seececil.org—with local information, events, and attractions

Accommodations

Fair Hill, MD, (410) 398-1246, offers primitive camping for recognized youth groups at several areas near Big Elk Creek.

Garden Cottage Sinking Springs Herb Farm
Elkton, MD
(410) 398-5566

Honorable Mentions

Compiled here is an index of great rides in Maryland's Piedmont region that didn't make the A list this time around but deserve recognition. Check them out and let us know what you think. You may decide that one or more of these rides deserves higher status in future editions, or perhaps you may have a ride of your own that merits some attention. Some of these rides are documented on our website, www .mtbdc.com.

D. Sugarloaf Mountain Bike Loop

In 1993, under the staff supervision of the Stronghold Corporation, groups of off-road cyclists, hikers, and Boy Scouts worked together to create a trail system that combined both forest roads and challenging singletrack. The result was a fantastic course ideal for mountain biking, hiking, and horseback riding. Unfortunately, the trail's popularity was far more than its narrow, twisting pathways could bear, as hundreds of cyclists each weekend saddled up and crowded its course. Land managers were forced to reassess the trail's design and concluded that, with parking spilling into nearby towns and the trail's capacity way overextended, limited access was the only answer. Currently, the Saddleback Trail (yellow blazed) is open to cyclists from June through October, Monday through Friday. It is not open to bikes on the weekends at any time of the year. While this may appear unfair and inconvenient to some, remember that Sugarloaf Mountain is a privately owned resource. Thankfully, the Stronghold Corporation is generous enough to allow the Saddleback Trail to remain open to cyclists at certain times. Access to the trail is available by the entrance to Sugarloaf Mountain along Comus Road. (www.sugarloafmd.com)

GPS coordinates: 39.251529, -77.393375.

E. Hashawa/Bear Run Nature Center

The Hashawa/Bear Run Nature Center trail system in Westminster, MD, is an up-and-coming and slightly underrated destination for mountain bikers. The system consists of a set of trails that intertwine between the nature center and the Union Mills Reservoir area. The trails in and around the nature center are easy, but as you venture off into the Union Mills area the trails get more difficult, with lots of twisty sections and "punchy" climbs. Hashawa still needs considerable work to bring it up to par with nearby trails, such as the new Emmitsburg network of trails at Rainbow Lake, but they are still a fun alternative in the area.

GPS coordinates: 39.663014, -76.986823.

F. Patapsco Valley State Park: Woodstock

There just isn't enough room in the book to detail all the great destinations in the region. The Woodstock trails at Patapsco Valley State Park are some of those I had to sacrifice in the name of space. The trails at Woodstock provide a connection point between the Daniels area (Ride 21) and the McKeldin area (Ride 20) of the park, and offer additional challenging and technical riding for the intermediate to advanced rider. They can be ridden as a loop, or if combined with one or both of the rides mentioned above, can extend your ride to more than 30 miles. The Woodstock trails are easily accessible from the parking area directly across from the Woodstock Inn (great place for an after-ride beer) along Woodstock Road in, you guessed it, Woodstock, Maryland. Or park farther down next to Saint Alphonsus Church on Old Court Road. If you register for one of the Patapsco Epic rides you'll get a chance to ride several of the trails in this area. Check www.mtbdc.com for additional information, including maps and downloadable GPS files.

GPS coordinates: 39.330995, -76.870485.

G. Loch Raven Reservoir

The Loch Raven Reservoir area has had a tumultuous history. Part of the reason I don't detail the trails in this phenomenal Baltimore destination is because of the shaky political climate that surrounded the area while I was working on this edition. After years of advocacy efforts, however, the landscape at Loch Raven is about to change dramatically. Shortly before publication of this guide, MORE, Bikemore, Bike Maryland, and the City of Baltimore's Department of Public Works (DPW) signed a historic Trail Stewardship Agreement. The agreement represents a new partnership between the City of Baltimore and regional volunteer organizations to assist in the maintenance of existing natural surface trails while improving the overall quality of Baltimore's drinking water supply. This landmark agreement opens the door to the development of new sustainable trails in the region. Volunteers, along with IMBA's regional chapter, MORE, will work to identify specific improvements while closing or re-routing unsanctioned trails. Loch Raven is where I first set wheels to dirt in the late 1980s and early '90s. It is where I discovered my love for mountain biking. The trails at Loch Raven, like Patapsco, are classic Piedmont ribbons, and offer intermediate to advanced riders the perfect playground to hone and improve their skills. If you are a local resident who enjoys riding the Loch Raven area I encourage you to get actively involved and help MORE's trail liaisons work with the DPW toward better sustainable trails. If you are unfamiliar with the trail I highly encourage you to connect with a local who knows what's open and what's not. The most popular access point to the trails at Loch Raven is along the intersections of Dulaney Valley Road and Seminary Road. Stay tuned to MORE's website (www.more-mtb.org) for additional information related to the agreement and the development of trails in the Reservoir area.

GPS coordinates: 39.424445, -76.596839.

H. Gunpowder Falls State Park: Jerusalem and Jericho

I simply ran out of time! Gunpowder Falls State Park, like Patapsco Valley State Park, covers a tremendous amount of space in Maryland's Piedmont region. In addition to the popular areas already detailed in this book, there is an expansive network of trails along the Little Gunpowder Falls River that can be accessed from Jerusalem Road (along Jerusalem Mill Village), or along Harford Road in the Gunpowder Falls State Park Central Area. The most popular loop along the Jerusalem Road trails will take you east to west along both sides of the river between Pleasantville Road to the northwest and the intersections of Jerusalem Road and Jericho Road to the east. Look for a detailed description of this trail system, including a map and directions on www.mtbdc.com.

GPS coordinates: 39.462821, -76.390062.

I. Gunpowder Falls State Park: Perry Hall

Riding the trails along the banks of the Gunpowder River is like stepping back in time. The large, towering trees, which frame the tamed Gunpowder River, provide shelter from the surrounding urban hustle and shade on hot sunny days. With little elevation gain, and close proximity to Perry Hall and the Baltimore Beltway, this trail is the perfect getaway for a quick off-road jaunt. From the Perry Hall parking area along the east side of Route 1 you can craft a short loop using the Lost Pond Trail

(blue) and the Sawmill Trail (yellow). Additional riding can be found on the west side of Route 1 along the white trail. From the main parking area go under the Route 1 tunnel and turn immediately left to go over the river (the trails straight ahead are closed to bikes). When you reach the backside of the Gunpowder Lodge, turn right. The trailhead is to the right of their patio area. The white trail will parallel the Big Gunpowder Falls all the way to Harford Road and beyond to Cromwell Bridge Road, where you can access the south side of Loch Raven Reservoir (HM G). The out-and-back to Harford Road is approximately 5 miles each way.

GPS coordinates: 39.427037, -76.442830.

J. Patuxent Research Refuge, North Tract

If you are looking for tight switchbacks and roller-coaster singletrack, this is not the place. But if you want to freely spin on wide-open gravel roads, this is your spot. The Patuxent Research Refuge's North Tract is the perfect place to get acquainted with the operation of your new bicycle and its components. It's also a good area to observe some of central Maryland's wildlife. This is a great ride for kids—especially if it's their first time off-road. The North Tract's several miles of gravel roads can be easily pieced together to create a 6- to 7-mile loop. This ride is documented in my other book, *Best Bike Rides Washington, D.C.*

GPS coordinates: 39.077988, -76.771606.

Coastal Maryland

T he state of Maryland has an immense variety of terrain available to mountain bikers, ranging in extremes from the rocky, technical, mountainous terrain of western Maryland (for hard-core riding) to the bay shores and sandy beaches of coastal Maryland, offering a uniquely pleasant environment in which to pedal one's steed. In between lies the Maryland Piedmont, with its fields, streams, and valleys.

Unlike the other regions of Maryland, coastal Maryland is generally flat. But don't let this fool you. A challenging variety of trails awaits the adventurous rider.

Mostly rural, coastal Maryland has several state forests and reserves open to and enjoyed by mountain bikers of all skill levels. Novice riders enjoy the generally wide and easy trails of the Patuxent Research Park. This park was once part of Fort George G. Meade, and many of the trails there today were once old army training grounds.

Farther south, near Waldorf, fat-tire enthusiasts enjoy the twisting singletrack trails in Cedarville State Forest and the new trails at Rosaryville State Park. Popular among cyclists of all levels, Cedarville is an ideal destination for novice cyclists. They can acquaint themselves with twisty narrow trails along with the luxury of flat terrain and plenty of escape routes back onto wide dirt roads. The relatively nonexistent elevation gain or loss in this part of the state makes these trails an inviting destination for riders of all ages.

Farther south in Maryland, riders can delight in the lakeshore trails of Saint Mary's River State Park. A bit more challenging than Cedarville and other coastal Maryland destinations, Saint Mary's is a preferred riding area for more advanced riders. Advocacy groups in southern Maryland work hard to keep this trail system open to cyclists. Their efforts are clearly visible in the trail's relatively good condition. Countless hours of maintenance have gone into these paths to ensure they are enjoyed by all for years to come.

The predominant landmark in southern Maryland is the Chesapeake Bay, a 200-plus-mile estuary harboring an exorbitant amount of wildlife and ecosystems. And to the east of the bay are the flatlands of the Eastern Shore. Bordered by the

Chesapeake Bay to the west and the Atlantic Ocean to the east, the Eastern Shore offers very little elevation change. But don't let this fool you into thinking there's nothing worth pedaling here. The relative flatness of the area lends itself to strong headwinds and thus the sense of going uphill all day long. And what places like Tuckahoe State Park lack in elevation they make up for with soft, sandy sections of trail that will make your legs work harder than will a Blue Ridge climb.

28 L. F. Cosca Regional Park

Readily accessible from the Washington Beltway, L. F. Cosca Regional Park is a deceiving place. Its small size and rather urban setting hide a great network of single-track. This regional park in Prince George's County has that specific ingredient that makes every ride better—singletrack. The variety of possible routes in this park will undoubtedly keep you busy for a couple of hours.

Start: L. F. Cosca Regional Park main parking area by the park office
Length: 5.1 miles
Ride time: About 1 hour
Difficulty: Easy to moderate
Trail surface: Singletrack
Lay of the land: Stream crossings and heavily wooded terrain around Cosca Lake
Land status: Regional park

Nearest town: Clinton, MD
Other trail users: Hikers and nature enthusiasts
Trail contacts: L. F. Cosca Regional Park, (301) 868-1397; Clearwater Nature Center, (301) 297-4575
Schedule & fees: Open daily 7:30 a.m. to dusk, year-round; small nonresident vehicle fee from Memorial Day to Labor Day

Getting there: From the Capital Beltway (I-495): Take exit 7 to MD 5 (Branch Avenue) toward Waldorf. Go approximately 4 miles to MD 223 (Woodyard Road). Turn right on Woodyard Road, taking it 0.6 miles to Brandywine Road. Turn left on Brandywine Road. Follow it south toward Clinton (0.75 miles), then turn right on Thrift Road. Thrift Road takes you south 1.5 miles to the park entrance on your right. Go right into the park and continue to the Tennis Bubble. Turn left into the main park office parking area.. The trailhead is adjacent to the Tennis Bubble. GPS coordinates: 38.739502, -76.909887.

The Ride

Things can often deceive you, disappoint you, and leave you feeling shortchanged. Louise F. Cosca Regional Park, just outside the town of Clinton in Prince George's County, is one such place that will, indeed, deceive you. It will not, however, leave you disappointed. For despite its small size, this park has everything off-road cyclists dream of: deep, wooded surroundings; stream crossings; a beautiful 15-acre lake; quick, rugged singletrack trails; and a variety of off-road possibilities.

The trails twist back and forth beneath the tall trees and, in the colorful fall season, can be breathtaking. Continuing around the perimeter of the park, the trails roll more gently back toward the start of the ride, allowing you to sit back and enjoy your wooded surroundings.

The trails at Cosca have been rerouted with cyclists in mind.

Miles and Directions

0.0 The ride at Cosca begins at the first trail marker by the road as you ride out from the main parking area by the park office. A large tennis bubble will be visible to your right. As you ride out of the parking area you'll see a trail marker with orange and white markers. Continue through the power lines to pick up the trail on the other side.

0.2 The trail comes out on the power lines again. You are at a highpoint and can see the creek below to your left. The trail will switch back down to the left a little farther down. As you cross the power lines you will see a trailhead on the other side. We'll come back to that one later. Ride down and to the left to parallel the creek.

0.4 As you reach the lake and the paved trail, make an immediate right and go over two bridges. After the second small bridge turn to the right.

0.9 Continue following the orange markers. The trails to the right and left are no longer in use.

1.1 Reach the green trail. You can go either way on the green trail and it will loop you back to this same spot. For now, take the left fork and continue to follow the green trail. Follow the green/orange and blue markers.

1.2 After a nice fast descent you'll reach a four-way intersection. Continue to follow the green arrows to the right/straight. If you look to the far right you'll see the remnants of the old green trail. The blue trail to the left takes you toward the nature center. Continue right on the green trail.

1.4 Continue following the green trail to the left over the small creek and then stay to the right to remain on the green trail. Continue following the green markers. A great section of trail follows.

L. F. Cosca Regional Park

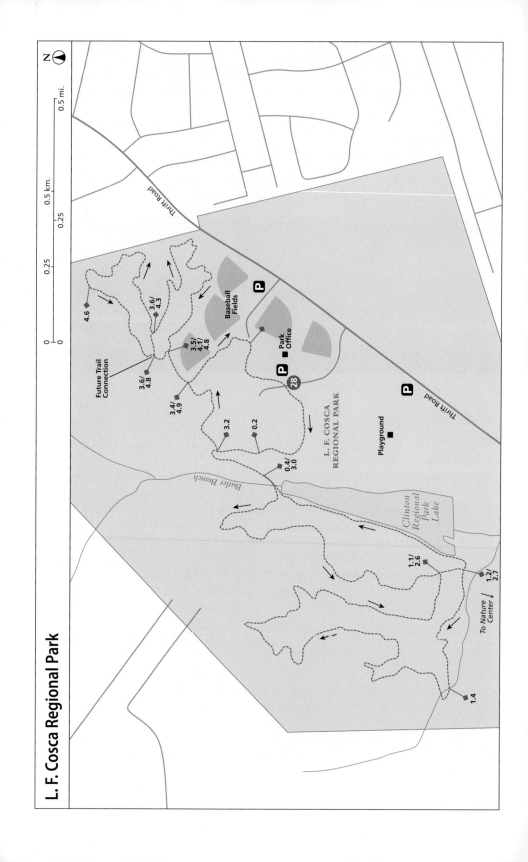

N

0   0.25   0.5 km.
      0.25

0   0.5 mi.

Thrift Road

4.6

3.6/
4.3

Future Trail
Connection

3.6/
4.8

3.5/
4.1/
4.8

Baseball
Fields

P

3.4/
4.9

3.2

0.2

P

Park
Office

28

P

0.4/
3.0

Butler Branch

L. F. COSCA
REGIONAL PARK

Playground

Thrift Road

Clinton
Regional
Park
Lake

1.1/
2.6

1.2/
2.7

To Nature
Center

1.4

2.6 You're back at the entrance of the green trail (1.1). Turn right again and double back down on the short descent. At the bottom make a sharp left and head toward the lake.

2.7 You'll come out on an open field. Turn left and follow the tree line to the left edge of the lake.

3.0 You're back at the two bridges we crossed at mile marker 0.4. Go over the bridges and backtrack to the left back to the power lines.

3.2 Cross the power lines and head into the orange/purple trail we bypassed at marker 0.2.

3.4 Continue straight past this intersection. (A right turn will take you back toward the starting point of the ride. We'll come back this way to finish out the loop.)

3.5 Reach a four-way intersection. Turn left and follow the purple-blazed trails. The next sections of trails will likely change slightly by the time you read this; lots of new trails will be going up in the near future.

3.56 Make a sharp right to continue following the purple blazes. By the time you read this there may be a new trail heading up straight ahead.

3.6 Continue straight through the next two intersections; you will return from the other side to complete a figure-eight.

4.1 You're back at the four-way intersection you came upon at mile marker 3.5. A left turn will take you back toward the starting point of the ride. Head right and double back for a short period of time to continue the figure-eight.

4.25 Stay to the right at the first intersection. Continue to double back on the trail and at the second intersection make a left turn.

4.6 Stay to left at this intersection. At the time I documented this ride the trail to the right was just starting to be built. That trail will take you to marker 3.56 of this ride, where we made the sharp right.

4.75 Follow the trail to the right and backtrack toward the four-way intersection.

4.8 Continue straight through the four-way intersection and backtrack toward the beginning of the ride.

4.9 Cross the doubletrack and head up the trail as it skirts the edge of the baseball fields to the right.

5.0 Turn right on the road.

5.1 Turn left and follow the sign to the Cosca Park office and the starting point of the ride. Or, turn right and start the loop all over again.

Ride Information

Local Information
Prince George's County Parks and Recreation
www.pgparks.com

Maryland-National Capital Park and Planning Commission
Riverdale, MD
(301) 699-2407

29 Rosaryville State Park

Avalon's little sister, nestled just outside the beltway in southern Maryland, is Rosaryville State Park. Conceived in partnership by the Mid-Atlantic Off-Road Enthusiasts (MORE) and Maryland's Department of Natural Resources (DNR), Rosaryville is one of the region's newest off-road destinations. The ride is similar to Patapsco, but with less of the extreme portion. There is a single 8-mile singletrack perimeter loop that circumnavigates the park with a short inner-extension technical loop that's bound to please the most demanding riders.

Start: Rosaryville State Park main perimeter loop parking area
Length: 8.3 miles
Ride time: About 1–2 hours
Difficulty: Easy/moderate
Trail surface: Mostly singletrack
Lay of the land: Fast, rolling, and twisty singletrack
Land status: State park
Nearest town: Waldorf , MD

Other trail users: Hikers, occasional equestrians
Trail contacts: Mid-Atlantic Off-Road Enthusiasts (MORE), www.more-mtb.org
Schedule & fees: Open year-round, sunrise to sunset. Sanctioned night rides in the winter; check the MORE website for details (www .more-mtb.org). Small vehicle fee on the honor system.

Getting there: From the Capital Beltway (I-495) take exit 11A for MD-4 S/Pennsylvania Avenue toward Upper Marlboro. Continue for approximately 2 miles and take the MD-223/Woodyard Road exit toward Clinton/Melwood Road and then make an immediate left onto Marlboro Pike. Marlboro Pike will become Osborne Road. Turn right on US 301 South and then right again onto West Marlton Avenue (the park entrance). Turn right at the first intersection, pay your fee, and continue straight and follow the signs to the Perimeter Loop Trail parking area. GPS coordinates: 38.78091, -76.802641.

The Ride

Rosaryville State Park is a relatively new riding destination in the Washington, D.C., capital region. Not long ago, off-road cyclists had very few options to ride in southern Maryland, Cedarville State Forest being one of them. Riders often had to make the trek across the beltway to neighboring Virginia or farther north in Maryland to find quality singletrack, but that all changed in 2000 when MORE member Austin Steo spied a small sign and locked gate at an undeveloped area of Rosaryville State Park. (In Ride 19, Fairland Regional Park, I write a little more about my friend Austin's vision and passion for cycling.) Austin was on his way to ride Cedarville with a group of friends when he noticed the tract of land, and later after inspecting some topographic maps of the area came to the realization that they could be the perfect location for a system of trails. Excited about the prospect, Austin borrowed my GPS

The trails at Rosaryville have become a regional favorite.

and headed out to do an initial survey of what was out there. He returned wide eyed as to the incredible potential the area offered. Soon after his discovery he started making a few calls and wound up in contact with Rosaryville Conservancy and members of the Maryland Department of Natural Resources, to whom he pitched the idea of building new sustainable trails and offered to put together a proposal to do so.

The Conservancy and DNR were intrigued and allowed Austin to proceed. Since Rosaryville was a little out of the way for him, Austin recruited another MORE member, Todd Brooks, to aid in the effort. After a brief meeting the two set out to explore and survey Rosaryville even further and determined that the potential for a 9-mile perimeter loop existed in the park. With two people excited about the prospect of new trails in the area the project began to gain steam. Todd and Austin then took Dan Hudson of IMBA and his wife, Karen Garnett, out to the park to show them what they had found. Dan recommended that they involve IMBA's trail-building guru, Rich Edwards, to advise and help with the planning. The involvement of Rich Edwards was critical in the development of the trails. By this time Austin had become MORE's Maryland advocacy director and had managed to help the club secure $75,000 in grants from the state of Maryland toward the development of trails in the region. Part of that money went into the building of trails at Rosaryville and the funding needed to have IMBA's Trail Solutions crew provide their expertise and mechanized equipment to bench-cut and build new trail. During the peak of construction, volunteers and IMBA's crew were building about 800 feet of trail per day.

The first build day was scheduled for November 12, 2002, and was attended by a myriad of volunteers that included not only MORE members but also DNR representatives and members of the Rosaryville Conservancy, including avid equestrians.

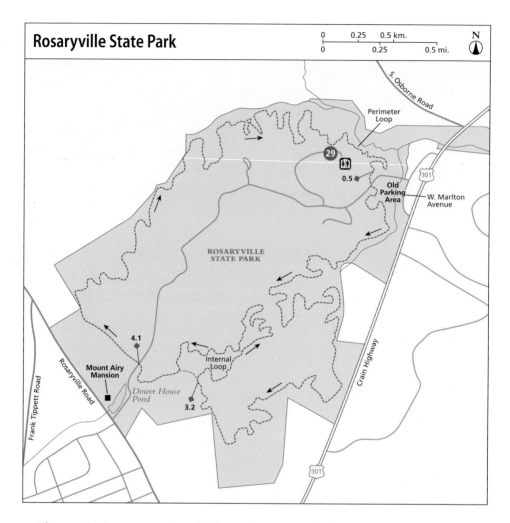

Rosaryville State Park

After nearly three years of work, the trail was completed in 2005, and today it has become an incredibly popular destination for cyclists in the region.

The perimeter loop runs for a little under 8 miles and offers cyclists of all levels a challenging and fun experience. The trails take complete advantage of the lay of the land and follow its contours in a natural and exciting fashion. Fast downhills, challenging climbs, and fun and twisty singletrack make for a ride that you'll want to head back to over and over. After the trail's completion an extension was added to the loop, but for some reason it has seen very little use over time—a testament, perhaps, to how well built and enjoyable the perimeter loop is.

The Rosaryville trail perimeter loop is clearly marked and very easy to follow. While I detail a clockwise loop here, the trail can be ridden in either direction. This is a two-way trail, so encountering other riders coming at you in the opposite direction is a real possibility. Please ride within your limits.

Miles and Directions

0.0 Start at the trailhead entrance. We will ride the perimeter trail in a clockwise direction. Shortly after entering, turn right at the T intersection.

0.5 Reach the original parking area. Go through it. The trail continues on the other side of the road as you exit the parking area and it is clearly marked.

3.2 Continue to the left following the perimeter trail. (The right fork will take you to the inside loop.)

3.9 Continue following the perimeter loop to the left. (The right fork will take you to the inside loop.)

4.1 Cross the road. A right turn along the road will take you toward the Rosaryville mansion.

8.3 Back at the T intersection. Turn right to complete the loop.

Ride Information

Local Information

Upper Marlboro
www.uppermarlboromd.gov

Mount Airy Mansion
www.mountairymansion.org

Bike Shops

Bike Doctor
Waldorf, MD
(301) 932-9980
www.bikedoctorwaldorf.com

Family Bike Shop
Crofton, MD
(410) 721-8244
www.familybikeshop.com

Where to Eat

Olde Towne Inn
14745 Main St.
Upper Marlboro, MD
(301) 627-1400
www.otitherestaurant.com

Moms Thai Kitchen
14710 Main St.
Upper Marlboro, MD
(301) 627-0011
www.momsthaikitchen.com

30 Cedarville State Forest

Tight, twisty singletrack is what you'll find when you visit Cedarville. There are more than 10 miles of singletrack and doubletrack in this 3,500-acre state forest just south of Washington, D.C. Its proximity to the nation's capital and its modest terrain have made Cedarville State Forest a popular cycling destination for riders throughout the region. Unlike those in neighboring parks to the north, the trails in Cedarville are generally hard-packed dirt with very few rocks. Occasional mud holes may slow you down, but this is otherwise one of the most enjoyable mountain-bike destinations in the area.

Start: Cedarville State Forest ranger station
Length: 13.2 miles
Ride time: About 2-3 hours
Difficulty: Easy due to flat, unimpeded trails
Trail surface: Flat, dirt trails and dirt roads
Lay of the land: Flat, woodland setting with a freshwater lake
Land status: State forest
Nearest town: Brandywine, MD

Other trail users: Campers, anglers, hikers, equestrians, and hunters
Trail contacts: Maryland Forest, Park, and Wildlife Service, (301) 888-1622
Schedule & fees: Open daily from 8 a.m. to sunset most of the year; winter schedule: 10 a.m. to sunset; small vehicle fee on the honor system

Getting there: From the Capital Beltway (I-495): Take exit 7 to MD 5 (Branch Avenue) toward Waldorf. Go 11.6 miles on MD 5 (which joins with US 301), then turn left on Cedarville Road. Go 2.3 miles, then turn right on the forest entrance road (Bee Oak Road). Park office and parking 1 mile down the road. Portable toilets are available. Water and telephones are not available. GPS coordinates: 38.647110, -76.830203.

The Ride

Here's an off-road ride that rolls along forest roads and wooded trails through Prince George's and Charles Counties' quiet state forest. There are no monuments, natural wonders, or sights of great historical significance in Cedarville State Forest. Even the name may leave you wondering, as cedars are uncommon to the immediate area. (The name, in fact, was taken from a nearby post office.) What this small state forest in southern Maryland offers instead is a network of wonderful wooded trails and dirt roads that guide visitors beneath tall stands of loblolly and white pine, around groves of holly and magnolia trees, past a four-acre lake, through the headwaters of Maryland's largest freshwater swamp, and across abandoned farmland with streams and springs once used for making moonshine.

The state acquired the land in 1930 during a period of farm abandonment and crop failures in southern Maryland. It planned to use this land to demonstrate

Unlike those in neighboring parks to the north, the trails in Cedarville are generally hard-packed dirt with very few rocks and little elevation change, the perfect combination for novice riders to hone their skills and advanced riders to work on their speed.

techniques in forestry, but the land is now managed for both recreation and business. You may notice, as you ride through the park, sizable areas that have been clear-cut or thinned. The cut timber, restricted to Virginia and loblolly pine, is sold to paper mills as far away as West Virginia and Pennsylvania.

This is a wonderful ride for novices and experts alike who have a passion for the great outdoors. Cedarville's terrain is mostly flat, as is most of southern Maryland, but the beauty of its wooded forest roadways rises high above most everything else in the area.

The orange trail trailhead is directly accessible from the parking area at the ranger station. We will begin measuring from the trailhead entrance. For this ride, we'll ride all the trails in the park in quick succession and in this order: Orange to blue to brown to green to blue to orange to white.

Miles and Directions

0.0 Enter the orange-blazed Holly Trail. At the T intersection, turn right, following the orange blazes.

0.4 Cross Bee Oak Road and continue following the orange blazes.

0.8 Cross Bee Oak Road.

1.0 Cross Bee Oak Road.

1.5 Turn left and continue following the orange blazes.

2.0 Cross Forest Road and continue following the orange blazes.

2.7 Turn left onto the doubletrack. The trail will continue to be blazed orange.

3.4 Reach the intersection of the orange and blue trails. Merge and continue onto the blue trail over the bridge.

3.7 Cross Forest Road and continue following the blue blazes on the opposite side.

3.9 Continue to the right. The trail to the left is an access point from the Charcola Kiln parking area. This marks the beginning of the white trail.

4.0 After a short descent you will be on the convergence of the orange, blue, and white trails; stay to the left and follow the blue blazes.

4.1 Turn right onto Sunset Road, and then immediately after crossing the short bridge turn left and continue following the blue trail.

5.3 Cross "Crossroads" and continue following the blue blazes.

5.7 Turn right on Forest Road to do a short loop along the brown and green trails. (You can, if you want, continue on the blue straight on the other side of Forest Road and bypass this section of the ride.)

5.8 The entrance to the Swamp Trail (green blazes) is to the right. We will return from that side. Continue following the road to the left toward the parking area. The entrance to the brown trail will be on the opposite side of the parking area to your left.

5.9 Enter the Plantation Trail, blazed brown.

6.4 Follow the brown blazes to the right.

6.5 Continue following the brown blazes to the right. You will be riding along the park's boundary line.

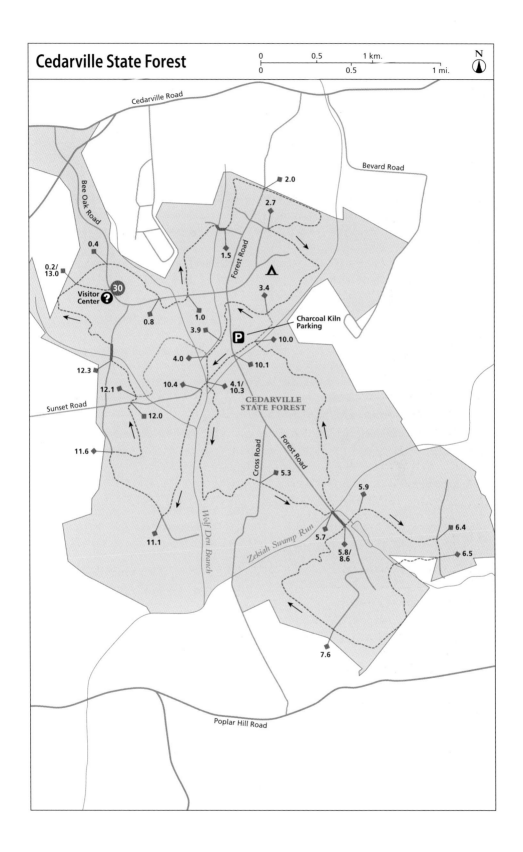

Cedarville State Forest

0   0.5   1 km.

0   0.5   1 mi.

N

Cedarville Road

Bevard Road

Bee Oak Road

2.0

2.7

Forest Road

1.5

0.4

0.2/
13.0

3.4

30

Visitor
Center

Charcoal Kiln
Parking

0.8   1.0

10.0

3.9

P

4.0   10.1

12.3

4.1/
10.3

12.1   10.4

CEDARVILLE
STATE FOREST

Sunset Road

12.0

11.6

Cross Road

Forest Road

5.3

5.9

Wolf Den Branch

Zekiah Swamp Run

5.7   6.4

11.1

5.8/
8.6   6.5

7.6

Poplar Hill Road

7.6 Continue straight at this intersection. You will now be on the green trail. (A right turn will take you straight down to Forest Road to the entrance of the green trail we saw at marker 5.8.)

8.6 Back at Forest Road. Turn left and then immediately right after the bridge to get on the blue trail.

9.5 Cross Crossroads and stay on the blue trail.

8.8 Cross Mistletoe Road. Forest Road is to the left. Continue following the blue blazes.

10.0 Turn left onto the orange trail.

10.1 Cross Forest Road and continue following the orange blazes. You are now on Sunset Road.

10.3 Reach the intersection of blue, orange, and white. You've been here before at mile marker 4.1. After riding over the small bridge continue straight on the white trail (unless you want to ride the blue trail again).

10.4 Follow the white blazes to the left. (Sunset Road continues to the right. You will converge back with Sunset Road farther up.)

11.1 Continue following the white blazes to the right.

11.6 Make a sharp right to continue on the white trail.

12.0 Continue following the white trail to the right.

12.1 Turn left to continue on the white trail. Straight will get you on Sunset Road and take you straight back down to marker 10.4. Immediately after making the left you will merge with the orange trail. Follow the orange blazes back to the starting point.

12.3 Turn right as the trail parallels Hidden Spring Road, and then make a left to cross the road. The orange trail continues on the other side.

13.0 Turn right at this intersection. The trail will lead you straight back to the parking area.

13.2 The loop is complete.

Ride Information

Local Information

Charles County's website has local information, events, and attractions: www.charlescountymd .gov

Accommodations

Structured campsites are available off Forest Road. Primitive camping is also available in the forest.

31 Saint Mary's River State Park

Boasting more than 8 miles of pristine singletrack, Saint Mary's Lake is an Eastern Shore destination. The ride's lack of serious elevation change makes this trail ideal for beginning to intermediate riders. The advanced rider should not be discouraged, however, as the winding singletrack trails make for great fun. Enjoy the variety of terrain that this trail has to offer.

Start: Saint Mary's River State Park main parking lot at the boat ramp
Length: 10.7 miles
Ride time: About 1.5-2.5 hours
Difficulty: Easy to moderate with flat, winding singletrack
Trail surface: Singletrack
Lay of the land: Wooded acres and fields, swamps, and small streams
Land status: State park
Nearest town: Leonardtown, MD

Other trail users: Hikers, anglers, hunters, and canoeists
Trail contacts: Saint Mary's River State Park, care of Point Lookout State Park, Scotland, MD, (301) 872-5688 or http://dnr2.maryland.gov/publiclands/Pages/southern/stmarysriver.aspx
Schedule & fees: Open 6 a.m. to sunset daily from March 1 through the third weekend in November; small vehicle fee from May to September

Getting there: From Waldorf: Take MD 5 south to Leonardtown. Continue for approximately 5 miles and turn left on Camp Cosoma Road (follow signs to Saint Mary's River State Park). Follow Camp Cosoma Road until it ends. Park at the far right corner (as you drive in) by the restrooms. A sign marks the trailhead. GPS coordinates: 38.251940, -76.542153.

The Ride

Southern Maryland does not usually conjure up images of great mountain biking terrain. However, near Lexington Park, north of Saint Mary's City in Saint Mary's County, is a small treasure not too many off-road cyclists know about—Saint Mary's River State Park. Located between Leonardtown and Lexington Park, near the mouth of the Chesapeake Bay, this remote park boasts more than 8 miles of pristine singletrack.

Making a short trip to Saint Mary's City, designated a national historic landmark, is well worth the time. On March 25, 1634, some two hundred colonists sent by Lord Baltimore of England landed on the shores of Saint Clements Island. Two days later, they sailed their ships, the *Ark* and the *Dove*, up what is now the Saint Mary's River and bought close to 30 square miles of land. This land, purchased from the local Native Americans, included the Yeocomico Village, establishing what is now Saint Mary's City.

Prior to the landing of England's colonists and as far back as 3,000 years ago, several Indian tribes, including the Piscataway-Conoy, Algonquins, and Susquehannocks,

The trails at Saint Mary's Lake will offer plenty of opportunities for you to work on your balance skills.

called this area home. Evidence of their existence can still be found along the banks of the river in the form of arrowheads, pottery, and ax heads.

As the first capital of Maryland and the fourth permanent English settlement in the New World, this area on the Eastern Shore was a busy pioneer community. In 1637, Saint Mary's County was established, and it became known as the "Mother County of Maryland." Saint Mary's County was also the first county to establish peaceful relations with the local Indians and was home to Maryland's first state house.

Today, much of what used to be Saint Mary's City no longer exists. By the time the state house was moved to Annapolis in 1695 and the American Revolution had ended, Lord Baltimore's capital was gone. However, during the commemoration of Maryland's 300th anniversary in 1934, the original Maryland state house was reconstructed. In 1984, for Maryland's 350th anniversary, other original sites were reconstructed. As time passes, more of Maryland's original buildings and points of interest are identified by more than 150 active archaeological excavations. Today, Saint Mary's City and County are living museums of Maryland's past.

In the 1970s, the state began purchasing land north of Great Mills, named for the mills operating along the banks of the Patuxent River. By 1979, it had completed a dam designed to protect the 5,600-acre watershed from spring floods. In 1981, this area was opened to the public as a state park.

Located on the northern edge of the Saint Mary's River watershed, the park is divided into two sites. Our ride is located on Site 1, which holds the 250-acre Saint Mary's Lake. This area has become a popular freshwater fishing spot and is currently designated as a trophy bass lake. Of more importance to cyclists, Saint Mary's Lake is circled by an 11.5-mile trail, of which 8 miles are mapped for your ride. As you pedal through the forest, notice the variety of habitats ranging from wooded acres and grass fields to swamps and streams.

Currently, the park is in its early stages of development, so read the main bulletin board for special announcements and information on areas that may be closed to the public. As you drive into the park, continue to the lower lot, to the left of the boat ramp. The trailhead is clearly marked. We will ride around the lake in a clockwise direction.

Miles and Directions

0.0 Start at the trail marker and head in to the singletrack, staying to the left. The trail is blazed white.

0.5 Stay to the right after the short climb. The trail to the left leads up to private property.

2.1 Immediately after crossing a narrow bridge with no railings the trail splits. Continue following the fork to the left. The right-side path is usually a muddy mess.

2.2 Continue to the left. The trail to the right simply takes you back to 2.1.

3.6 Turn left at this intersection to get on the Pine Trail. (The white path continues straight following the perimeter of the lake.) We will return to this intersection after riding a figure-eight through some of the other lake trails.

4.0 Stay to the right and on the Pine Trail.

4.2 Cross over the Forest Road trail and continue following the sign to the "new trail." A right turn on Forest Road will take you back down to the white trail.

4.6 Turn left to join the Lake Access Trail.

4.7 Turn right on the white path. (If you want to bail, take a left to cut the ride short and complete the lake loop.) We'll come back to this intersection in a bit.

5.4 Turn right at this intersection. You'll now ride up Forest Road to the entrance of the Pine Trail and then back to the white path (marker 3.6).

5.7 Turn right to hop on the Pine Trail, blazed red. (Continuing straight will take you up to the point where we crossed Forest Road the first time.)

6.2 Turn left at this intersection. You will now begin backtracking along the Pine Trail back to the white path.

6.6 Cross over Forest Road again and continue back to the white path.

6.8 Stay left to continue on the Pine Trail.

7.2 Turn left on the white path. You'll stay on this perimeter trail for pretty much the remainder of the ride.

7.9 Continue to the right. Forest Road is to the left.

Saint Mary's River State Park

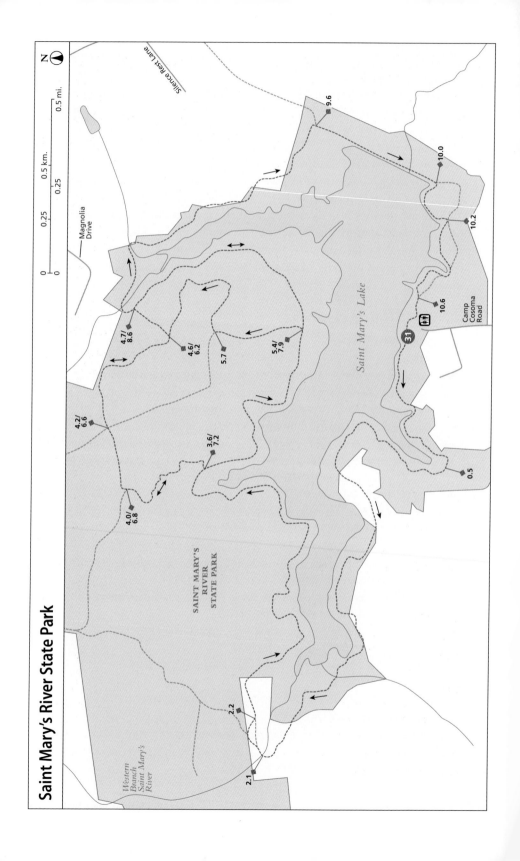

IN ADDITION: CHESAPEAKE BAY

Certainly, one of the most prominent features in this region is the Chesapeake Bay—the largest inlet on the Atlantic coast of the United States. The unique character and identity of eastern Maryland and Virginia are woven inextricably around the bay's coastal environment and economy, giving this region a flavor all its own.

The Patuxent River, along which the Patuxent River Park is located, travels nearly 100 miles to reach the bay and is one of the many broad, deep tidal rivers to pour into this vast waterway. Other major rivers feeding the bay are the Susquehanna, Patapsco, Severn, Potomac, Rapahannock, York, and James. The Chesapeake Bay is actually the "drowned" river valley of the lower part of the Susquehanna River, which pours into the bay at its head near the Maryland/Pennsylvania border.

In all, the bay measures nearly 195 miles long, ranges from 3 to 25 miles wide, and is deep enough to accommodate oceangoing vessels. It has about 27,000 miles of shoreline and covers 3,237 square miles of water. The Chesapeake Bay is considered one of the most important commercial and sportfishing grounds in the United States. It is famous for its oysters, crabs, and diamondback terrapins.

Another unique feature associated with the bay is the Chesapeake Bay Bridge-Tunnel, stretching between Cape Charles (the southern tip of Virginia's Eastern Shore) and a point east of Norfolk, Virginia. The bridge-tunnel carries motorists over and under 17.6 miles of uninterrupted ocean.

One of the nice things about traveling to Patuxent River Park is the classic eastern Maryland scenery and character that you are bound to experience along the way. As you drive down US 301, you should have plenty of opportunities to purchase fresh blue crabs from roadside vendors or to stop at one of the many seafood restaurants serving nothing but the freshest catch.

8.6 Stay to the right. The Lake Access Trail is to the left.

9.6 Turn right to go over the dam along the St. Mary's River Park Dirt Road.

10.0 Immediately after crossing the dam, turn right to continue on the singletrack that follows the edge of the lake. The trail will connect with the dirt road a little farther down.

10.2 Make a sharp right to reconnect with the white path and head down toward the lake. At this point there are two trails (white and yellow) that parallel each other along the edge of the lake and will take you back toward the main lot. Continue following the white path, but you can also follow the yellow-blazed trail in the same general direction.

10.6 Come out on the main gravel lot. Continue to the lower lot and the beginning of the ride.

10.7 The loop is complete.

Ride Information

Local Information

Historic Saint Mary's City
St. Mary's City, MD
(301) 862-0990

Local Events and Attractions

Southern Maryland Online—a local website with information about events and attractions in St. Mary's, Charles, and Calvert Counties: www.somd.com

Accommodations

Myrtle Point B&B
California, MD
(301) 862-3090

Local motel and hotel references: www.somd.com/travel

32 Tuckahoe State Park

Located just east of Maryland's Bay Bridge in Talbott County, Tuckahoe State Park has a surprisingly great trail system. The park has two main sections of trails. The first and longest is located below the dam and travels parallel to Tuckahoe Creek. This trail switches between hiking trails, equestrian trails, and a wide hard-surfaced path. The second trail is far shorter and runs along the creek above the lake. This section is far more challenging than the lower trail, offering more obstacles and a few sharp drop-offs with steep sections along gullies.

Start: Parking area along Cemetery Road on the southern edge of Tuckahoe State Park
Length: 10.6 miles
Ride time: About 1–2 hours
Difficulty: Easy
Trail surface: Mostly singletrack and doubletrack
Lay of the land: Streams, forest, and wetlands along Tuckahoe Creek
Land status: State park

Nearest town: Hillsboro, MD
Other trail users: Hikers, equestrians, anglers, boaters, and canoeists along the Tuckahoe Creek
Trail contacts: Tuckahoe State Park, (410) 820-1668, www.stateparks.com/tuckahoe_ state_park_in_maryland.html, http://dnr2 .maryland.gov/publiclands/Pages/eastern/ tuckahoe.aspx
Schedule: Open year-round sunrise to sunset

Getting there: Take US 50 East toward Ocean City, Maryland. Turn left on MD 404 East and continue for 7 miles. Make a U-turn on Ridgely Road and then take the first right onto Cemetery Road. The parking area will be to your immediate left before the cemetery. GPS coordinates: 38.922573, -75.943567.

The Ride

Tuckahoe State Park has transformed considerably since I last visited for the previous edition of the book. Since the last time, new trails have been developed, rerouted, and updated to offer cyclists greater opportunities within the park.

The park is divided by Tuckahoe Creek, which runs the entire length of the park's 3,800 acres. Trails are available on either side of the creek and offer hikers, equestrians, and mountain bikers a vast array of easy, rolling trails to play on. Don't be fooled by the lack of elevation, though. Because of its proximity to the bay and Maryland's shore, the soil in the park tends to be sandy and soft in sections, making it challenging to negotiate. The vast majority of trails are hard packed, so they offer riders the perfect surface to roll their bikes across the quiet and serene landscape of the park.

Tuckahoe has approximately 15 miles of trails, and our ride will take advantage of most of them. With the exception of the Little Florida Trail, which requires a fording of the Tuckahoe Creek, we will ride most of the park's inventory.

Pee Wee's trail will make you want to "scream your head off!" Super fun.

Tuckahoe, like many of the areas along the eastern Maryland shore, is rich in history. Its most early inhabitants were the Alonquin Indians who lived off the land and the riches of the bay, the creeks, and the eastern shore. It wasn't until later in history, however, that the area where Tuckahoe State Park is located made its mark. It is strongly believed that this tract of land served as a safe passage for runaway slaves to find refuge in the safe houses of Harriet Tubman's Underground Railroad.

Tuckahoe was also the birthplace of a prominent former slave, Frederick Douglass. Douglass was an instrumental member of the abolitionist movement and staunch supporter of women's rights. He was an influential orator who used his own experience as a slave, and subsequent escape into freedom, to support abolitionist movements.

As you ride through the park you'll see very little evidence of Tuckahoe's past; however, the relatively quiet and pristine surroundings will offer you a glimpse of the vast diversity of Maryland's flora and fauna. As you ride along the creek, or near the sixty-acre lake, you'll likely spot some of the park's residents, including bald eagles, blue herons, and osprey. If you have time, take a side trip to the main park office to get a glimpse of some of the predatory birds that live in the park's small aviary.

Miles and Directions

0.0 Start heading north toward the cemetery along Cemetery Road.

0.2 Continue through the gate; this marks the entrance to Tuckahoe State Park. You'll be on the blue trail, but will make an immediate left under the power lines to get onto the Creek Side Cliff Trail.

0.4 Turn right into the woods to continue on the Creek Side Cliff Trail.

1.3 Either fork will take you to the same place. The left branch is a little easier; the right side includes a short and technical rooty descent.

1.6 Reach the intersection of the Turkey Hill Trail (to the left) and the Tuckahoe Valley Trail (straight and right). Continue straight through this intersection. A right turn would take you back to Cemetery Road.

1.8 Continue following the blue trail up and to the left past the creek crossing. Shortly after, the trail will split. Both forks will take you to the same place. The left fork climbs gradually while the right side is more severe.

2.0 Turn right and continue along Wilbur's Cut-off Trail. You'll return from the left side.

2.2 Turn right onto the Office Spur Trail.

2.5 Turn left and follow the signs for the Arboretum Spur Trail. (Continuing straight will take you to the park office. Adjacent to the office is an aviary with several predatory birds. It's worth a quick side trip.) At this point you are entering the Adkins Arboretum. The only trail open to bikes here is the blue-blazed Tuckahoe Valley Trail; please respect this.

2.6 Turn right onto the blue trail. (A left turn will take you back toward Wilbur's Cut-off.)

3.1 Go past the first intersection to the left and continue to the T intersection. Turn left onto Upland Walk, still blazed blue.

3.4 Continue left at this intersection to stay on the blue trail. Upland Walk continues to the right.

3.7 Continue straight through this intersection. Nancy's Meadow Loop is to the right.

3.8 Go over the bridge and continue following the trail to the left.

4.3 Cross over Crouse Mill Road. You'll head up past the recycled-tire playground and do a quick out-and-back on the Lake Trail. Immediately after passing the playground you'll hit a paved path. The trailhead is up ahead to the left. The trail is blazed blue. You can skip this and continue left on the road toward the Tuckahoe Creek Spillway.

5.0 Reach the Cherry Lane picnic area. Turn around and head back to the recycled-tire playground and Crouse Mill Road.

5.7 Turn right onto Crouse Mill Road and follow it over the spillway. After the spillway continue following Crouse Mill Road to the left.

6.9 As Crouse Mill Road begins to curve to the left you'll see the entrance to Pee Wee's Trail along the tree line to the left. Follow it. Continue following the orange blazes.

8.1 Come out of Pee Wee's Trail into a semi-open area. Continue following the trail over the bridge to the left. Once you cross the bridge you will be back on the blue-blazed Tuckahoe Valley Trail. A right turn will begin your journey back to the starting point. We'll extend the ride a little and go left.

8.6 Turn right at this intersection. If you continue straight you'll end up back at the Office Spur Trail. A left turn will take you back toward the Arboretum.

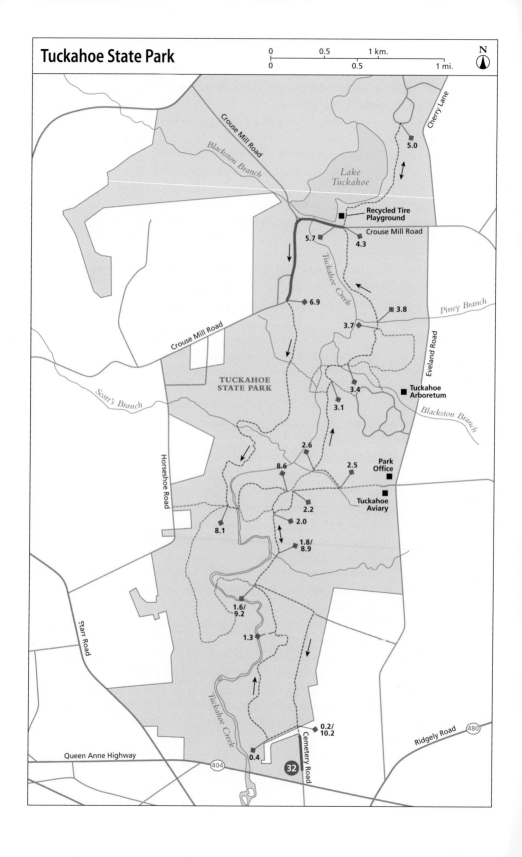

Tuckahoe State Park

0   0.5   1 km.

0   0.5   1 mi.

N

Crouse Mill Road

Blackston Branch

Cherry Lane

Lake
Tuckahoe

5.0

Recycled Tire
Playground

Crouse Mill Road

5.7   4.3

Tuckahoe Creek

Piney Branch

6.9

3.8

3.7

Eveland Road

Blackston Branch

3.4

Tuckahoe
Arboretum

TUCKAHOE
STATE PARK

3.1

Scott's Branch

2.6

Park
Office

8.6

2.5

Horseshoe Road

2.2

Tuckahoe Aviary

8.1

2.0

1.8/
8.9

1.6/
9.2

1.3

Starr Road

0.2/
10.2

Tuckahoe Creek

Cemetery Road

Ridgely Road

480

Queen Anne Highway

0.4

404

32

8.7 Make a sharp left and begin a short, loose climb and then make an immediate right at the top to continue on the blue trail. (Wilbur's Cut-off Trail is to the left and would take you right back to the bridge crossing.) Begin backtracking for a short time.

8.9 Reach a fork in the trail (opposite side of marker 1.8). Either branch will do.

9.2 Reach the intersection with the yellow trail. Continue to the left along the blue trail.

10.2 Continue straight through this intersection and onto Cemetery Road and make your way back to the starting point.

10.6 The loop is complete.

Ride Information

Local Information

Queen Anne County, Maryland
www.queenannesguide.com

Bike Shops

Bike Doctor of Kent Island
www.bikedoctorki.com
410-604-6096

Easton Cycle and Sport
www.eastoncycleandsport.com
410-822-7433

Local Events and Attractions

Adkins Arboretum
www.adkinsarboretum.org

Highland Aerosports
www.aerosports.net

Where to Eat

Hot Off the Coals
Queen Anne, MD
(410) 364-9494

Honorable Mentions

Compiled here is an index of great rides in coastal Maryland that didn't make the A list this time around but deserve recognition. Check them out and let us know what you think. You may decide that one or more of these rides deserves higher status in future editions, or perhaps you have a ride of your own that merits some attention. Some of these rides are documented on our website, www.mtbdc.com.

K. Naylor Mill Park

The trails at Naylor Mill Park are a little, unknown gem in the Eastern Shore. Packed in a relatively small space that's enclosed by the Henry S. Parker Athletic Complex to the east, Leonard Pond Run to the west, and Naylor Mill Road to the south, it is virtually impossible to get lost. The 5 miles of twisty, interconnecting trails will keep you busy for a few hours. Despite the lack of elevation, the trail builders have added lots of technical features to keep your ride interesting and fun. Check out ESIMBA's website at www.esimba.org for additional information on this trail system and upcoming events.

GPS coordinates: 38.412695, -75.590312

L. Pocomoke River State Forest

The trails at Pocomoke River State Forest are rather easy to negotiate. Like most of the destinations in Maryland's Eastern Shore, Pocomoke's trail system offers very little elevation change. Despite that, however, this network of trails is challenging, especially on a hot summer day when the overgrowth and myriad of cobwebs will keep you on your toes; for that reason I recommend visiting this destination in the fall or winter. Several old logging roads have slowly been reclaimed by the forest and have now become narrow doubletrack and singletrack trails. The trails on the east side of Blades Road are mostly doubletrack, while the trails that venture out along the east side are mostly singletrack. Overall there are about 7 miles of trails to enjoy.

GPS coordinates: 38.118844, -75.467148

M. Pocomoke YMCA

The Pocomoke YMCA Bike Trail system is a shining star in the region. Built and maintained by ESIMBA, they offer tight and twisty singletrack riding in a relatively compact place. All of the trails are well marked and accessible from the YMCA's main paved loop, a local favorite with joggers and walkers. ESIMBA has an accurate high-quality map that you can use to guide you easily through this system. Park behind the YMCA building and you'll see the ESIMBA trail marker. Hop on the main loop to ride it counter-clockwise and after a short distance along the paved path you'll reach the first trail, Dash Z. Simply turn right onto it until it brings you back out on the

The trails at the Pocomoke YMCA are clearly marked and easy to follow.

main loop. Continue repeating this procedure as you reach the system's other trails, including Whispering Pines (my favorite), The Ripper, Will's Woods, Keydawg, Turtle Ponds, and Bush Hog. Please respect the facility's confidence obstacles and do not climb on or play on them; this will ensure continued access to this trail system.

GPS coordinates: 38.080926, -75.538583

Northern Virginia

T raffic! Is there really anything more to say about Northern Virginia? Most of us in the Northern Virginia area are stuck in it going one direction, the other, or both, and it's only getting worse (do they really think building more roads will solve the problem?). So what's the deal? Can you really find a good place to ride a bike in this overdeveloped suburb of D.C.? Absolutely!

Look no farther than Wakefield Park and Lake Accotink, just 0.25 mile off the Beltway. Here you'll find great off-road riding for a variety of skill levels, including everything from taxing singletrack to sluggish dirt paths. The ride is guaranteed to keep cyclists who are just leaving work, tired of rush hour, and in need of a quick fix before heading home, in just the right mind-set.

But that isn't all. Northern Virginia is actually loaded with great places to pedal off-road. Some of the rides are in fairly standard places, such as Burke Lake Park with its meandering pathway around the lake, great for novices and families. Other mountain-bike trails had to be built, such as the trails in Fountainhead Regional Park, planned by the Northern Virginia Regional Park Authority in close collaboration with the Mid-Atlantic Off-Road Enthusiasts (MORE). The stacked trail system at Fountainhead is a great circuit of tightly wound singletrack going up and down the hilly banks of the Occoquan Reservoir through a lush canopy of woods.

So even though it may take you a few nerve-wracking hours to drive 10 miles through Northern Virginia traffic just to get to some of these rides, once you get out on the trails described in this book, all that frustration and energy will be well served on what is certainly some of the most fun riding in the region.

33 Elizabeth Furnace

This is by far one of the most difficult rides in the book, but one of the most rewarding. I won't sugarcoat it—this ride is demanding, technical, steep, fast, and dangerous. If the ride itself doesn't do you in, a bear might. When you finish, you'll ask yourself "Why?" And then, out of nowhere, you'll start planning your return, or researching other rides in the forest—there are plenty, more than 400 miles of singletrack to choose from. This demanding and technical ride has become a rite of passage for mountain bikers in the Washington, D.C., region and serves as the perfect introduction to the type of trail you'll find elsewhere in the George Washington National Forest and the Catoctin Mountains to the north.

Start: Massanuten Mountain/Signal Knob parking area
Length: 11.7 miles
Ride time: About 2–3 hours
Difficulty: Difficult
Trail surface: Mostly singletrack; one section of gravel road

Lay of the land: Rugged trails of the Appalachian Mountains
Land status: State forest
Nearest town: Front Royal
Other trail users: Hikers
Trail contacts: GWNF Supervisor's Office, (540) 265-1000 (information only)
Schedule: Open year-round

Getting there: From Washington take 66 West toward Front Royal. Take exit 6 for US 340/US 522 South toward Front Royal. Turn right on US 55W, Strasburg Road, and then left onto Fort Valley Road. The parking area will be to your right and clearly marked as you enter the George Washington National Forest. GPS coordinates: 38.924428, -78.332176.

The Ride

I remember the first time I ventured out into the George Washington National Forest (GWNF). . . . I thought it would be the last. I headed out west of Washington on Route 66 to Front Royal with a group of friends from the Mid-Atlantic Off-Road Enthusiasts (MORE) group to ride Elizabeth Furnace for the first time. I had already been riding my mountain bike in the region for several months and had ridden Wakefield, Patapsco, and Loch Raven Reservoir to the north in Baltimore, and all the other usual spots. But none of those rides would prepare me for what I was about to experience in the foothills of the GWNF and the Appalachian Mountains.

The first part of our ride will follow a gravel road that was once used to transport the pig iron created in the furnace below to the other side of Massanutten Mountain. Iron ore was mined in the area and then brought to the Elizabeth Furnace, where it was purified. Unfortunately not much is left of the furnace that produced nearly three tons of pig iron daily until the Federals burned it during the Civil War. The

The trails at Elizabeth Furnace are very challenging.

furnace was rebuilt shortly after the war, but it only stayed in operation for a short time and then never operated again. Today some of the structure remains, but it is in disrepair and often covered by overgrown vegetation during the spring and summer months.

Once past the dirt road, which really is a pleasant climb, we will enter the canopy and begin a journey toward the Strasburg Reservoir and Signal Knob. The singletrack trails continue in an upward direction and offer a series of highly enjoyable technical sections with several creek crossings. They are technical enough to keep you focused on the ride and what lies ahead. The beauty of this ride is that at its midpoint you can veer right and visit Strasburg Reservoir, and during a hot summer day, take a dip in its cool waters before confronting the hike-a-bike to Signal Knob, the high point of the ride.

▶ **The Appalachian Mountains are more than 450 million years old and were once as tall as the Alps and the Rocky Mountains.**

To get to Signal Knob, however, you must endure one of the toughest 0.5-mile sections of trail in the region. Once up high you'll be treated to fantastic panoramic views of the valley below. It's no surprise that Confederate soldiers climbed the very same trail you will use to observe Union troop movements and

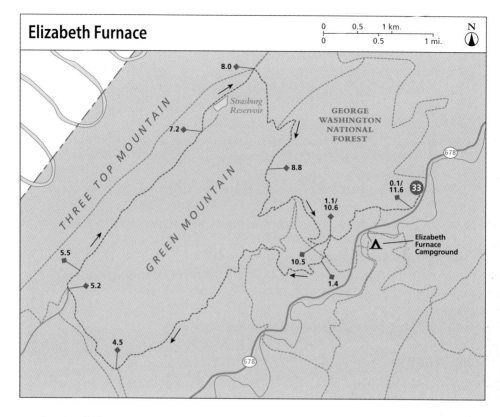

relay signals from its peak to their counterparts. After enjoying the view and recovering your strength you'll descend on what is perhaps one of the best downhill runs in the region. Boulder gardens that will tame the most seasoned mountain biker will open up and treat you to one of the most technical and rewarding downhills you'll ever experience, and before you know it deliver you to the starting point of the ride. You'll likely spend a quarter of the time in this last section, and although exhausted you will undoubtedly be asking for more.

If more is what you want, don't fret. There are literally hundreds of miles of trails in the forest. My good friend Chris Scott, owner of the Stokesville Lodge and Shenandoah Mountain Touring in Harrisonburg, VA (www.mtntouring.com), can tailor a tour for you to show you some more of the best riding in the area. Don't hesitate to contact him so he and his crew can guide you through some of the best trails in the region.

Miles and Directions

0.0 Start from the Massanuten Trail, Signal Knob parking area. The trailhead is on the west side of the parking area. Enter the trail and stay to the left.

0.1 Stay to the right as you reach the group camping sign. The trail will be blazed orange.

0.4 Stay to the right and follow the blue blazes.

1.1 Turn left at this trail intersection. Massanuten Mountain West is on the right fork; this is the direction we will be returning in.

1.4 Turn right on the fire road and get ready for a nice grinder up the mountain.

4.5 The fire road ends. Enter the singletrack and then stay to the right at the trail fork.

5.2 Cross Mudhole gap and then turn right on the gravel road. Continue following the orange blazes.

5.5 Continue straight through the gate on the gravel road.

7.2 Turn left and follow the signs for Signal Knob. (If you continue straight, less than 0.25 mile ahead is the Strasburg Reservoir. On a blistering hot day you can take a dip in the reservoir.)

8.0 Turn right into the blue trail. This is the beginning of the last, and most brutal, climb of the ride.

8.8 You've reached the top. I highly suggest you take a break and prep yourself for the downhill ride. The trail is to the left and blazed blue.

10.5 Stay left at this intersection and continue on the blue trail.

10.6 Stay to the left at this intersection. (You can turn right and do the entire loop again if you want.) At this point we'll be backtracking on the trail we initially started on.

11.6 Stay to the left.

11.7 Turn right to return to the parking area and close out the loop.

Ride Information

Local Information

Front Royal, VA
www.discoverfrontroyal.com; www.frontroyal
chamber.com

Bike Shops

Element Sports
Winchester, VA
(540) 662-5744
www.elementsport.com

Hawksbill Bicycles
Luray, VA
(540) 743-1037
www.hawksbillbicycles.com

Local Events and Attractions

www.discoverfrontroyal.com

Where to Eat

Jalisco Mexican Restaurant
Front Royal, VA
(540) 635-7348

34 Conway Robinson State Forest

Although short, the ride will certainly be a pleasing one. It has quickly become a favorite destination for my daughter and I to visit. The relatively flat trails and smooth surface make it a perfect destination for novice to intermediate riders. A short section of trail has been crafted to please more experienced riders and can easily be bypassed if you are not up to the challenge.

Start: Main Conway Robinson parking area
Length: 3.3 miles; additional if you ride the internal trails
Ride time: About 0.5–1 hour
Difficulty: Easy
Trail surface: Doubletrack and singletrack trails
Lay of the land: Pine and old-growth hardwood stands

Land status: State forest
Nearest town: Gainesville and Manassas, VA
Other trail users: Hikers, equestrians, and hunters
Trail contacts: Virginia Department of Forestry: www.dof.virginia.gov
Schedule: Open year-round, sunrise to sunset

Getting there: Follow Route I-66W to exit 43B, US 29 N. Follow 29 North and make an immediate left on University Blvd. into the park's parking area. The trailhead is to the left of the main picnic area (as you face it). GPS coordinates: 38.803490, -77.587845.

The Ride

Conway Robinson State Forest is adjacent to the Manassas National Battlefield, and as such, played an important role during the Civil War. Situated in Prince William County and near the junction of the Alexandria and Manassas Gap Railroads, it served as a key link to the South. Confederate generals recognized the geographic significance of the area and stationed their troops to protect and maintain possession of the railroad junction. Allowing the Union to control it would mean they could lose a key access point to the South's capital, Richmond, Virginia.

Only a few months had passed since the start of the Civil War when Northern citizens began clamoring for an advance on Richmond. They thought that by taking the South's capital city, they would quell the rebellion and hostilities would come to a quick end. Yielding to pressure from the public, and from political leadership, Brigadier General Irvin McDowell led his inexperienced army across Bull Run, and through much of the area where Conway Robinson State Forest is today, toward Manassas. Their aim was to capture Manassas Junction, the pivotal railroad town next to Brentsville that would give the North an overland route to the South's capital.

The southern army met the "surprise" attack planned by the North with determination and conviction on July 21, 1861. Led by a relatively unknown officer from the Virginia Military Institute (VMI), Thomas Jackson, the Southern forces held their ground and drove the northern forces back toward Washington, D.C. It was in that first battle that Jackson earned his nickname, "Stonewall." Jackson's brigade suffered considerable casualties that day, but they stopped the Union's assault and helped drive it back. It was another officer in the Southern forces, Brigadier General Barnard Elliott Bee Jr., who uttered the words that earned him and his brigade their nickname: "Look at Jackson standing there like a stonewall." It was also the first time that Union soldiers heard the Rebel Yell. It was Jackson who instructed his troops to "yell like furies" when they advanced and charged the enemy.

The trails at Conway Robinson State Forest are perfect for kids and novice riders.

Both the South and North suffered great casualties in the First Manassas, and both armies came to the realization that the war would be longer, more arduous, and more brutal than they had ever anticipated. Nearly 5,000 men died in the battle, proving how difficult the war would be. Years later, more than half a million Union and Confederate soldiers would lose their lives in battle. The Second Battle of Manassas in late August of 1862 was of greater scale. More than 100,000 men fought in the fields of Prince William County, and more than 12,000 died, most from the Union. Ultimately the North prevailed and today, Manassas and the areas adjacent to Conway Robinson State Forest are simple historic reminders of a painful past that has long been gone, but one that shaped the county, the state, and our nation as a whole.

Today, Conway Robinson State Forest offers us a glimpse in to the past. Acquired by the state in 1938, Conway Robinson State Forest is an urban oasis dedicated to the preservation of the natural woodland within it. Named after Conway Robinson, a 19th-century prominent Virginian, the 444-acre parcel remains one of the largest undeveloped parcels of land amid the suburban jungle of Northern Virginia. Hikers, cyclists, equestrians, and hunters can now enjoy an environment that has been

IN ADDITION: BIKING WITH KIDS

Shortly after my daughter was born, I could not wait to take her out on the trail with me. Now that she can ride without training wheels we head out regularly to ride both on and off-road. Here are a few simple tips to remember when riding with young kids:

Start early. I've found that my daughter will ride farther when we go out in the morning. In the afternoon she generally tires quickly.

Invite a friend. If you have a friend who is also trying to get his daughter (or son) out on the bike, ask them to tag along. Kids tend to have more fun when there is someone of their own age with them. MORE has recently begun a sMOREs (small MORE members, aka kids) program; check out their calendar at www.more-mtb.org for regularly scheduled rides. All of the clubs mentioned in the book have some kind of kids' program to get lots of children riding together.

Take your time. When out with kids, a 4-mile ride may take up to 2 hours. This is all about them getting to know their bikes and having fun.

Take breaks. Plan your route; if you know there is a playground or other interesting kid-friendly landmark along the way, fit it into your ride to add a little variety and to give your child a break. It will keep them interested and entertained, plus they'll get a rest.

Bring snacks and plenty of water, and make sure you eat and drink them. When I ride with my daughter one of our rituals is to find a nice spot to sit down and have our snacks.

Be prepared. Bring whatever tools you may need. Always carry your phone and some cash in case of an emergency and always let someone else know exactly where you'll be and how long you plan to be away. This tip applies to riding with adults as well, and especially when riding on your own.

Have fun. Be enthusiastic and encouraging. Always praise whatever little accomplishment your child makes on the bike and express pride in what they do—it will make them want to come back and ride with you again and again.

Be safe. Don't ride above your ability or allow your child to take unnecessary risks. After all, we want to ride again tomorrow.

carefully managed through passive silviculture techniques—the practice of controlling the growth, composition, and quality of forests.

We will ride the Conway trails in a clockwise loop. Although Conway has many intersecting trails, these tend to be very muddy, even long after rain has passed.

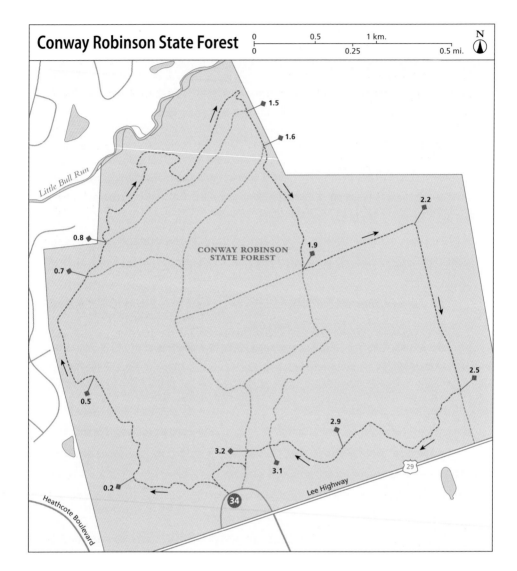

Conway Robinson State Forest

0   0.5   1 km.

0   0.25   0.5 mi.

N

CONWAY ROBINSON
STATE FOREST

Little Bull Run

Heathcote Boulevard

Lee Highway

Miles and Directions

0.0   The trailhead is to the left of the pavilion as you look at the pavilion from the parking area. The trail is blazed blue. Immediately upon entering the trail, stay to the left.

0.2   Cross the doubletrack to stay on the blue trail.

0.5   Stay to the right. The left branch is a neighborhood connector.

0.7   Stay to the left to continue to follow the blue loop.

0.8   Turn left onto the orange trail. The orange trail is the most technically difficult portion of this ride. You can bypass it and continue straight if you want.

1.5   Reach the blue loop again. Turn left to continue on the blue loop; right will simply take you back to the entry to the orange trail.

1.6 Continue following the blue trail as it curves to the left.

1.9 Turn left to continue following the blue blazes under the pines.

2.2 Turn right on the doubletrack. When I documented this ride the forest service had done a controlled burn on the woods to the left.

2.5 Turn right to continue on the blue and the singletrack. Straight ahead will take you to VA 29.

2.9 Go over the bridge.

3.1 Stay to the left to stay on the blue trail. The red trail to the right is notoriously muddy and best avoided.

3.2 Turn left on the yellow trail. This doubletrack will lead you back to the parking area. We will immediately turn right to hop on the blue and ride behind the picnic pavilion. At the T intersection, turn left on the blue to complete the ride, or turn right and do the whole loop again.

3.3 The loop is complete.

Ride Information

Local Information

The city of Manassas is rich in history and there is a lot to do in the area year-round. Check out visitmanassas.org for regional attractions and the City of Manassas website for additional information: www.manassascity.org.

Bike Shops

Bull Run Bicycles
Manassas, VA
(703) 335-6131
www.bullrunbicycles.com

A-1 Manassas Cycling
Manassas, VA
(703) 361-6101
www.a1cycling.com

Local Events and Attractions

Manassas National Battlefield Park
www.nps.gov/mana/index.htm

Where to Eat

Okra's Cajun Creole Restaurant
Manassas, VA
(703) 368-3427
www.okras.com

City Square Cafe
Manassas, VA
(703) 369-6022
www.citysquarecafe.com

35 Lake Fairfax Park

The trails at Lake Fairfax have seen a considerable transformation over the last few years. What were once soggy and boggy unsustainable tracts have been converted to a network of sustainable ribbons across this Fairfax County destination.

Start: Michael Faraday Court parking area adjacent to and behind the Skate Quest Ice Rink
Length: Up to 12 miles
Ride time: About 1.5–3 hours
Difficulty: Easy/intermediate
Trail surface: Mostly singletrack, some doubletrack
Lay of the land: Rolling trails through the dense forest of Lake Fairfax Park

Land status: County park
Nearest town: Reston, VA
Other trail users: Hikers
Trail contacts: Fairfax County, Virginia, www.fairfaxcounty.gov/parks/lakefairfax; Mid-Atlantic Off-Road Enthusiasts, www.more-mtb.org
Schedule: Open year-round sunrise to sunset

Getting there: From I-495 take VA 267 (tolls) west for approximately 6 miles and exit onto Hunter Mill Road (exit 14). Make an immediate left onto Sunset Hills Road to continue west toward Reston. Continue on Sunset Mills Road for approximately 1.2 miles and turn right onto Michael Faraday Court. Cross the Washington & Old Dominion trail (W&OD) and continue straight to the far end of the parking area. The trailhead will be to your left as you drive in. GPS coordinates: 38.950733, -77.331256.

The Ride

When we first documented the trails in the vicinity of Lake Fairfax there was very little to talk about. Initially we had set out this destination as a point-to-point ride, taking riders from the southeast of VA 7 to the Difficult Run parking area, where Ride 38 of this edition begins. Along the way riders would pass what's now the starting point of this loop.

Back then there were very few trails to choose from, and the best alternative was to send riders along Colvin Run along the water's edge. That route, historically, was often soggy, muddy, and otherwise susceptible to damage from heavy use.

The Mid-Atlantic Off-Road Enthusiasts (MORE) set out to change the landscape of the area, and in collaboration with Fairfax County worked to develop new sustainable trails along Lake Fairfax, repair unsustainable ones, and work on maintaining and improving the trails along Colvin Run to offer all users additional opportunities in the park. Today, there are more than 10 miles of easy to intermediate trails around Lake Fairfax that can be tied together with the Washington & Old Dominion rail-trail (W&OD, a paved bike path), and the Cross County Trail (Ride 38) to craft a longer loop. In fact, in 2014, MORE held the annual NoVa Epic, and used most

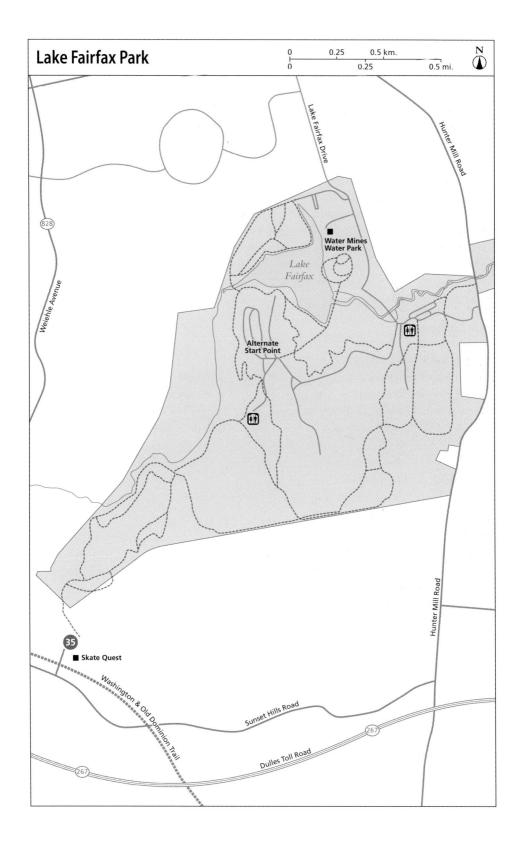

Lake Fairfax Park

0   0.25   0.5 km.

0   0.25   0.5 mi.

N

Lake Fairfax Drive

Hunter Mill Road

828

Weiehle Avenue

Water Mines
Water Park

Lake
Fairfax

Alternate
Start Point

35
Skate Quest

Washington & Old Dominion Trail

Hunter Mill Road

Sunset Hills Road

267

Dulles Toll Road

267

of the trails in this Northern Virginia destination to piece together a 25-mile loop through mostly singletrack trails.

Lake Fairfax is compact, and there are a lot of trails to the south of the lake that crisscross each other to create a maze of trails. Much like the trails at Lake Accotink Park in Annandale, Virginia (Ride 40), it is difficult to piece together and give you directions for an actual loop. For that reason, I'm only providing you with a starting point and general guidance on where to head. It's hard to get lost within the park, and once you've ridden the network of trails that meander under its canopied forests, you'll be able to craft a loop of your very own.

MORE holds regularly scheduled rides in this park for riders of all levels. Check their events calendar regularly for upcoming rides at Lake Fairfax, including a spring/summer kids ride series, sMOREs. The best way to learn the system is to follow along on one of their guided rides.

Despite all of the progress made by MORE to build and maintain these trails to be sustainable, please do not ride them when wet, especially after heavy rains.

Miles and Directions

Start your ride from the parking area at the end of Michael Faraday Court and behind the Ice Skating Rink. As you drive into the parking lot you'll see the trailhead to the left. Chances are there will be lots of other riders in the vicinity as well, so getting someone to point you in the right direction should not be a problem. Once you enter the park, the trail splits into three branches, all of which will take you northwest toward the lake. My personal preference is to follow the furthermost right trail and take that in a counter-clockwise direction to the lake, returning then along the banks of Colvin Run. Doing so will provide you with a sense of the system's perimeter. There are lots of other trails within these boundaries to play in.

Ride Information

Local Information
Visit the Fairfax County website for information on events and things to do in Reston, Virginia: www.fxva.com/our-community/herndon-reston/things-to-do-va

Bike Shops
The Bike Lane
Reston Town Center
Reston, VA
(703) 689-2671
www.thebikelane.com

Bikenetic
Falls Church, VA
(703) 534-7433
www.bikenetic.com

Where to Eat
Pollo Peru
Reston, VA
(703) 707-8484
www.facebook.com/polloperu

36 Fountainhead Regional Park

This ride will take you through one of the region's most successful off-road cycling projects. Originally conceived by a band of riders from MORE in early 1994, and redesigned with the International Mountain Biking Organization (IMBA) in 2010–2012, the new Fountainhead Trail is challenging, fun, and an incredibly rewarding system of trails. The once straight and steep climbs and downhills that crossed the park have been replaced with challenging switchbacks and screaming berms. Fountainhead is a glorious playground in which to take your mountain-biking skills to the next level.

Start: Fountainhead Park
Length: 14.8 miles (green 2.2 miles, blue 4.7 miles, black 3.9 miles)
Ride time: About 1.5–3 hours
Difficulty: Moderate to difficult
Trail surface: Technical singletrack and doubletrack
Lay of the land: Wooded and hilly
Land status: Northern Virginia Regional Park
Nearest town: Springfield, VA

Other trail users: None; this loop is mountain-bike specific
Trail contacts: Northern Virginia Regional Park Authority, (703) 352-5900; Fountainhead Regional Park, (703) 250-9124, www.fountainheadproject.org; Mid-Atlantic Off-Road Enthusiasts (MORE), (703) 502-0359
Schedule: Open daily from dawn to dusk, March to November

Getting there: From the Capital Beltway (I-495): Take exit 5 west onto Braddock Road. Head south on VA 123. Continue past Burke Lake Park to the Fountainhead Regional Park sign on the right side of the road. Turn right at this sign on Hampton Road. Follow Hampton Road to the park entrance on the left. Park in the first parking lot on the right. The trailhead is to your left. GPS coordinates: 38.724367, -77.330382.

The Ride

When I first included Fountainhead Regional Park in this book, I wrote, "the Fountainhead Regional Park Mountain Bike Trail was opened in the spring of 1997. Before then, bicycles were not permitted on any of the trails within the park. The Fountainhead Regional Park Mountain Bike Trail represents an important opportunity and major breakthrough in the Washington Metropolitan area. It was planned by the Northern Virginia Regional Park Authority (NVRPA) in close collaboration with the Mid-Atlantic Off-Road Enthusiasts (MORE) and initially funded, in large part, by REI (Recreational Equipment, Incorporated). This flagship mountain bike trail project was designed specifically for mountain bikers and will serve as a real litmus test for other park officials who are interested in constructing and maintaining mountain-bike-specific trail ways at their parks."

Suffice it to say, I think the litmus test proved to be a success. Since it was opened, the trails at Fountainhead have evolved considerably, and after a period of transformation are better than ever. The original loop, which was roughly 4.5 miles, has more than doubled in length, and the trails are far better than what was originally laid out. Today, with the help of the International Mountain Biking Association (IMBA) and careful planning, the trails are an off-road cyclist's dream. Tight switchbacks, rock outcroppings, banked turns, technical drops, and fast descents are but a few of the features that have recently been incorporated into the improved trail design. Drainage issues and a variety of troublesome erosion issues have been addressed, and

The entrance to the new black diamond loop at Fountainhead is particularly hard . . . for a reason.

the entrance and exit to the trail have been divided so that there is no longer a two-way-traffic trail. The entire loop continues to be a directional loop, which ensures that you'll never run into a rider going in the opposite direction. This makes riding the new downhill and banked turns extremely fun.

Additional improvements have also been made at key intersections. Additionally, a new boardwalk and bridge leads riders to a new exit trail, and midway through the ride you can hang out and play around in a technical section that was designed to improve your handling skills.

Initially there was a little bit of an uproar when announcements were made that Fountainhead would receive a facelift. Some riders felt that the goal of the New Fountainhead Project was to "dumb down" the trails and take away its challenging sections. On the contrary, the new Fountainhead continues to be a challenging trail that has been made longer.

Of particular pride to me is that the original name of Shockabilly Hill has been retained. Back during the first Fountainhead project, one of the sponsors for the trail was FAT City Cycles, a custom frame builder from Massachusetts and makers of one of my first "real" mountain bikes. My relationship with FAT helped us secure a

YOU MAY RUN INTO: LARRY CAUTILLI

Larry's quest for fitness led him to buy a bike in early 1985. Then, a few years later he added another, a mountain bike. It was with that mountain bike that Larry began racking up the miles. "It became an addiction," Larry said. "The more I rode, the more I wanted to ride. I really can't pinpoint what one thing I love about cycling, but if I had to, it is just being on the bike."

That need to just "be on the bike" has been to our benefit. In early 1996 when MORE was beginning to work on the first loops at Fountainhead, Larry used most of his two hundred hours of "use or lose" vacation time to work on the trails manually. Over the years he has seen the loops evolve. Most recently, due in large part to Larry's dedication, the trails at Fountainhead have been transformed into a regional mountain-biking destination.

Larry loves to ride Gambrill State Park in Frederick and the Frederick Watershed, but you'll undoubtedly find him spinning the trails at Wakefield and now, more than ever, over the fruits of his efforts at Fountainhead. If you see him, say hello and make sure you thank him for a job well done. He certainly deserves it.

Shockabilly frame set to raffle off during one of several events promoted by MORE in support of the project. Having that prize helped MORE to raise the funds necessary for the project. In exchange, my friend Valerie Dosland, a MORE board member, suggested to FAT that we would name one of the trails after their bike. They agreed to the deal, so we coined the steepest part of the trail (at the time) Shockabilly Hill (SOB). As you close out the ride you'll come to an intersection giving you the option of riding old Shockabilly or the new, improved version (SAB).

Fountainhead is a closely monitored trail. When conditions are not favorable for riding, the trail gates are closed and access is denied to the system. Do not bypass the gates. If the trail is closed, please respect the closure and come back another day. Bypassing the gates only threatens access for other users. Before heading out to Fountainhead I highly suggest you check the trail's status. Park managers and project leads have set up a Facebook page (www.facebook.com/thefountainheadproject) where they promptly post trail conditions, and a ride line (703-250-9124) is also available to obtain more information.

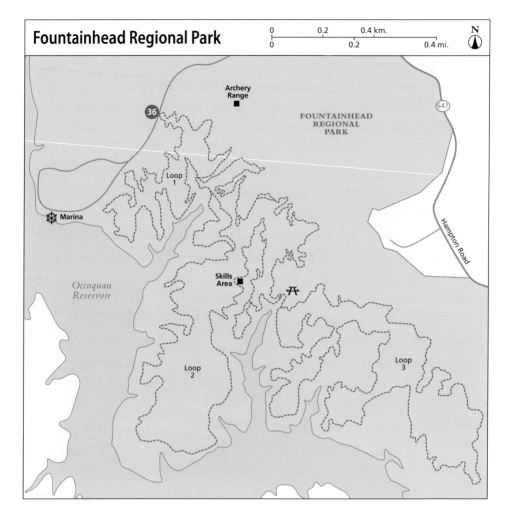

Fountainhead Regional Park

Fountainhead continues to be a showpiece for the Mid-Atlantic region. From its early ambitious beginning, to its successful redesign, Fountainhead is certainly bound to bring a smile to your face.

Miles and Directions

Fountainhead Regional Park is an easy trail to follow. As part of the new design, the trail has been adequately marked, and all intersections are clear and easy to understand. The trail is unidirectional to avoid any collisions, and it is mountain-bike specific, so you will be unlikely to run into any other trail users. Do watch your speed, though, and ride within your abilities.

Fountainhead is a "stacked" system. The first, green loop, is the easiest and closest to the parking area. If you have difficulty riding that, I suggest you skip the blue and black loops. If you enjoy the green loop then continue on to the blue loop, which offers additional challenges. The blue loop will take you farther away from the parking area. Finally, if you have no troubles with the green or blue loops, than hammer away at the black. Be warned, though, the entrance to this loop has been made hard for a reason, because you will most definitely encounter lots of challenging and technical sections beyond what you experienced in the green or blue loops. And the black loop will take you farther away from the lot.

Ride Information

Local Information

Occoquan's website for local information: www .historicoccoquan.com

Fairfax County Convention and Visitors Bureau (800) 7FAIRFAX, www.visitfairfax.org

Bike Shops

The Bike Lane
Springfield, VA
(703) 440-8701
www.thebikelane.com

Olde Town Bicycles
Woodbridge, VA
(703) 491-5700
www.oldetownebicycles.com

Village Skis & Bikes
Woodbridge, VA
(703) 730-0303
www.vsbsports.com

Local Events and Attractions

Historic town of Occoquan
www.historicoccoquan.com

Harbor River Cruises in Occoquan
(703) 385-9433

Historic Occoquan Spring Arts & Crafts Show
(703) 491-2168

Accommodations

Bennett House Bed & Breakfast
9252 Bennett Dr.
Manassas, VA
(703) 368-6121

Sunrise Hill Farm B&B
5590 Old Farm Inn
Manassas, VA
(703) 754-8309

37 Great Falls National Park

Great Falls National Park is a natural haven for thousands of Washingtonians seeking solitude from the daily grind of gridlock and government. Trails abound throughout this park on the river, offering cyclists, hikers, and equestrians alike rugged terrain. Some portions of the park's trails are wide, dirt carriage roads dating back through history and meandering through the scenery, while others are steep, rocky, and narrow, keeping even agile cyclists on the tips of their seats. Come one and all to this park of presidents, dignitaries, and commoners and enjoy what folks throughout time have been enjoying along the rapids of the Potomac.

Start: Great Falls National Park visitor center
Length: 6.8 miles
Ride time: About 1–1.5 hours
Difficulty: Moderate due to occasional steep, rocky singletrack
Trail surface: Rocky, dirt trails and carriage roads
Lay of the land: Wooded, rocky, and hilly terrain along the banks of the Potomac River

Land status: National park
Nearest town: McLean, VA
Other trail users: Hikers, equestrians, climbers, kayakers, and tourists
Trail contacts: National Park Service, (703) 759-2915
Schedule & fees: Park is open from 7 a.m. to sunset; small entrance fee

Getting there: From the Capital Beltway (I-495): From exit 13 northwest of McLean, take VA 193 (Georgetown Pike) west toward Great Falls. Go about 4 miles, then turn right on Old Dominion Road, which becomes the park entrance road. Go 1 mile to the end of this road and park at the visitor center. Telephones, water, food, restrooms, and information available inside the visitor center. GPS coordinates: 39.003029, -77.256459.

The Ride

Great Falls is one of the nation's most popular national parks. How appropriate then for it to be located just 14 miles from our nation's capital. And what a thrill for cyclists to know that mountain biking is not only allowed at the park—it's welcome. Along with hikers, historians, rock climbers, and kayakers, off-road cyclists come in droves to enjoy the park's public resources. There are more than 5 miles of designated trails to enjoy in this park, all of which conveniently intersect to create hours of off-road adventure. The trails vary in intensity, ranging from rolling forest roads beneath tall oaks and maples to steep, rocky singletrack overlooking the dramatic Mather Gorge. The park's unequaled beauty, proximity to Washington, and accessible trails combine to make Great Falls National Park Northern Virginia's most popular off-road cycling haven.

The ride begins at the visitor center parking lot and travels south along Old Carriage Road through the middle of the park. Old Carriage was used in the 1700s to carry settlers to their dwellings at Matildaville, ruins of which still stand. Henry Lee, a Revolutionary War hero and friend of George Washington's, developed this small town. Named after Lee's first wife, Matildaville lasted only three decades before fading into history.

The route bends deep into the park and travels up and down the rocky pass along Ridge Trail. During the winter months, breathtaking views of the gorge show through deciduous trees. The trail then descends quickly to the Potomac (another great view) and follows along Difficult Run before heading north again back toward the start.

Great Falls has always been a popular place to visit for locals and world tourists alike. Some have come to survey the river's rapids. George Washington formed the Patowmack Company in 1784 to build a series of canals around the falls. Theodore Roosevelt came to Great Falls to hike and ride horses during his presidency. Today, thousands come to enjoy Great Falls as well. But they don't come to build canals, develop towns, make trade, or seek solitude from the presidential office. They come only to ride the park's great trails, kayak the rapids, climb the steep cliffs, and bear witness to the magnificent scenery at Great Falls National Park.

Miles and Directions

0.0 Start at Great Falls Visitor Center. Follow the horse/biker trail south along the entrance road.

0.4 Bear right at the restrooms and go around the steel gate on Old Carriage Road (unpaved).

1.1 Bear left down the trail to Sandy Landing.

1.3 Arrive at Sandy Landing, a beautiful spot along the river, great for viewing Mather Gorge. Return to Old Carriage Road.

1.5 Turn left, continuing on Old Carriage Road. Begin a steady uphill.

1.9 Turn left near the top of this climb on Ridge Trail.

2.7 Turn left after the steep descent on Difficult Run Trail. Head toward the Potomac.

2.9 Arrive at the Potomac River. This is another great spot to view Sherwin Island, where Mather Gorge and the Potomac River converge. Turn around and follow Difficult Run Trail west along Difficult Run Creek toward Georgetown Pike.

3.6 Turn right on Georgetown Pike. Be careful with traffic and ride on the dirt shoulder.

3.8 Turn right on Old Carriage Road. This is the first dirt road you come to along Georgetown Pike. Go around the gate and begin climbing.

4.0 Turn left on Ridge Trail. Follow this toward the entrance road.

4.7 Reach the park entrance road (Old Dominion Road). Turn around and continue back on Ridge Trail.

5.4 Turn left on Old Carriage Road.

6.4 Go through the gate at the beginning of Old Carriage Road and head back to the parking lot at the visitor center.

6.8 Arrive back at the visitor center and parking lot.

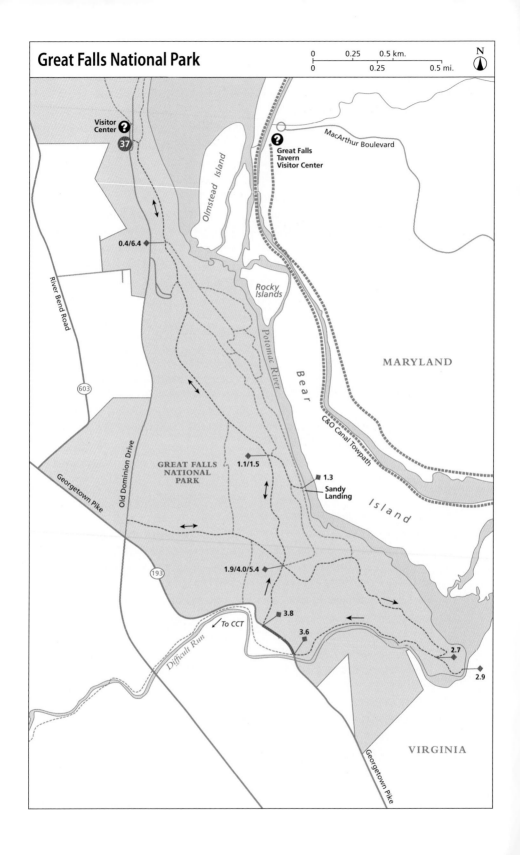

Great Falls National Park

0   0.25   0.5 km.

0   0.25   0.5 mi.

N

Visitor
Center ❓
37

Great Falls
Tavern
Visitor Center ❓

MacArthur Boulevard

Olmstead Island

0.4/6.4 ◆

Rocky
Islands

Potomac River

River Bend Road

603

MARYLAND

C&O Canal Towpath

Bear

1.1/1.5 ◆

GREAT FALLS
NATIONAL
PARK

1.3 ■
Sandy
Landing

Island

Georgetown Pike

Old Dominion Drive

193

1.9/4.0/5.4 ◆

3.8 ■

To CCT

3.6 ■

2.7 ◆

2.9 ◆

Difficult Run

Georgetown Pike

VIRGINIA

Ride Information

Local Information

Fairfax County Convention and Visitors Bureau
(800) 7FAIRFAX
www.visitfairfax.org

Local Events and Attractions

Colvin Run Mill
(703) 759-2771

Wolf Trap Farm Park for the Performing Arts
(703) 255-1800

Where to Eat

Great Falls Village Centre
Great Falls, VA
(703) 759-2485

Pio Pio Pollo
Great Falls, VA
(703) 865-7700
www.greatfallspiopiopollo.com

38 The Cross County Trail

This ride will take you on the Cross County Trail (CCT) from its northern terminus in Great Falls, Virginia, to its southern end at Occoquan Regional Park. Along the 40 miles we will travel past several other rides included in this book making it possible to create a "mega" epic ride, should you have the legs for it.

The CCT includes a combination of singletrack, dirt, bike paths, gravel roads, and on-road surfaces and is best completed on a mountain bike or reliable cross bike. I generally ride it on a rigid mountain bike with "slicks" (street tires). The trail is well marked with brown plastic pylons throughout its entirety, but there are certain intersections and points where it is not very obvious. Just follow the directions here and you should be fine. While on the trail, look for the distinguishable CCT markers. If you don't see one, chances are you've veered off course. For the most part, all branches out of the CCT are feeder trails into the CCT.

Start: Difficult Run Parking Area, Great Falls
Length: 39 miles one way
Ride time: About 3–5 hours
Difficulty: Difficult due to distance
Trail surface: Combination of singletrack, dirt, bike paths, gravel roads and on-road surfaces
Lay of the land: Wooded trails and roads of Fairfax County, Virginia

Land status: Public land
Nearest town: Great Falls at the starting point and Occoquan at the terminus
Other trail users: Hikers, equestrians, and vehicle traffic in some sections
Trail contacts: Fairfax County, Virginia, www.fairfaxcounty.gov/parks/cct
Schedule: Open year-round

Getting there: From Maryland, take I-495 South over the American Legion Bridge and take exit 44 onto Georgetown Pike (MD 193) toward Langley/Great Falls. The Difficult Run parking area will be to your left in approximately 3.7 miles. From Virginia, take I-495 North to exit 44 and follow the same directions as above. GPS coordinates: 38.978311, -77.249293.

The Ride

The Cross County Trail (CCT) is a unique achievement for Fairfax County. It is a trail nearly 40 miles in length that connects the county from one end to another. Along its path it links hills and valleys, streams and meadows, and intersects urbanized landscapes and neighborhoods. Its very creation was a catalyst that united government agencies with citizen activists, environmental groups, trail enthusiasts, and private-sector organizations, and has been serving as an example of what can be achieved regionally when everyone puts differences aside and works together toward a common goal.

The trail was conceived in the mid–1990s when Fairfax resident and hiking enthusiast Bill Niedringhaus approached the county with an idea to connect existing trails

There are lots of stream crossings along the CCT.

in an effort to create one long corridor from Great Falls to Occoquan Regional Park. Park staff was extremely busy back then but they entertained Niedringhaus's idea. With support of the county, Niedringhaus and a few friends created the Fairfax Streams and Trails group and did considerable research on his proposal before presenting it to the County Board of Supervisors in 1998. Then-chairman Gerry Connolly realized that Niedringhaus was on to something great, so he presented a resolution to create the Cross County Trail, which the board unanimously approved. The county then sought and later received additional resources and federal support for the project.

Shortly thereafter, other groups became involved. The Mid-Atlantic Off-Road Enthusiasts (MORE) and the group Fairfax for Horses jumped in, and by early 2000 construction to connect several portions of the trail began. By December of 2005 the entire route was mapped and completed, and today, the CCT is a jewel in Fairfax County.

Much of the trail follows the stream valleys of Difficult Run and Accotink Creek. The northern portion of the system begins near Great Falls and follows the Difficult Run into the heart of Fairfax. Because the county has banned construction in floodplains, the trail offers a linear park that stretches

▶ **This is a shuttle ride, unless you really want to make it an out-and-back and double the distance. A couple of things to confirm before you start: Have plenty of water and make absolutely sure that each driver in the shuttle chain has their respective vehicle keys—trust me on this one . . .**

for nearly 15 miles. Most of the traffic here is via off-road singletrack trails. As you reach the southern portion of the system you'll have to ride on a short section of road before rejoining the trail. At this point the trails split between natural surface and paved paths, yet it does not lose its character as it continues to follow streams en route to Occoquan.

Along the way you can access several other parks and trail systems in the region. From the CCT you can access Wakefield Park (Ride 40), Laurel Hill (Ride 41), the Washington & Old Dominion rail-trail (W&OD), Lake Accotink, and with a little extra effort places like Fountainhead Regional Park, Burke Lake, Holmes Run, and the Custis trail. This makes the CCT yet another valuable natural resource and a backbone trail from which to launch your very own cycling adventures.

Miles and Directions

0.0 Start from the Difficult Run Parking Area in Great Falls, Virginia. Look for the CCT sign to the right of the lot as you drive in. Head southwest on the CCT.

0.6 Reach the first of many stream crossings along the CCT.

1.0 Stay to the right at this intersection to continue on the CCT.

1.3 Come out onto Leigh Mill Road. The CCT continues to your right shortly before the bridge that crosses over Difficult Run.

1.7 You have a couple of options here. Stay on the bridle path as it circles to the right or climb up on the singletrack. For this ride, climb up over a series of short and steep switchbacks to the left. When you come up on the road turn left and as you reach the small court look for the trailhead to the right.

1.9 Turn left into the doubletrack. If you had stayed to the right at the previous marker this is where you would have ended up.

2.0 Stream crossing number two.

2.5 The trail comes out into a small parking area and continues on a paved road. Continue on the paved road until you reach Colvin Run Road.

2.7 Turn left and cross Leesburg Pike (VA 7) and then turn left into the clearly marked CCT shortly after you cross VA 7.

3.0 Stay to right to continue on the CCT.

3.8 Reach Browns Mill Road. You can cross Browns Mill and then turn immediately left to cross the Difficult Run River, or turn left and then pick up the CCT to the right. For now, skip the river crossing and turn left and then right into the CCT. The CCT is now paved.

3.9 Turn right at this intersection to continue on the CCT.

4.3 Turn right into the gravel path to continue on the CCT. The left fork is a feeder trail.

4.4 Ride under the Dulles Toll Road.

4.7 Stay to the right to go over the bridge and continue on the CCT.

4.9 Turn left to go over another bridge, then turn right. Continue to follow the "worn" trail.

5.9 Continue to the left as you come out on the field.

6.0 After leaving the field and crossing a small bridge, turn left onto the gravel path and then into the singletrack.

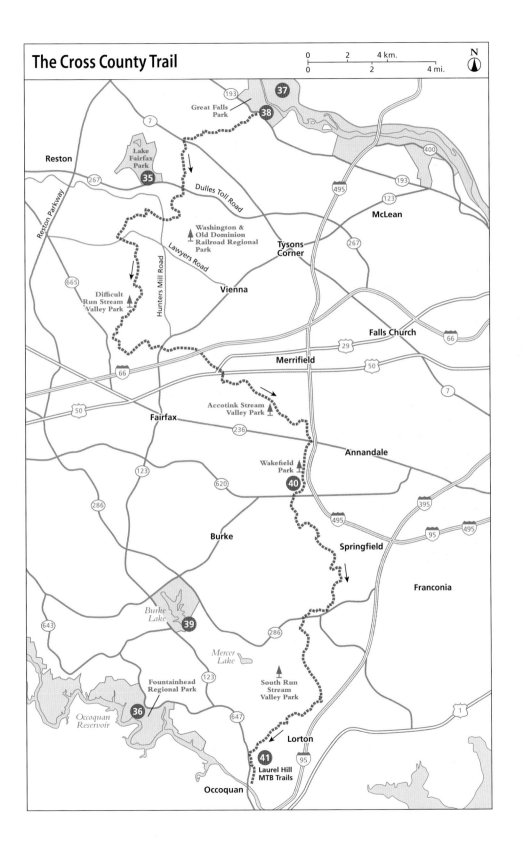

The Cross County Trail

0   2   4 km.

0   2   4 mi.

N

37

38

Great Falls
Park

193

7

McLean

400

193

Lake
Fairfax
Park

35

Reston

267

Dulles Toll Road

495

123

Reston Parkway

Washington &
Old Dominion
Railroad Regional
Park

Tysons
Corner

267

665

Hunters Mill Road

Lawyers Road

Vienna

Difficult
Run Stream
Valley Park

Falls Church

66

66

29

Merrifield

50

50

7

Fairfax

Accotink Stream
Valley Park

236

Annandale

123

Wakefield
Park

40

620

395

286

495

95

495

Burke

Springfield

Franconia

Burke
Lake

39

643

Mercer
Lake

286

Fountainhead
Regional Park

123

South Run
Stream
Valley Park

1

Occoquan
Reservoir

36

647

Lorton

95

Laurel Hill
MTB Trails

41

Occoquan

6.1 Stay right at this T intersection. You are now on the W&OD, affectionately known as the WOD trail.

6.3 Use caution when crossing Hunter Mill Road.

6.9 Turn left into the CCT. This intersection is easy to miss since you will be heading down fast on the W&OD. Don't hang out on the WOD at this intersection since riders from the opposite side of the WOD will be barreling down in your direction and could easily crash into you.

7.1 Turn right and head over the small wood bridge. (Note: At the time of this writing, this entire section was under significant construction and this area may be considerably different than what you are reading. It is safe to say, however, that the trail will be clearly marked and in better shape since the construction is a trail improvement project.)

7.5 Stay left and then right to continue on the CCT.

7.9 Reach Twin Branches Road. Cross the road and turn left to pick up the CCT on the other side. This section of the trail is called the Turquoise Trail. As you enter the trail stay to the right.

8.5 After crossing the bridge turn left at the T intersection.

8.6 Stay right at this intersection to continue on the CCT.

8.7 Cross Lawyers Road and continue on the CCT to the right. Then after a short, steep gully continue to the left.

9.2 The trail continues to the right on the other side of the creek (Little Difficult Run).

9.5 The trail descends to the right and then switches back to the left. At the bottom turn right to follow the CCT marker.

10.0 Cross this intersection and continue following the wood fence line to the right.

10.6 Cross Vale Road and turn left on the CCT as it parallels Vale Road.

10.9 Turn right to continue on the CCT.

11.0 Cross the Rocky Branch and continue straight.

11.1 Cross a small bridge and stay to the right.

12.2 Turn right at this T intersection to continue on the CCT.

12.9 Turn right at this intersection to continue on the CCT.

13.0 Stay to the left after a short singletrack downhill and then cross the next intersection.

13.3 Power up a short, steep climb and come out onto Miller Heights Road. Turn right on Miller Heights Road.

13.6 The entrance to the CCT is clearly marked with a crosswalk and a trail marker. Turn left into the trail.

14.1 Follow the Oak Marr Golf Course fence line to the right.

14.7 Turn right onto the paved CCT and continue following the golf-course fence line. The CCT is paved again. At this point all the singletrack portions of the ride are behind you. From now on you ride on the road (3.2 miles on a combination of paved and doubletrack gravel paths).

14.9 Turn left on Jermantown Road and follow the trail along the sidewalk for a short distance. At the corner of Elmendorf Road, cross Jermantown and continue in the same direction on Jermantown Road.

15.2 Jermantown becomes Blake Road, and then Pickett after crossing Fairfax Boulevard.

15.3 Cross Chain Bridge Road.

16.6 Cross Route 66.

17.3 There's a 7/11 to the left—a perfect place to replenish and get some water.

17.6 Cross Fairfax/Arlington Boulevard.

17.9 Turn left into Pickett Park and then left into the parking lot. The CCT picks up at the far right corner on the backside of a small baseball field. Turn right into the CCT. You will now follow the trail as it parallels and crosses Accotink Creek for about 20 miles, along the way riding past Lake Accotink.

18.6 Turn right into the gravel doubletrack to continue on the CCT.

19.0 Cross Barkley Drive and enter into Sally Ormsby Park.

19.5 Cross Prosperity Avenue.

19.8 Stay to the right at this intersection. The path is now paved.

20.3 Cross Woodburn Road. Make a quick right into the CCT and then a quick left to continue on the CCT.

21.2 Stay right at this intersection.

21.4 The CCT curves to the right. You can start to hear the Capital Beltway traffic. This section of the CCT will run near the nation's busiest thoroughfare.

22.1 The trail comes out from the Little River Turnpike Beltway and underpasses under a set of power lines. Continue following the trail to the left as it curves around the outfield of the baseball field to left. When it reaches the pavement, turn left to head into the tree cover.

22.4 As the road curves to the right the CCT picks up straight ahead.

22.6 Continue following the trail to the right to cross the creek and then immediately after crossing the creek turn to the left.

22.8 Turn left to go over a bridge and then right immediately after you cross it. You are now in Wakefield Park and riding parts of the Wakefield Park ride (Ride 40).

22.9 You have the option of continuing straight at this intersection to remain on the CCT or following the path to the left toward the Audrey Moore RECenter. I'll take you that way since water and restrooms are available in case you need them.

23.1 After turning left, follow the trail to the right as it follows the edge of the tennis courts. Come out into the parking area and head straight to the rec center beyond the skate park to the right. When you reach the rec center continue following the parking area to the left and pick up the CCT again at the far end. Turn right into the CCT at mile marker 23.6. After turning right you'll go over a small bridge. To the left is the Wakefield area commonly known as "The Bowl," a small playground of intertwined singletrack trails. Continue on the doubletrack and come out into the athletic fields parking area. The trail picks up at the opposite far corner of the parking lot to the right.

23.9 Enter the CCT and go over the small arched bridge and continue following the paved path to the right.

24.1 Stay to the left and then to the right to go under Braddock Road.

24.6 Continue straight at this intersection and follow the signs to the Lake Accotink Marina. You are now on the Lake Accotink Trail.

25.7 Stay to the right at this intersection.

26.3 Pass the marina and turn right on the road and head toward the dam and the railroad overpass.

26.5 The road will curve to the left and head under the railroad viaduct. Follow it into the parking area to the right. The CCT continues at the far end to the right.

28.0 Continue following the CCT to the right. You'll pass several baseball fields to the left.

28.5 Ride under Old Keene Mill Road. The trail turns to gravel.

28.7 Continue following the trail to the left.

29.5 Continue straight past two intersections, and at the third one follow the path to the right up a steep climb to Hunter Village Drive. Cross Hunter Village and continue in the same general direction on the path along the road.

30.2 As Hunter Village Drive curves to the right you'll reach a crosswalk. Use it to cross the road. Climb up the ramp and cross Rolling Road. Immediately after crossing, turn right and ride along the sidewalk that parallels Rolling Road for a short distance.

30.4 Turn left into the CCT. You'll be riding along the backside of some townhouses.

30.6 Turn right along the Fairfax County Parkway.

30.8 At the light, turn left to cross the Fairfax County Parkway and then right on Hooes Road immediately after you cross.

30.9 Turn left into the CCT—thankfully it is right before the ominous climb you see up ahead.

31.1 The trail turns sharply to the right.

31.2 After crossing the creek turn left and up to continue on the CCT.

31.3 After a steep climb follow the trail to the left.

31.5 Stay left at this intersection, go over the small bridge, and continue following the Pohick Creek. You'll now ride parallel to and cross Pohick Creek several times before we finish.

32.8 After a short creek crossing, turn right and then go through the creek again. You'll see a house up high to the right as you ride under the power lines. Continue straight through the next intersection.

33.1 Cross the creek again. This crossing seems to be the deepest of all of the ones we've encountered thus far.

33.3 Continue straight following the creek.

33.9 Shortly before you reach the underpass for Pohick Road, turn left and shoot straight up to continue on the CCT. Once you reach Pohick Road turn right to go over the overpass. The CCT will now parallel Pohick Road for a short distance.

34.1 Turn left to cross Pohick Road. Then, immediately after crossing, turn left again to stay on the CCT. The trail will actually follow the sidewalk as it heads toward Creekside View Lane.

34.2 Turn right to continue on the CCT.

34.4 Continue to the left.

35.1 Cross Bluebonnet Drive and then turn right at the T intersection to cross Laurel Crest Drive.

35.4 Cross Paper Birch Drive and hop on White Spruce Way to cross over Silverbrook Road. You can now see the old Lorton Penitentiary up ahead. After you cross Silverbrook Road, continue straight toward Lorton's other gated community, Spring Hill. The trail entrance is to the left as you reach the community gates.

35.5 Enter the CCT again and follow it as it circles the old penitentiary to the left.

36.0 Stay to the left and continue following the perimeter of the penitentiary. As you reach the last tower veer right to continue on the CCT. The trail is marked with paint on the pavement and continues down the hill to the left. The Laurel Hill Ride (Ride 41) begins on the parking area to the left.

36.4 Continue straight and go over the bridge that spans Giles Run. After crossing the bridge you'll see the Giles Run Meadow Trail trailhead to the left.

36.6 Stay left at this intersection.

36.8 The Barrett House parking area is to the right. Continue straight under the arched bridge.

37.0 Turn left on the road and head down to the stop sign to cross Lorton Road. Use caution at this intersection. The CCT continues on the other side of the road. Immediately after crossing the road stay to the right. (To the left is the entrance to the Laurel Hill trails.) Continue following the trail southwest as it parallels Lorton Road until you reach Ox Road (VA 123).

37.5 Turn left on VA 123. The Lorton Workhouse Arts Center will be to your left.

37.9 Turn left to enter the Occoquan Regional Park. The CCT will run parallel to the road shortly after you enter the park. Follow it to the bottom.

39.0 The ride is complete.

Ride Information

Local Information

The CCT bisects Fairfax County from north to south, beginning at Great Falls and ending in Occoquan Regional Park.

Local Events and Attractions

Great Falls Park Falls Walk: A great way to learn about Great Falls from the rangers at Great Falls Park is through this regularly scheduled tour. Visit www.nps.gov/grfa for additional information and event schedules

Local Fairfax County events
www.fairfaxcounty.gov

Lorton Workhouse Arts Center
www.lortonarts.org/calendar.php

Historic Occoquan
www.historicoccoquan.org

Bike Shops

The Bike Lane
11943 Democracy Dr.
Reston Town Center
Reston, VA
www.thebikelane.com

Spokes Etc.
10937 Fairfax Blvd.
Fairfax, VA
(703) 591-2200
www.spokesetc.com

Where to Eat

Cock & Bowl
302 Poplar Alley
Occoquan, VA
(703) 494-1180
www.cockandbowl.com

39 Burke Lake Loop

This ride isn't designed for thrill seekers and singletrack lovers. Instead, it reveals the lighter side of off-road bicycle riding, leading cyclists on a pleasant trip past flower gardens and lakeside vistas. The route is mostly flat and smooth, traveling along well-maintained dirt paths around Burke Lake or meandering along South Run on a paved bicycle path. There's plenty for off-road cyclists to do along this easy route to and from Burke Lake, so bring the family and enjoy the ride.

Start: South Run District Park
Length: 7.5 miles
Ride time: About 1–1.5 hours
Difficulty: Easy
Trail surface: Asphalt and dirt trails
Lay of the land: Wooded and flat
Land status: Regional park
Nearest town: Springfield

Other trail users: Hikers, boaters, anglers, naturalists, and picnickers
Trail contacts: Fairfax County Park Authority, (703) 324-8700; Burke Lake Park, (703) 323-6601
Schedule & fees: Open daily from dawn to dusk, mid-March to mid-November. Trail is open year-round; small fee on weekends and holidays for nonresidents

Getting there: From the Capital Beltway (I-495): Take I-95 south toward Richmond. Go only about 0.5 miles and take Springfield exit 57, VA 644 (Old Keene Mill Road). Follow Old Keene Mill Road west 3 miles, then turn left on Huntsman Boulevard. Follow Huntsman Boulevard 1.5 miles to the Fairfax County Parkway. Turn right on the Fairfax County Parkway, travel about 0.3 miles, and turn left into South Run District Park. Parking, water, phones, restrooms, and showers are available at the South Run Recreation Center. GPS coordinates: 38.747708, -77.275922.

The Ride

> *This spring the government chose Burke for the new airport. The whole town was shocked. 4,500 acres has been condemned. The town hasn't been the same since. Over 100 families are forced to find new homes by May 1, 1952.*
>
> *Virginia Lee Fowler*
> *October 11, 1951*

It's hard to imagine what the mood was like in the 1950s in the vicinity of what is now Burke and Mercer Lakes. After World War II, the aviation industry around the country was thriving. One particular area of the country to benefit from this boom was the Washington, D.C., area. The federal government saw the need for a second airport to service the region. That second airport, it was decided, would be built in the town of Burke and the area where Burke Lake currently sits. The proposed location of the new international airport would occupy nearly 4,500 acres and would displace hundreds of families. According to a June 14, 1951, article in the *Evening Star*, the proposed airport would be completed by 1955 and would "dwarf both Washington National and Baltimore's Friendship terminals."

Understandably, Burke residents vehemently opposed the proposal, and thanks to some great leadership from the town, the federal government reconsidered, and in 1958 decided instead to build its planned modern-age facility farther to the west in the town of Willard, what is now present day Chantilly. That airport, as we all know it today, is Washington Dulles International Airport, perhaps one of the busiest international airports in the country.

With the airport battle behind them, Fairfax County acquired the land the federal government had set aside for the airport project at auction in 1959. Instead of an airport, the county opted to follow the suggestions of its citizens to create a recreational area, including a public fishing lake. In 1961, after identifying a suitable location and completing dam construction, the Fairfax County Park Authority began the process of filling in the 218 acres that would become Burke Lake. Nearly 2,000 people attended the facility's opening ceremonies on May 25, 1963. Today, that lake is surrounded by nearly 900 additional acres of wooded parkland, making it one of the county's largest lakes and also one of its most beautiful. It is a peaceful place to spend time, and lucky for us, it includes a bike trail around its perimeter. From the trail you can catch a glimpse of an elusive bald eagle or one of the many waterfowl that call the lake home, and who live on Vesper Island, a state refuge.

The lake is extremely popular during the spring and summer months, primarily because of its family-oriented attractions, including camping, several picnic areas, a playground, and a Frisbee golf course. The park also operates a miniature railroad that has been running for more than forty years. It's not uncommon to see parents who as kids rode the train themselves enjoying it with their children. The second miniature replica of the Central Pacific Steam Engine chugs around the 1.75 miles of track in about ten minutes. There is also an old-fashioned carousel for further enjoyment. And, if you tire of everything the park has to offer, you can take a quick ride over 123 to the adjacent driving ranges and golf courses, which include a school for aspiring golfers of all ages, or farther south to the Lorton Arts Center, where local artists have studios open to the public.

This ride does not have to start from South Run District Park, and can easily be altered to begin at Burke Lake. But be prepared for a per-car fee for nonresidents of Fairfax County.

Surrounded by wooded parkland, it's easy to agree that Burke Lake, Fairfax County's largest lake, is also one of the region's prettiest, most peaceful places for a bike ride.

Miles and Directions

0.0 Start at South Run District Park behind South Run Recreation Center (main building at the park). Follow the paved path, starting behind the fieldhouse, down the hill into the woods.

Burke Lake Loop

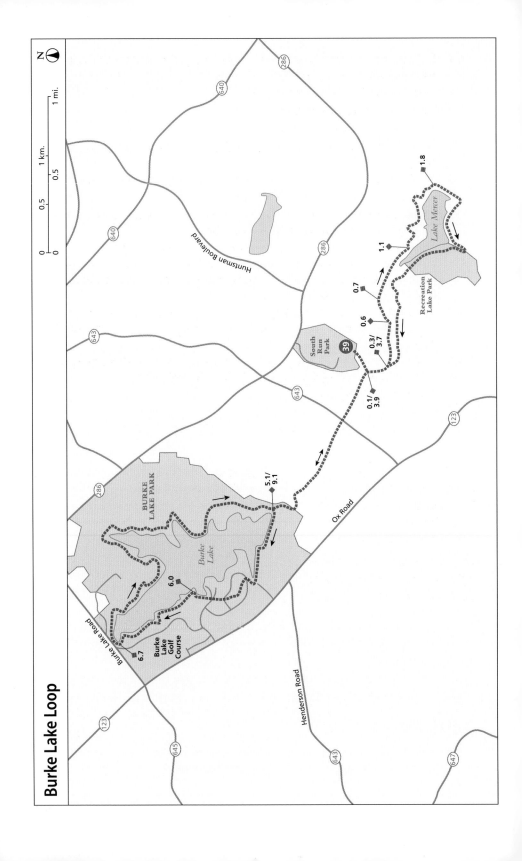

0.2 Reach the bottom of the hill and follow the asphalt bike path to the right along South Run. The stream should be on your left.

0.4 Cross underneath the power lines.

0.6 Cross underneath Lee Chapel Road.

1.5 Arrive at Burke Lake and turn left, crossing the dam.

1.7 Reach the other side of the dam. Continue along the gravel bicycle and walking path, following the park trail signs.

2.0 Reach a small parking lot and boat ramp at the end of the cove. Follow the park trail signs.

2.2 Cross a small open field. Stay to the right side of the field. The trail picks up on the other side. (Trail markings are obscure here, so keep a sharp eye.)

2.4 Cross the park road leading to Burke Lake Park's marina. Follow the park trail signs across the road, back into the woods. A concession stand with food and drinks, boat rentals, restrooms, and more is available at the marina. To continue on, stay left on the trail, going around the Frisbee golf course.

3.3 The trail drops out on the paved park road. Turn right on this road, cross the bridge, then reenter the trail back into the woods. (Burke Lake Road is on your left.) Continue following the trail around the lake.

6.0 Reach the dam. The loop around Burke Lake is complete. Stay to the left and follow the asphalt bicycle path along South Run back to South Run District Park.

7.1 Cross underneath the power lines.

7.3 Bear left up the asphalt path to South Run Park.

7.5 Reach South Run Park's recreation center.

Ride Information

Local Information

Fairfax County Convention and Visitors Bureau
(800) 7FAIRFAX
www.visitfairfax.org

Local Events and Attractions

Burke Lake Park offers fishing, boating, and a great Frisbee golf course.

Bike Shops

The Bike Lane
Springfield, VA
(703) 440-8701
www.thebikelane.com

40 Wakefield Park/Lake Accotink Trail

Wakefield Park is quite possibly the most popular mountain-bike destination in the Metro Washington, D.C., area. Its close proximity to the Capital Beltway makes it a popular destination for all the northern Virginia suburbanites who live and/or work inside the beltway. On any given afternoon, the parking lots of Wakefield Park are brimming with activity from people using the soccer fields, Audrey Moore RECenter, skate park, tennis courts, and the extensive network of bike trails that run parallel to Accotink Creek and the nearby power lines.

Start: Audrey Moore RECenter parking area
Length: 5.5 miles
Ride time: About 1 hour
Difficulty: Moderate
Trail surface: Singletrack and dirt trails
Lay of the land: Wooded and relatively flat, next to the Capital Beltway
Land status: County parks

Nearest cities: Annandale, VA; Alexandria, VA
Other trail users: Hikers
Trail contacts: Fairfax County Park Authority, (703) 324-8700; Lake Accotink Park, (703) 569-7120; Wakefield Park, (703) 321-7081
Schedule: Open daylight to dark all year; night riding is allowed only on designated MORE rides on Tuesday and Thursday

Getting there: The park is less than 0.5 mile from the Capital Beltway off Braddock Road in northern Virginia. Exit west on exit 54A, Braddock Road, and turn right in less than 2 miles into Wakefield. Drive straight for approximately 0.5 mile and then turn left where the tarmac ends into the main Audrey Moore RECenter parking area. Park adjacent to the recycling bins to the right. GPS coordinates: 38.817901, -77.223256. GPS coordinates (Accotink Trails): 38.801682, -77.234768.

The Ride

Sometimes it's interesting to see where you will find challenging trails. More often than not, Washingtonians and nearby D.C. suburbanites have to venture far out to the west or north of the city to find natural-surface trails that crisscross the forested spaces of Frederick County in Maryland and the George Washington National Forest in Virginia. But, as it turns out, there are surprising opportunities closer to home for dirt lovers to enjoy. One such location is the network of trails that exists only minutes from the Capital Beltway in Wakefield Park. For those nature enthusiasts who can't afford to venture out and drive over an hour to distant trail networks, Fairfax County's Wakefield Park has become an oasis for indoor and outdoor recreational activities.

Wakefield Park is the home of the Audrey Moore RECenter, a facility that includes a multitude of activities for Fairfax County residents and visitors alike. The rec center—dedicated to longtime Fairfax County politician Audrey Moore—measures in

Wakefield is home to the Wednesdays at Wakefield summer races.

at nearly 76,000 square feet, houses a 50-meter pool with various diving boards and spectator seating, a spacious sundeck, locker rooms, saunas, and showers. There is also a large gym with multiple basketball hoops and volleyball nets. The rec center also includes a cycle studio, should you feel compelled to cycle indoors. If you want to mix in a strength workout before or after your ride, there is also a spacious fitness center with a multitude of cardio equipment, free weights, and a stretching area.

On the outside you'll find seven well-maintained athletic fields, including five softball fields, a football field, and a soccer field. You'll also see a basketball court, a skate park, and eleven lighted tennis courts to go along with the more than 6 miles of natural-surface singletrack mountain-biking trails.

The trails at Wakefield have been through a drastic transformation over the past decade. The early popularity of mountain biking in the mid-1990s and subsequent

> **The Cross County Trail (CCT) runs through Wakefield Park and area riders often combine this ride with other CCT accessible trails to create "epic" loops easily exceeding the century mark.**

2000s brought a tremendous number of riders into the park. Unfortunately, the original power line and wooded trails that existed within its boundaries were not designed for off-road cycling, thus they suffered considerably with the number of riders that used them on a daily basis. Park managers and the Mid-Atlantic Off-Road Enthusiasts (MORE) recognized the problem and took action to improve and preserve the network of trails.

With the help of the International Mountain Biking Association's trail crew, the muscle of local area volunteers, and the support of the Fairfax County government, regional riders set out to improve the trails of this Beltway destination. Thanks to the efforts and dedication of those biking advocates, today the park in Wakefield houses more than 6 miles of sustainable, enjoyable, and challenging trails, all within 0.5 mile from the Capital Beltway.

Our loop will take you through those renovated trails and partially through part of the popular Wednesdays at Wakefield (W@W) summer series of mountain-bike races race course. While challenging, it is a ride that can be easily conquered by beginner riders and enjoyed by accomplished dirt lovers alike. I highly recommend you change directions on this loop or change it around to make it your own. To add a little distance to your ride, also venture out and include sections of "The Bowl," a small area of the park that lies between the Beltway and the park entrance road that offers a couple of extra miles of singletrack. You may also want to give the trails a shot at night. Thanks to a well-crafted partnership between Fairfax County and MORE, night riding is allowed in the park on Monday, Tuesday, and Thursday nights from dusk to 10:30 p.m. Bear in mind that night riding is not allowed in any other Fairfax County Parks, and, to ensure this privilege remains, please don't ride the trails during any non-designated nights.

> **The Accotink Trail was once part of the Orange and Alexandria Railroad's original roadbed, built in the early 1850s.**

The ride outlined below is a suggested route. My advice is just to go out and explore all the trails around the power lines to find the loop that you like best. I have not included The Bowl in this writeup, but you can easily add 3 more miles to your ride by riding it. MORE also hosts regular Tuesday and Thursday evening rides for all ability levels. Check out MORE's website (www.more-mtb.org) for additional information.

Miles and Directions

0.0 Start immediately adjacent to the recycling bins and turn left on the gravel road toward the pedestrian bridge that spans over the Capital Beltway.

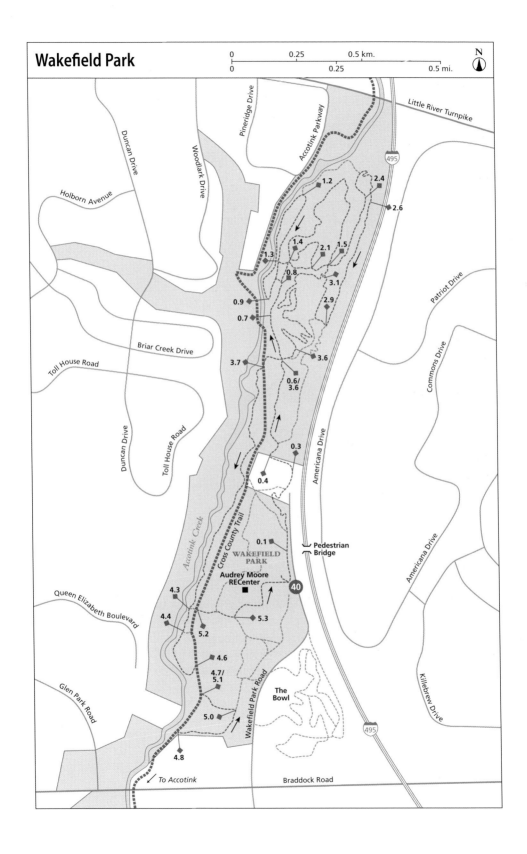

Wakefield Park

0   0.25   0.5 km.

0   0.25   0.5 mi.

N

Little River Turnpike

Pineridge Drive

Accotink Parkway

495

Duncan Drive

Holborn Avenue

Woodlark Drive

1.2
2.4
2.6

1.4
2.1
1.5
1.3
0.8
3.1

0.9
2.9

0.7

Patriot Drive

Briar Creek Drive

3.7
3.6

Toll House Road

0.6/
3.6

Duncan Drive

Toll House Road

Commons Drive

Americana Drive

0.3

0.4

Accotink Creek

Cross County Trail

0.1

Pedestrian
Bridge

WAKEFIELD
PARK

Audrey Moore
RECenter

40

Americana Drive

Queen Elizabeth Boulevard

4.3

5.3

4.4

5.2

4.6

4.7/
5.1

Killebrew Drive

Glen Park Road

5.0

Wakefield Park Road

The
Bowl

495

4.8

To Accotink

Braddock Road

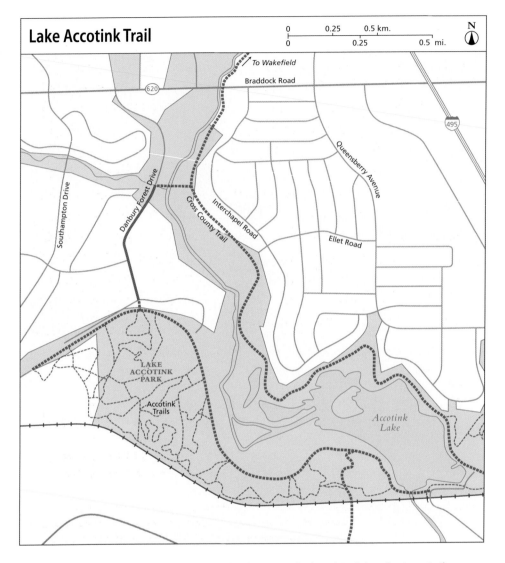

0.1 As you reach the pedestrian bridge take the narrow singletrack trail that shoots up to the left. Follow this trail as it zigzags through this small section of woods.

0.3 Cross the dirt road and ride on the singletrack that runs parallel to I-495. When the trail splits, take the fork to the left along the perimeter of the power station.

0.4 Continue on the singletrack trail toward the left after crossing the small creek. The trail will then veer to the right slightly before reaching the CCT. Continue on it over the short boardwalk and rock section, and then immediately head into the woods to continue on the trail that runs parallel to the power lines.

0.6 Cross over the creek and continue straight across this intersection. Get ready for a short burst

0.7 Continue straight past this intersection and continue the short climb.

IN ADDITION: NIGHT RIDING

The loop I detail above encompasses the trails around the power lines. You can also access The Bowl, a small area with about 3 miles worth of trails, from the same starting point. Instead of turning left on the gravel road at the starting point, turn right and head on the road as if exiting the park. The Bowl trailhead will be to your left where the wood line begins along the I-495 buffer wall.

You can also access the extensive network of trails at Lake Accotink from this location. The Lake Accotink trails are a complex network of interconnecting singletrack trails framed by the railroad tracks and the Accotink Lake trail. The easiest way to access them is to take the CCT under Braddock Road to the Lake Accotink Marina. Once at the marina, follow the paved path over the dam and under the railroad bridge. Immediately after a short, steep climb you'll see the first of several trails that shoots to the left and the singletrack network. I highly suggest you join one of MORE's regularly scheduled Tuesday or Thursday evening rides so that knowledgeable trail users can guide you through this maze.

0.8 After a short downhill turn left and then immediately left again into the main trail (basically a big U-turn).

0.9 Turn immediately right into the creek trail.

1.2 Continue bearing to the right (follow the yellow arrows) to return to the main trail.

1.3 Turn left at the first intersection. There is a yellow arrow marker clearly visible here. Follow the trail to the right for a short climb until it ends at the next intersection.

1.4 Turn left and pass one intersection, the exit of Phase 4. We'll be back at this point shortly.

1.5 Turn left. This is the second intersection and the entrance to Phase 4. Remain on Phase 4 and go over eight small wood bridges.

2.1 Turn left onto the trail we were just on. This time continue straight past the entrance to Phase 4 and out into the power lines. The trail will veer to the left under the power lines. At this point you'll ride toward and around the back of the second set of towers visible from where you are.

2.4 The trail veers to the left as you reach the second tower and then back to the right and behind the tower. After a short switchback climb you'll emerge on the top adjacent to the two towers.

2.6 You are now at the base of the two towers. Follow the trail as it runs parallel to the Beltway back in the direction you came from. This time ride back toward the second set of two towers from which you originally came from.

2.9 Turn right to ride the trail on the inside of the two towers. Immediately after passing the second tower (single pylon) turn right to head back down a series of jumps that end with a sweeping left-hand berm turn into the woods at 3.0.

3.1 Continue following the trail to the left for approximately 0.5 mile. The right fork takes you back to the entrance of Phase 4. This trail will gradually climb and then descend via a series of switchback berm turns along the power lines.

3.6 Turn right before the trail shoots out into the open and then immediately right again. You'll see the creek, which we crossed at mile marker 0.6. Continue straight until you reach the CCT and turn left at 3.7.

3.7 After turning left on the CCT go over a small bridge and immediately turn right onto the Creek Trail. You will now remain on the Creek Trail for nearly a mile.

4.3 Stay to the right to remain on the Creek Trail.

4.4 Stay to the right to remain on the Creek Trail.

4.6 The Creek Trail comes out of the power lines and veers to the left and back and intersects the CCT. Make a sharp right. Our return trip will bring us back to this intersection shortly.

4.7 Continue to the right and cross the creek.

4.8 Turn left on the CCT. A right turn will take you to Lake Accotink.

5.0 Immediately before reaching the parking area, turn left to follow the trail along the outfield fence line.

5.1 Turn right to return to the trail you were just on a few minutes ago, and then right again when the trail comes out into the power lines.

5.2 Go over the bridge and turn right to remain under the power lines. As soon as you reach the two large towers, turn right to head up to the soccer fields and the Audrey Moore RECenter.

5.3 Turn right on the paved trail that runs around the perimeter of the soccer field and then right again to head up between the skate park and the rec center to reach the parking area.

5.5 You're back at the lot and the starting point of the ride.

Ride Information

Local Information

Fairfax County Convention and Visitors Bureau
(800) 7FAIRFAX
www.visitfairfax.org

Local Events and Attractions

Wakefield Farmers Market: Wednesdays, May 2 through October 31, 2 to 6 p.m.

Mountain-bike races are conducted throughout the summer, including the Wednesdays at Wakefield (W@W) Mountain Bike Race series.

Trail-running races are conducted within Wakefield Park as a part of the Backyard Burn race series coordinated by Ex2Adventures in the spring and fall.

Bike Shop

The Bike Lane
8416 Old Keene Mill Rd.
Springfield, VA
(703) 440-8701
www.thebikelane.com

41 Laurel Hill

The ride through the hills and meadows of Laurel Hill will take you through a parcel of land that was once home to a Revolutionary War hero, thousands of reformatory inmates, and a magazine of intercontinental ballistic missiles.

Start: Giles Run Meadow Trailhead parking lot by the playground; alternate start points: Barret House, Lorton Workhouse Arts Center Parking Area; alternate parking area: Equestrian parking lot
Length: 10.9 miles; optional 1.7-mile reformatory loop (good for kids)
Ride time: About 1–2 hours
Difficulty: Easy/moderate

Trail surface: Mostly doubletrack and single-track trails with a short section of hard surface on the CCT trail
Lay of the land: Rolling, open fields with some wooded section; former site of D.C. Penitentiary
Land status: County park
Nearest town: Occoquan, VA
Other trail users: Hikers, equestrians
Trail contacts: Fairfax County, www.fairfax county.gov/parks/laurelhill
Schedule: Open year-round, dawn to dusk

Getting there: Laurel Hill is in Lorton, Virginia, approximately 20 miles south of Washington, D.C. From I-95, take the Lorton Road exit. Head west at bottom of ramp (a right turn whether coming north- or southbound on I-95). The Giles Run entrance is on the right in about 0.25 mile down Lorton Road. Follow the driveway up until you see the prison complex. The parking lot is on the left, next to the playground. GPS coordinates: 38.709430, -77.239068.

The Ride

Laurel Hill, located in Lorton, Virginia, is a relatively new addition to a growing list of off-road cycling trails in Fairfax County. Named after the original hometown of one of the area's first settlers, Joseph Plaskett, Lorton has a very colorful history. And Laurel Hill, the geographic area where this ride takes place, is no different. The ride will take you through what was once the home of a Revolutionary War hero, thousands of the most hardened criminals, and a magazine of six Nike intercontinental ballistic missiles aimed toward the Soviet Union.

Lorton's history starts well before the arrival of Joseph Plaskett in the mid-1800s. The area had been home to the Powhatan people, a confederation of tribes that farmed and hunted the lands of the coastal plains and tidewater region. Like in so many regions in the east, it didn't take long for the Native Americans to be displaced by the arriving settlers. Yet it really wasn't until Joseph Plaskett added a post office to his popular country store that Lorton was finally placed on the map.

Roughly around the same time that Lorton gained postal recognition, another prominent American and contemporary to both George Mason and George

Brisk winter days are the best time to visit the trails at Laurel Hill.

Washington settled in the area, giving it prominence. William Lindsay, a major in one of Virginia's militias during the Revolutionary War and a presumed aide to George Washington himself, built a home for his family on a hilltop overlooking his 1,000-acre plantation and named it Laurel Hill after what is believed to have been the original Lindsay family estate in Ireland. In 1871 Lindsay suffered severe wounds in the battle of Guilford Courthouse and returned home, where he spent his last decade alongside his wife and sixteen children. Upon his death, the major was buried in the estate, where his grave remains visible to this day. Over the years his home was renovated and expanded, and was even once occupied by the superintendent of the Lorton prison. Today, unfortunately, it stands in disrepair.

The area remained in the shadows until the early 20th century, when then-President Theodore Roosevelt commissioned the building of a progressive penitentiary and reformatory for the District of Columbia in the meadows of Laurel Hill. Roosevelt firmly believed that the natural surroundings of the area and exposure to nature and hard work provided an ideal environment suitable for the rehabilitation of prisoners. With that in mind, the Lorton Reformatory and Penitentiary was built, and at its peak grew to accommodate more than 7,000 inmates within nearly 3,000 acres of land. The prison's dwindling popularity, changing attitudes, and the sprawl of the late 20th century toward the Virginia suburbs forced its closure and transference from the federal government to Fairfax County by the beginning of the 21st century.

▶ **At its peak, the Lorton penitentiary and reformatory held more than 7,000 prisoners. On November 19, 2001, amid little fanfare, the last handful of prisoners left the correctional facility for transfer to other federal facilities across the country.**

Lorton's proximity to Washington, D.C., also made Lorton the perfect location for a Nike missile site. During the peak of the Cold War, when the arms race between the United States and the Soviet Union was at its height, the army acquired thirty acres from the federal government on the grounds of the penitentiary and built a double pad with six Nike missile magazines. The site maintained operations until the early 1970s when Secretary of Defense James R. Schlesinger ordered its closure. As a result, most of the missile structures were razed and today very little evidence of their existence remains.

Prior to acquiring the land from the federal government, Fairfax County was mandated to develop a "Reuse Plan that would maximize use of land for open space, parkland or recreation." In 1999 a citizen task force was appointed to develop the plan, which was later adopted by the County's Board of Supervisors and presented to Congress. Then, by November 2001, with the transfer of the last of the prisoners from the penitentiary complete, the Lorton prison was officially closed. By July 2002, after an extensive survey, more than 2,000 acres of land in the facility were transferred to Fairfax County at a cost of $4.2 million and thus began the renovation of the Lorton facilities.

Today the area is most commonly referred to as Laurel Hill to honor the legacy of William Lindsay and to preserve its historical significance. The phased approach toward development outlined in the Reuse Plan is well underway and over the past decade the facilities have seen a dramatic change. Several of the old penitentiary buildings have been restored and now house a thriving community of artists and craftsmen that host cultural and community events. An environmentally oriented eighteen-hole golf course is up and running, and, luckily for cyclists, an extensive system of trails has been built and is now open for the enjoyment of the community. Future plans include the restoration of the original 18th-century Lindsay home and additional work to the penitentiary and reformatory buildings to include residential units, restaurants, retail shops, and educational facilities.

Miles and Directions

0.0 Start the ride from the far end of the parking area where the paved path begins by the small playground with the climbing apparatus. Head down the path and turn left to enter the singletrack. The trail will then turn right and head toward the Meadow Pond.

0.1 Pass the Meadow Pond. The trail is easy to follow and well marked from here on.

0.4 Cross the creek and continue on the other side to the right. The trail will curve left and then right as it climbs to the wood line.

0.9 Stay right at this intersection to continue on the Giles Run Meadow Trail.

1.3 Turn left on the doubletrack. You are now on the Cross County Trail (CCT).

1.5 Stay left to continue on the CCT.

1.7 Right before the Barrel Arch Bridge there is a trail to the right. This is a short connector that will take you to the Barret House and an alternate starting point for this ride. Continue straight under the barrel bridge and past the trail intersection to the left.

1.9 Turn left on the pavement and cross Lorton Road. Use Caution. The trail is clearly visible on the other side of the road. Follow it and turn left at the first intersection, then follow the trail to the right.

2.2 Turn left at this intersection and then immediately right at the bottom and left again to enter the Slaughterhouse loop.

2.3 Pass the Slaughterhouse and turn right to follow the trail as it climbs to the top of the hill via a series of switchbacks.

2.7 You're back where you started the Slaughterhouse loop. Exit and head back up the way you came in. Upon exiting turn right and then immediately left to climb back up to the Workhouse loop.

2.8 Turn left. Follow the arrow labeled "To CCT."

3.0 Turn right on the CCT and continue back to the point where you started this first loop. If you turn left on the CCT it will take you to the Lorton Workhouse, an alternate starting point for the ride.

3.1 Turn right and then immediately left to head down into the other side of the Workhouse loop.

3.3 Continue straight. You will take the trail to the left on your way out.

3.8 Stay to the left at this intersection to head toward the yellow (Pasture loop). Cross the road, pick up the trail, and then turn left to follow the yellow loop (alternate parking area/ starting point).

4.3 Turn left at this intersection to head up toward Furnace Road and the Apple Orchard loop. After the Apple Orchard loop you'll return to this spot.

4.4 After crossing the road you'll be in the Apple Orchard loop. You can go either direction. For now, go left and follow the loop in the clockwise direction. There are a couple of well-marked intersections on the loop; just make sure to stay to the right on both (left if you're heading counter-clockwise).

6.0 Back at the entry point of the Apple Orchard loop. Turn left to head back to the Pasture loop.

6.1 Turn left on the Pasture loop (yellow trail) and head south toward the incinerator.

6.3 Veer left at this intersection to enter the Power Station loop.

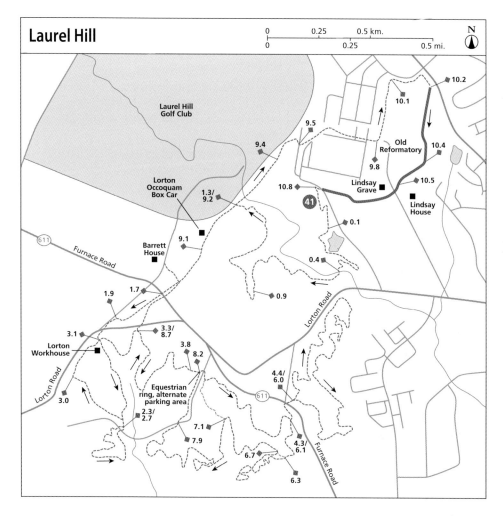

Laurel Hill

0   0.25   0.5 km.
0   0.25   0.5 mi.

N

Laurel Hill
Golf Club

9.5

9.4

Lorton
Occoquam
Box Car

1.3/
9.2

10.8

41

0.1

Old
Reformatory

10.1

10.2

10.4

9.8

Lindsay
Grave

10.5

Lindsay
House

611

Furnace Road

Barrett
House

9.1

0.4

0.9

Lorton Road

1.9   1.7

3.1

3.3/
8.7

3.8

8.2

Lorton
Workhouse

Lorton Road

3.0

Equestrian
ring, alternate
parking area

2.3/
2.7

7.1

4.4/
6.0

611

7.9

6.7

4.3/
6.1

6.3

Furnace Road

6.7 Turn left to continue on the Pasture loop.

7.1 Continue following the trail to the left to enter the Dairy Barn loop. If you were to turn left and head back up you would reach the Workhouse loop.

7.9 Cross the dirt road and pick up the Workhouse loop directly across the road to the left. If you head down the road to the left you would reach the Slaughterhouse loop. To the right is the entrance to the Pasture loop (mile marker 3.8 above).

8.2 Stay left at this intersection. You'll double back on the Workhouse loop for a short distance before making your way back to the Giles Run Area (alternate parking area/starting point).

8.7 Turn right at this intersection to cross Lorton Road and head back toward the CCT.

8.8 Turn right on the CCT and head back the way you initially came in. The Barrel Arch Bridge will be to your immediate right.

9.1 Stay to the right to continue on the CCT. The old Lorton Occoquan Boxcar will come up on your left.

9.2 To the right is the intersection of the Giles Run Meadow Trail. Continue straight over the bridge. (Or you can head back up and ride it in the opposite direction to your vehicle if you wish.)

9.3 Immediately after crossing the bridge stay to the left to go on a quick sightseeing loop around the perimeter of the penitentiary. (The short hill to the right will take you back to the parking area.)

9.4 Continue to the left and circle the pond in a clockwise direction, heading up to the path you see along the side of the reformatory.

9.5 Turn right and then immediately left to go around the reformatory. If you continue straight after turning right you'll end up in the parking area.

9.8 Continue following the path to the left. The main prison wall will be to your right.

10.1 The blacktop ends. Turn right on the sidewalk and follow it to the stop sign. At the stop sign turn right and follow the dirt path around the next watchtower.

10.2 Turn left on the road when the dirt path ends. The prison wall will now be immediately to your right.

10.4 The wall ends. Continue following the fence line along the perimeter of the road.

10.5 You'll get a good glimpse of the Lindsay house to the left and his grave immediately to the right by the prison gates. Continue straight on the road.

10.8 Turn left into the parking lot and head back toward the playground and the starting point of the ride.

10.9 The loop is complete.

Optional Maximum Security Prison Loop

This loop is excellent for kids or if you're looking to do a quick run after or before your ride.

0.0 Start at the Giles Run parking area by the playground. Start measuring from the first access point to the parking lot, by the yellow pylons. Exit the lot by turning right and then follow the left fork along the perimeter of the reformatory. You'll now be on the Cross County Trail (CCT).

0.3 After a short down and up, you'll reach the first watchtower. To the right is the Lindsay house, to the left his grave.

0.5 Reach the second watchtower. There is a gap in the fence that allows access to the athletic fields. You can get a closer look at the facilities around here. Continue following the road that runs along the reformatory wall.

0.6 At the time of this writing there was a chain-link fence blocking the road. Turn right as you reach the fence and then follow the dirt path to the left to continue riding along the perimeter of the reformatory.

0.7 Turn left on White Spruce Road. Stay on the near sidewalk, which will put you on the paved blacktop trail. Turn left on the path to follow the perimeter of the reformatory. If you're lucky you'll get a glimpse of the new prison residents. Virtually every time I ride through here I have seen gophers, groundhogs, and red foxes running around.

1.0 Turn right on the brick path.

1.3 You have three options here. Turn left to head back to the parking lot. Follow the middle path to head down to the CCT. Or turn right and quickly left to take a slightly longer route to the CCT. For now, turn right and then immediately left and follow the path around the pond.

1.4 Turn right.

1.5 Don't cross the bridge. Make a sharp left and head back up toward the parking lot.

1.6 Follow the path toward the right between the watchtower and the guard house to complete the loop; or, turn left and do the loop in the opposite direction. I'd opt for the latter.

1.7 Complete the loop.

Ride Information

Local Information

Town of Occoquan
www.occoquanva.gov

Lorton, VA
www.virginia.org/Cities/Lorton

Bike Shops

The Bike Lane
Springfield, VA
(703) 440-8701
www.thebikelane.com

Olde Town Bicycles
Woodbridge, VA
(703) 491-5700
www.oldetownebicycles.com

Village Skis & Bikes
Woodbridge, VA
(703) 730-0303
www.vsbsports.com

Local Events and Attractions

Lorton Workhouse Arts Center
www.lortonarts.org

Historic Occoquan
www.historicoccoquan.org

Where to Eat

Antonelli's
Lorton, VA
(703) 690-4500
www.antonellis-pizza.com

Cock and Bowl
Occoquan, VA
(703) 494-1180
www.cockandbowl.com

42 Meadowood Recreation Area

This ride will take you through mature hardwood forests in the Mason Neck Peninsula. The trails we'll be riding are relatively new and chances are, by the time you are reading this, the 3.1-mile loop will be transformed into a larger and longer network of mountain-bike trails. Plans are in motion to nearly double the length of the existing mountain-bike loop with a directional trail that will take advantage of the terrain's natural features and offer cyclists a challenging and enjoyable ride.

Start: Old Colchester Road parking area
Length: 3.1 miles
Ride time: About 0.5–1 hour, longer if you do multiple loops
Difficulty: Easy/intermediate
Trail surface: Mostly singletrack, with elevated boardwalks and berms
Lay of the land: Mature hardwood forest of the Mason Neck Peninsula

Land status: BLM park
Nearest town: Occoquan, VA
Other trail users: Hikers and equestrians
Trail contacts: Bureau of Land Management, www.blm.gov/es/st/en/fo/lpfo_html/recreation.html
Schedule: Open year-round

Getting there: Take the Capital Beltway (I-495) toward northern Virginia and follow the signs for I-95 South. Take exit 163 for VA 642 toward Lorton and turn left onto Lorton Road. Follow Lorton Road for approximately 1 mile and turn right on US 1 south. In 2.1 miles turn left on Hassett Street and then left onto Old Colchester Road. The parking area will be clearly marked to your right. GPS coordinates: 38.680545, -77.219717

The Ride

The Meadowood trails and recreation area are a relatively new leisure destination operated by the Bureau of Land Management (BLM). The nearly 800 acres of meadows, ponds, and hardwood forests where the trails currently lie were transferred in a land swap between Pulte Home Builders, Fairfax County, and the federal government in 2001. In late October of the same year, the land was assigned to BLM, which currently manages it to ensure it is used as an open space for recreation and environmental education.

Before the land was acquired and transferred to the BLM, it had been a working farm with horse stables. It also included a series of wooded trails that were in varying states of disrepair. Many of the trails were along steep lines, causing erosion and posing safety and water issues. Once the BLM took over the day-to-day management of the location, they fixed some immediate problems and developed an integrated activity plan in which they outlined their vision for the area and identified the potential use scenarios. These included hiking, fishing, horseback riding, and cycling (mountain

The wood features of the Boss Trail are an absolute blast to ride.

biking). The plan also identified and recognized that the legacy all-terrain vehicles and old farm equestrian trails should be abandoned and replaced with new sustainable routes.

Meadowood is physically divided into two distinct areas by Belmont Boulevard. The east side of the system, and closest to the Meadowood Field Station (management offices) and adjacent to the existing horse boarding stables, is primarily an equestrian destination; bikes are not allowed there. The west side had remained undeveloped, and since mountain biking would be one of the allowed activities in the system, the BLM worked with International Mountain Biking Association (IMBA) representative and trail specialist Dan Hudson to lay out a potential biking and hiking loop. The area surveyed included some of the old farm trails, and it was recommended that many of these be rerouted or rebuilt.

In 2009 the BLM, using American Recovery and Reinvestment Act (ARRA) funds, hired two term staff members, Doug Vinson and David Lyster, with trail-building experience to oversee the recommendations made by Dan Hudson and IMBA. After a period of additional planning, Vinson and Leyster begin building the recommended loop in early 2011. By January 2012 they had completed the South Branch Trail.

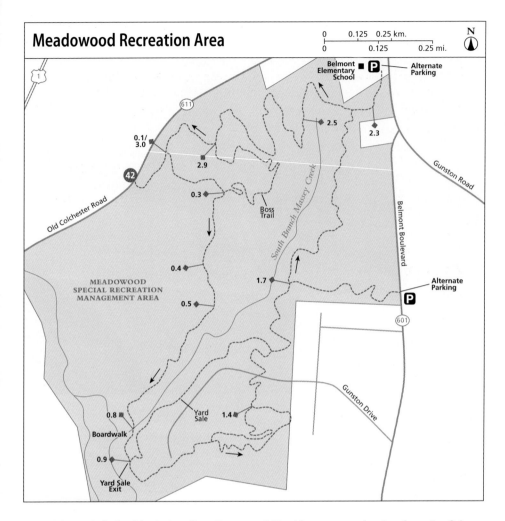

Meadowood Recreation Area

0   0.125   0.25 km.

0   0.125   0.25 mi.

N

Belmont Elementary School

Alternate Parking

2.5

2.3

0.1/ 3.0

2.9

Gunston Road

42

0.3

Old Colchester Road

Boss Trail

South Branch Massey Creek

0.4

MEADOWOOD SPECIAL RECREATION MANAGEMENT AREA

0.5

1.7

Belmont Boulevard

Alternate Parking

601

0.8

Yard Sale   1.4

Gunston Drive

Boardwalk

0.9

Yard Sale Exit

Not satisfied with their effort, Doug and David set out to begin phase 2 of the Meadowood project. Enlisting the help of volunteers and the Mid-Atlantic Off-Road Enthusiasts (MORE), they began to solicit and raise funds for several extensions to the loop. Again, with the help of IMBA, they crafted a design that added three additional trails, accessible from the South Branch trail. The new trails, Boss Trail, Stinger and Yard Sale, have more advanced trail features, including banked turns, rock outcroppings, narrow log crossings, jumps and steep climbing turns.

Miles and Directions

0.0   Start at the parking area of Old Colchester Road. Mileage measurements start at the gate. Immediately after crossing the gate, turn left to enter the South Branch Trail. The trail is very well marked and easy to follow. You'll ride it in a counter-clockwise direction.

0.1   Turn right to begin the loop.

0.3 Reach the entrance to the Boss Trail. I suggest you run the entire loop first and then come play here. Great stuff.

0.4 Continue straight through this intersection.

0.5 Continue to the left. You'll come up through a series of three additional trail junction points. Remain left at all of them and follow the clearly marked South Branch Trail.

0.8 Reach the boardwalk. Cross it and continue straight and up on the trail.

0.9 Yard Sale's exit is to the left.

1.4 Continue straight into the singletrack at this intersection.

1.7 Continue straight through the next two intersections. The trail to the right will take you to Belmont Boulevard, an alternate starting point.

2.3 Make a sharp left. Straight will take you to Gunston Elementary and an alternate starting point.

2.5 Bench; the trail continues to the right.

2.9 Boss Trail's exit point. The Boss Trail is directional—don't even think about making a left.

3.0 Continue to the right. The left will start the loop again (mile marker 0.1).

3.1 The loop is complete.

Ride Information

Local Information

Town of Occoquan
www.occoquanva.gov

Lorton, VA
www.virginia.org/Cities/Lorton

Bike Shops

Olde Towne Bicycles, Inc.
Woodbridge, VA
(703) 491-5700
www.oldetownebicycles.com

Village Skis & Bikes
Woodbridge, VA
(703) 730-0303
www.vsbsports.com

Where to Eat

Antonelli's
Lorton, VA
(703) 690-4500
www.antonellis-pizza.com

Cock and Bowl
Occoquan, VA
(703) 494-1180
www.cockandbowl.com

43 Lodi Farms

The trails at Lodi Farm have been around for quite some time. They used to be known as Hollywood Farm, but it really wasn't until the Frederick Area Mountain Bike Enthusiasts (FAMBE) got involved that the trails took the shape they hold today.

Start: Lodi Farms main trailhead parking area
Length: 9.5 miles
Ride time: About 1.5–3 hours
Difficulty: Intermediate
Trail surface: Mostly singletrack
Lay of the land: Wooded farmland along the Muddy Creek

Land status: Private property.
Nearest town: Fredericksburg, VA
Other trail users: Hikers
Trail contacts: Fredericksburg Area Mountain Bike Enthusiasts, FAMBE (fambe.org)
Schedule: Open year-round
Fees: Daily use/ride pass $5; annual pass $30

Getting there: Take I-95 South to exit 133A, US 17 South, Warrenton Road. Continue on 17 South for approximately 1.8 miles and make a right on Route 1 South, Cambridge Street. Immediately after getting on Route 1, veer off to the right onto West Cambridge Street and follow it to the left onto River Road. Continue on River Road for 1.3 miles and turn left on Kings Highway, VA 3. Continue on VA 3 for approximately 8 miles and turn left onto Hollywood Farm Road (601). Immediately after crossing the railroad tracks, turn right into the gravel road and continue to the trailhead parking area. GPS coordinates: 38.4327117, -77.4171381.

The Ride

The trails at Lodi Farm began gaining popularity with the annual 12 Hours of Lodi, an endurance mountain-biking event that's been held on the property since 1996 and draws hundreds of riders from the D.C., Richmond, and Baltimore regions. The race originally started as a 12 a.m. to 12 p.m. event, and over the years it's evolved into a 10 a.m. to 10 p.m. event.

The trails at Lodi are pretty easy to follow. There is a main 9.5-mile loop with several short connector trails that allow you either to shorten the loop or extend it. The builders have maximized their resources and managed to fit a lot of trail in a small area; for that reason, there are lots of twists and turns. But this is precisely what makes Lodi so unique and fun. The twists and turns, coupled with the classic rooty east-coast

▶ **Lodi Farm is private property and requires a daily use/ride pass ($5) or an annual membership pass ($30) to enjoy the trails. Either bring cash with you to drop in the appropriate container at the trailhead or your annual pass card to display on your windshield while you enjoy the trails. Please use these trails responsibly, police your trash, and obey all posted rules. This will ensure continued access. Visit www.fambe.org for additional information.**

The wood features at Lodi get you through some of the marshy spots.

singletrack we've all become accustomed to, make it a phenomenal playground you'll want to ride again and again.

The trails run along the east and west side of the Muddy Creek, Muddy being the operative word; stay away from Lodi after hard rains. Although the latest iteration of the Lodi network has been rebuilt and rerouted to make it more sustainable, there are sections that tend to hold water.

Miles and Directions

Start from the trailhead parking area and head straight into the woods. We will follow the trail system in a generally counterclockwise direction, although you'll actually be traveling in all directions! Immediately upon entering you'll encounter a split. Stay to the right to enjoy more trail. The left fork is simply a quick shortcut. The trail will twist and turn like nothing you've ever ridden. I like to call it the "Lodi Factor." There are very few straight lines here, but when you do encounter them, they are great.

Study the map closely; there are three short connector trails you can use to shorten the loop (why would you?) should you choose to. The first is roughly at mile marker 0.5, the second around 0.6, and the third at around 3.5. The vast majority of the trails

Lodi Farms

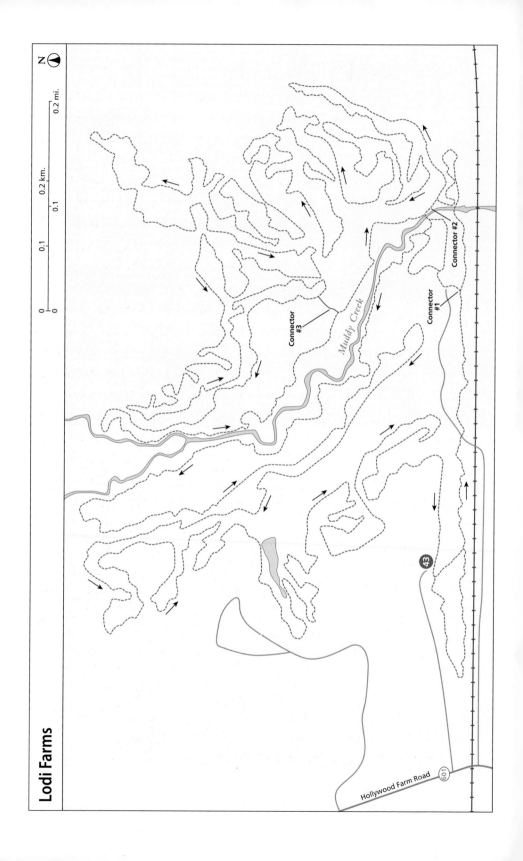

Connector #3

Muddy Creek

Connector #1

Connector #2

N

0.2 km.

0.2 mi.

0.1

0.1

0

0

43

Hollywood Farm Road

601

YOU MAY RUN INTO: ROBERT MAPLE

Rob and I met online when I started doing research for the fifth edition of this book. Until then I had ridden several of the trails in the Fredericksburg area, where he lives, with little knowledge of who had a hand in building or maintaining them. Over the years I had seen how Lodi evolved to the system it is today, and knew that whoever had worked in their development had a keen perception of what a good ride was supposed to be. His work in the trail system, along with that of other volunteers, and his rapport with the landowner have ensured that Lodi remains open for all to enjoy. It is through his direct involvement that I am able to include this ride in the book.

It is also through those rides at Lodi and at the Fredericksburg Quarry trails that I discovered and joined the Fredericksburg Area Mountain Bike Enthusiasts (fambe.org), Rob's creation. If you visit fambe.org, one of the first things you'll notice is the quality of the maps the group (Rob) has put together of area trails. His love for cartography, coupled with his passion for riding singletrack trails, put him on a quest to accurately map all the trails between D.C. and Richmond. "This quest has opened the door to so many great things, events, people, and places," he told me. "Luckily, there is much work to do, so I have a lot more riding to do."

Rob's favorite destination is the trails at Lodi, and you'll understand why. The twists and turns of this trail system give him a whole new meaning to the word freedom. "As a prior soldier, I know that freedom isn't free," Rob says. "Well, getting past the purchase of my bikes, gear, and all the supplements, riding my bike is freeing. Riding my bike by myself is

great, but riding my bike with others trumps solo rides in spades. Every ride is different, even while on the trails I always ride, and experiencing this with others brings it all together. Mapping the trails, and making them available to others, helps me share that feeling."

His quest for trails has led Rob to compete in various endurance races, some over 100 miles, but his proudest accomplishment continues to be the creation of FAMBE. There are a couple of rides that are not included in the book for one reason or another, but which you can find details for on fambe.org. Go check them out and print out one of the maps Rob has so expertly crafted

PHOTO COURTESY MIGUEL DÍAZ HANSEN

for you. Better yet, join FAMBE for one of their scheduled rides or scheduled workdays, and give this veteran a big pat on the back, not only for the service he's given our country, but for the continued efforts he makes so others can enjoy the Fredericksburg area trails. (You can also follow him on Twitter, @fambe2012.)

at Lodi are tight and twisty singletrack, so if you find yourself riding on anything other than that, you probably took a wrong turn. Don't fret, though, the system is tightly enclosed in a small area, so getting lost is virtually impossible.

Ride Information

Local Information
Fredericksburg, VA
www.fredericksburgva.gov
www.virginia.org/Cities/Fredericksburg

Bike Shops
Olde Towne Bicycles
www.oldetownebicycles.com
Fredericksburg, VA
(540) 371-6383

Bike Works
Fredericksburg, VA
www.bikeworks.us
(540) 373-0836

Local Events and Attractions
Visit Fredericksburg.com for regional information. The website has a comprehensive event
calendar at calendar.fredericksburg.com.

The 12 Hours of Lodi mountain-bike endurance
race is held every year in the spring. Additional
information can be found at www.newfred
events.wordpress.com.

Where to Eat
Blue and Gray Brewing Company
Fredericksburg, VA
(540) 371-7799
www.blueandgraybrewingco.com

Capital Ale House
Fredericksburg, VA
(540) 371-2337
www.capitalalehouse.com

Honorable Mentions

Compiled here is an index of great rides in Northern Virginia that didn't make the A list this time around but deserve recognition. Check them out and let us know what you think. You may decide that one or more of these rides deserves higher status in future editions, or perhaps you may have a ride of your own that merits some attention. Some of these rides are documented on our website, www.mtbdc.com.

N. Freedom Center

Home of the popular mountain-bike races Snotcycle and Hotcycle. Located in Loudoun County, and on private property, the Freedom Center was conceived and built by the guys from Mountain Bike Loudoun County (MTB LoCo, www.mtbloco.org). The trail offers intermediate riders a mixture of tough climbs, flowy singletrack, and fast downhills within the Freedom Center's property. A small pond provides a perfect spot to take a break and enjoy the rural setting of the facility. MTB LoCo maintains the trails and a short pump track on the property and often schedules organized rides to show you around. Check MTB LoCo's website for additional information, including their plans to design, build, and maintain a new multi-use system of trails in Loudoun's Evergreen Mills Park.

GPS coordinates: 39.228722, -77.550227

O. Locust Shade Park

Located just outside the gates from Quantico is a small county park with a series of short singletrack trails perfect for novice mountain bikers. If you are ever headed south along I-95 and are stuck in the dreaded corridor's evening traffic, and have your bike with you, take a quick detour to kill some time while the traffic dies down. My good friend Scott Scudamore, to whom this guide is dedicated, had a big hand in this system's development. The trail totals no more than 3 miles, but it is a perfect place to take young kids who are getting their mountain-biking skills into shape. A couple of short climbs will be difficult for them, but the rest of the system is easy to navigate and negotiate.

GPS coordinates: 38.531300, -77.351904

P. Marine Corps Base Quantico

The trails at Marine Corps Base Quantico have been around for several years and have seen a dramatic transformation. The primary reason I do not detail this network of singletrack goodness is because of its location, an active military installation. Quantico's access could very well go away with the blink of an eye, but because of the efforts of an active mountain-biking community within the base, the Quantico Mountain Bike Club (QMBC), the chances of that happening are very slim. For years the trails were accessible to the general public, but a couple of incidents involving cyclists and training marines changed that, and the trails remained closed for nearly a decade until they were opened again. To access the trails you will need a valid QMBC membership card, easy to obtain from the club, or a valid Department of Defense ID. Once in, you will be able to enjoy a great, challenging system of trails that will test all of your abilities. The trails at Quantico are clearly marked and easy to follow. The QMBC club has placed directional arrows at key intersections to guide you on one of three loops, an easy, intermediate, and difficult course. To learn more about the trails at Quantico, and to join the QMBC, please visit them on Facebook at www.facebook .com/groups/QMTBClub.

GPS coordinates: 38.533711, -77.332655

Q. The Fredericksburg Quarry

The trails at the Fredericksburg Quarry have been around in one way or another since the late '80s, but it wasn't until the mid '90s that the mountain-biking community began to lay claim to the network of trails and take interest in their development and maintenance. Unfortunately, that interest resulted in several uncoordinated efforts that did a little more damage than good to the trail system. Shortly after Hurricane Isabelle cut through Virginia in 2003, a small group of dedicated volunteers set out to transform the area and coordinate the various efforts in an attempt to reclaim the trails, help sustain them, and protect the environment around them, in the process ensuring continued access to mountain bikes.

That group organized and formed the Fredericksburg Area Trail Management and User Group, FATMUG. Today, FATMUG's organization and overall efforts have resulted in a system of well-designed environmentally sustainable trails. Today, the focus at the Quarry is to improve and maintain the trails for maximum sustainability. The primary reason I do not document this system of trails in the book is because a vast majority of them cut through private property. I do, however, provide additional details on my website (www.mtbdc.com) including a detailed cue sheet, GPS download, and map you can use for your own outings. For additional information on this regional Northern Virginia destination, visit www.fambe.org or www.fatmug.org.

GPS coordinates: 38.316643, -77.485698

R. Motts Run Reservoir

The first trails at Motts Run Reservoir were carved between the time I submitted my manuscript for publication and the moment the book went to print. For that reason I was unable to include a detailed write-up of the system. However, by the time you have this guide in your hands, there will be at least 3 miles of trails in this Fredericksburg destination. The first loop slated for opening at Motts Run is a 3-mile beginner designated trail. From there, the Fredericksburg Area Trail Management User Group (FATMUG) plans to build an additional 9–10 miles of intermediate to advanced trails for a total of nearly 12–13 miles of singletrack. You can easily access the new trails from the main parking area at Motts Run Reservoir.

GPS coordinates: 38.317296, -77.556361

Washington, D.C.

I t's tough to say a whole lot about mountain biking in the city, as no more than two rides originate here and just one, offered here as an honorable mention, finishes in D.C.—and in Anacostia at that! But surprisingly, both of these trails offer up some of the best off-road adventures in the book.

Starting in Georgetown, the C&O Canal is the longest and perhaps most scenic uninterrupted off-road ride not only in the state of Maryland but quite possibly in the whole East Coast, measuring just under 185 miles long. Despite the fact that it's a dead-flat ride along the Potomac River from Georgetown to Cumberland, Maryland, cyclists who have pedaled the distance throughout the years have logged miles and miles of countless sights and adventures. Cruising the C&O Canal in its entirety can be a real endeavor, so take it in pieces and ride it one section at a time. Or simply pedal this scenic national historic landmark along the same section day after day. Whatever you do, you won't be disappointed.

The Fort Circle Park ride is quite different from the C&O Canal, both in its location and its topography. This ride rolls along a hilly greenway through southeast D.C. and Anacostia, connecting a number of old Civil War forts, once part of a series of fortifications surrounding the city in defense against the South. Fort Circle Park, an oasis that cuts through the heart of Anacostia, will surprise most any cyclist who pedals through deep green woods along the hilly and well-maintained hike/bike trail. The history of the area isn't bad, either, so don't forget to make a stop at Fort Dupont Park to learn more.

D.C. is too small and too crowded to host many mountain-bike trails. And besides, who wants to ride over suspect terrain with all those lawyers around? But don't overlook what it does have to offer off-road enthusiasts and make sure to give both these rides a try.

I detail a slew of other rides in and around Washington, D.C., in my other guidebook, *Best Bike Rides Washington, D.C.* (*BRDC*). If you are up for some pavement, or simply a change of pace, give it a look. Several of the rides in *BRDC* wind in and out of Washington's neighborhoods, while others explore the rural suburbs around the nation's capital.

44 Chesapeake & Ohio Canal

Here's a ride for those slow-twitch-muscle types who can ride on and on and on and on without so much as a need to stop and fill up the water bottle once or twice. With 185 miles of off-road riding in one fell swoop (and this is just one way), the C&O Canal Towpath is one ride sure to challenge those who thrive on endurance activities. But few (in fact, almost none) of the cyclists who take to the canal each year attempt to ride the entire distance at once. However, anyone looking for a great trip along the Potomac River (leaving right from Georgetown) with virtually no elevation gain in sight should love this ride. Try it in sections, camp overnight, stay at some of the inns along the way to Cumberland, Maryland, or just ride up and down the canal near the city. Either way, it's a jewel for cyclists looking for an endless trip off the beaten path that leaves right from town.

Start: C&O Canal visitor center
Length: 184.5 miles one way
Ride time: Varies, depending on distance covered each day
Difficulty: Easy due to flat terrain
Trail surface: Crushed-stone and dirt towpath
Lay of the land: Flat canal towpath along the Potomac River

Land status: Maintained by the National Park Service
Nearest town: Washington, D.C.
Other trail users: Hikers, equestrians, and campers
Trail contacts: C&O Canal headquarters, (301) 739-4200
Schedule: Open from dawn till dusk every day of the year

Getting there: From the White House: Take Pennsylvania Avenue Northwest toward Georgetown. Go 11 blocks to M Street, turn left into Georgetown, then go 2 blocks to Thomas Jefferson Street. Turn left on Thomas Jefferson Street. The Georgetown C&O Canal visitor center is here.
   From the Metro: Take the Metro to the Foggy Bottom Metro station (Orange and Blue lines). Go north on 23rd Street 2 blocks to Washington Circle. Go counter-clockwise on Washington Circle to Pennsylvania Avenue Northwest. Take Pennsylvania Avenue Northwest 5 blocks to Georgetown. From here, follow the directions above. GPS coordinates: 38.904172, -77.067828.

The Ride

In 1828, on a hot Fourth of July in Washington, D.C., ground was broken and the challenge to see who would reach the "western frontier" (Wheeling, West Virginia) first was underway. The competitors: the Chesapeake & Ohio Canal Company versus the Baltimore & Ohio Railroad. Both started digging the same day. Through high costs, floods, land-access problems, 185 miles of rugged earth along the Potomac River, and twenty-two years of backbreaking labor, the C&O Canal finally reached Cumberland, Maryland—eight years after the B&O. Nevertheless, eleven stone aqueducts, seventy-four lift locks, and 185 miles of canal were complete. (The remainder

The C&O Canal is a great national resource.

of the route to Wheeling, West Virginia, would be by road.) Unfortunately, not only did the railroad reach the west first, but it was also faster and more reliable, as floods, freezes, and drought often handicapped the canal. Losing money to the railroad and regularly repairing costly flood damage, the C&O Canal was forced to close its gates in 1924, less than one hundred years after its completion.

Today, however, it is one of the most successful and reliable resources in the nation. Its success comes not in profits, though, but in the pleasure it provides to the thousands who hike, bike, or horseback ride along the crushed-stone and dirt towpath each year. It is a reliable treasure chest of sights and wonders, delightful scenery, peace and solitude, and miles of serenity each day of the year. One of the best ways to enjoy the C&O Canal is to ride it in sections, beginning from different starting points. But there are plenty of campsites along the towpath to accommodate a one-shot effort from Washington, D.C., to Cumberland, Maryland.

The surface of the towpath is mostly dirt or crushed stone and remains in excellent condition. Due to floods, freezes, and tree roots, however, you should be prepared for some bumpy trails. Also be aware that after heavy rainfall and times of high water, some sections might be impassable. Keep this in mind before heading out on a long weekend of riding.

With regard to the maps, don't be fooled by this ride's profile. It looks like an uphill battle all the way to Cumberland. Over 185 miles, however, a 600-foot elevation gain is virtually unnoticeable, and the trail will feel absolutely flat.

Miles and Directions

0.0 Start at the C&O Canal visitor center at the corner of Thomas Jefferson Street and M Street in Georgetown.

3.1 Pass Fletcher's Boat House on the left through the tunnel. Bike rentals and repairs are available.

14.3 Great Falls Tavern visitor center.

22.8 Seneca Creek Aqueduct.

30.8 Edwards Ferry. Not in operation.

35.5 White's Ferry. Last operating ferry on the Potomac.

42.2 Monocacy Aqueduct. The largest aqueduct along the canal.

44.6 Nolands Ferry.

48.2 Point of Rocks. Food available along Clay Street (MD 28).

55.0 Town of Brunswick. Phone, food, and groceries.

60.8 Harpers Ferry. C&O Canal Park headquarters. Phone, food, and grocery store. Cross Appalachian Trail.

69.3 Antietam Creek Aqueduct. Ranger station and camp.

72.7 Shepherdstown. Phone, food, and groceries.

99.8 Williamsport. Phone, food, and groceries.

124.0 Hancock. Visitor center. Phone, food, and groceries.

Chesapeake & Ohio Canal

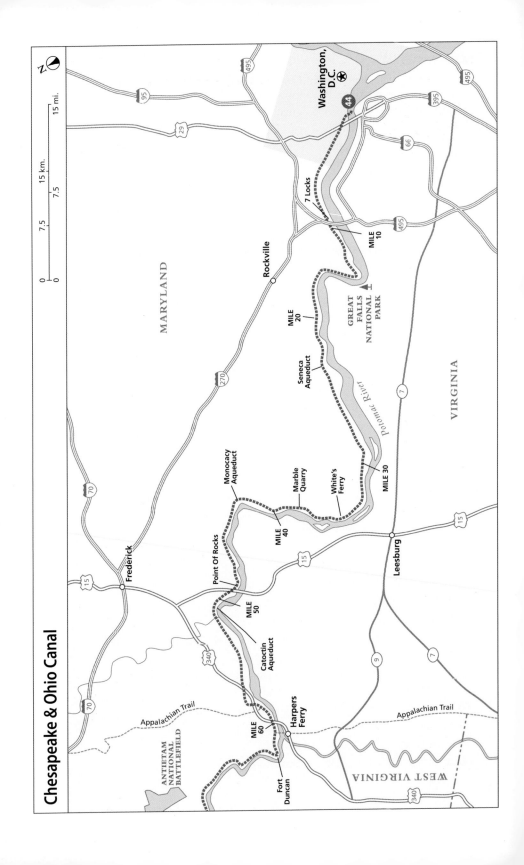

156.0 Paw Paw Tunnel.

184.5 Reach Cumberland. C&O Canal Towpath ends here. Phone, food, groceries.

Ride Information

Local Information

Chesapeake & Ohio Canal
www.nps.gov/choh/index.htm

Honorable Mention

S. Fort Circle Trail

Winding through a forested oasis, Fort Circle Trail is both a pathway through history and a greenway into the future of park systems. This dirt and gravel trail system travels up and down the hilly terrain east of Anacostia River, connecting a series of old Civil War fortifications built to protect Washington, D.C., during the war. The greenway is a surprisingly well-maintained park, kept up by the National Park Service, slicing through the heart of D.C.'s Anacostia neighborhoods. Allow plenty of daylight for this ride (you don't want to get caught here at night) and bring along a good map. Despite its location, visitors to this greenbelt will love it here.

GPS coordinates: 38.856714, -76.976530

Gravel Grinding

One of the great things about two of the areas I cover most in the book, Northern Virginia and Montgomery County in Maryland, is that in addition to the great trails riders have access to, there are also plenty of opportunities for riders to hit gravel roads and escape from the perils of traffic. Gravel grinding, a type of riding that has gained tremendous popularity over the past few years, is defined as a ride that takes place mostly on gravel roads. The ride itself can contain pavement and sections of singletrack, but its majority—more than 50 to 60 percent, must take place on dirt and gravel roads, hence the name.

Riding gravel roads presents a completely new challenge for cyclists. These are not quite mountain-bike rides and are not really road rides either, despite being mostly on roads.

The advent of 29er mountain bikes (mountain bikes with larger-diameter wheels) has several people advocating that a good mountain bike is all you need. Others, on the other hand, argue that a comfortable road bike outfitted with wider and stronger tires will do just the trick. Then, there are those who prefer cross bikes, a type of bike that borrows from both the road and mountain world.

At first sight a cross bike could be easily mistaken for a road bike but key differences in geometry and componentry make it more suited for the type of riding one would find on a gravel grinder. Cross bikes are more relaxed than road bikes—their geometry places riders in a position that permits them to use their body to absorb more of the types of shocks one would find off-road. Their wheelbase is also greater than a road bike's and more akin to a mountain bike, which allows for greater control over rough terrain. They still, however, retain some of the more aggressive geometry features of their road cousins, allowing riders to benefit from some of the performance aspects of a road bike that are not found in their off-road siblings.

Cross tire clearances are also greater than road bikes. This allows riders to choose and use larger tires. Encountering mud on a road bike would bring you to a halt and clog up your fancy caliper brakes, whereas a cross bike would do just fine. Finally, cross bikes are often fitted with a combination of off-road and road components making them less susceptible to damage during off-road outings. Cross bikes are generally fitted with cantilever brakes, and in some cases even disc brakes, providing more stopping power in "cruddy" conditions.

Ultimately you can ride any bike you want on a gravel grinder, but you'll get the most performance from a quality cross bike outfitted with the right components or a dedicated gravel grinder. For more info, visit your local bike shop. There are plenty of quality cross bikes on the market in various price ranges, and a few dedicated gravel-specific bikes. Given the rise in popularity of this type of riding it won't be long until manufacturers begin cranking out gravel-grinding-specific models to your local bike shop showroom floors.

Presented here are several of my favorite local grinders for you to sample. If you really take to it, there are several web resources that will take you even farther. A gravel-specific website by my good friend, Single Speed Outlaw David Kegley (www .grindinggravel.blogspot.com), details routes in Maryland, Virginia, Pennsylvania, and West Virginia.

A̅A̅ River Ride

This easygoing loop along the Potomac River connects two places that, at one time, signified an age when the ferry was the most convenient means across the river. The ride begins at White's Ferry and travels south along flat dirt roads to Edward's Ferry, which quit operations in 1936. You'll head back to White's Ferry along the C&O Canal, preserved now as a national historic park.

Start: White's Ferry
Length: 10 miles
Ride time: About 1–1.5 hours
Difficulty: Easy; flat pedaling with no technical challenges
Trail surface: Hard dirt (towpath); unpaved roads
Lay of the land: Hardwood scenery along the banks of the Potomac River

Land status: National historic park and public roadways
Nearest town: Poolesville, MD
Other trail users: Hikers, horseback riders, and automobiles
Trail contacts: C&O Canal headquarters, (301) 739-4200
Schedule & fees: Open year-round; small fee for ferry

Getting there: Maryland—from the Capital Beltway (I-495): Take I-270 north and go 10.5 miles to MD 117 West. Turn left at the second stoplight on MD 124 (Quince Orchard Road). Go 2.8 miles on Quince Orchard Road, and then make a right at the stoplight on MD 28 (Darnestown Road). Bear left after 6 miles on MD 107 (Fisher Avenue, then White's Ferry Road). Continue for 11.3 miles to White's Ferry on the Potomac and park in the parking lot on the right.

Northern Virginia—from the Capital Beltway (I-495): Take exit 10, US 7 (Leesburg Pike), all the way west to Leesburg (22 miles). Just before Leesburg, take US 15 (James Monroe Highway) north. Go approximately 3.5 miles on US 15, then make a right turn on White's Ferry Road. This will take you down to the ferry. You must pay a toll and cross the river to park and begin the ride. GPS coordinates: 39.155222, -77.518205.

The Ride

At one point, back in the 1700s, there were at least seven ferries carrying Loudoun County residents across the Potomac. Records of the county court show that by the end of the 18th century, not long after the signing of the Declaration of Independence, five ferries crossed the Potomac to connect the Maryland and Virginia shores. One of them was Edward's. White's Ferry, formerly known as Conrad's Ferry, began operations in 1836, carrying horse-drawn wagons, merchants, and supplies from shore to shore. Later in the 19th century, White's and Edward's Ferries served quite different purposes, however, and the results were often disastrous.

During the Civil War, both Union and Confederate troops used the ferries to carry troops back and forth across the Potomac. In one instance, on the night of October 20, 1861, Union troops under General Stone's command at Edward's Ferry

This relatively short and flat ride is a perfect introduction to gravel grinding.

and White's Ferry reported a Confederate camp near Leesburg. In an attempt to intimidate the Confederates to leave the area, General Stone set in motion events that ultimately resulted in the Battle of Ball's Bluff (see Ride DD, Canal Ride/River Grinder), costing the Union a severe and gruesome loss. Alternately, Confederate General Jubal A. Early, for whom the present ferryboat at White's Ferry is named, used both Edward's Ferry and White's Ferry in retreat after his daring attack on Washington in July 1864.

Today, White's Ferry is the last of the ferries to carry customers across the Potomac, operating seven days a week from 6 a.m. to 11 p.m. In fact, it's the only place between Point of Rocks, Maryland, and the Capital Beltway to cross the river—a stretch of 40 miles.

As you ride back along the C&O Canal Towpath, be sure to notice Harrison Island on your left. During the Civil War, the island served as a temporary hospital to care for the Union's wounded soldiers after their dramatic loss at the battle on Ball's Bluff. One of the wounded taken to Harrison Island was a recent Harvard graduate and a future Supreme Court justice, First Lieutenant Oliver Wendell Holmes Jr. He was shot through the leg and the small of the back but was diagnosed on the island as "doing well."

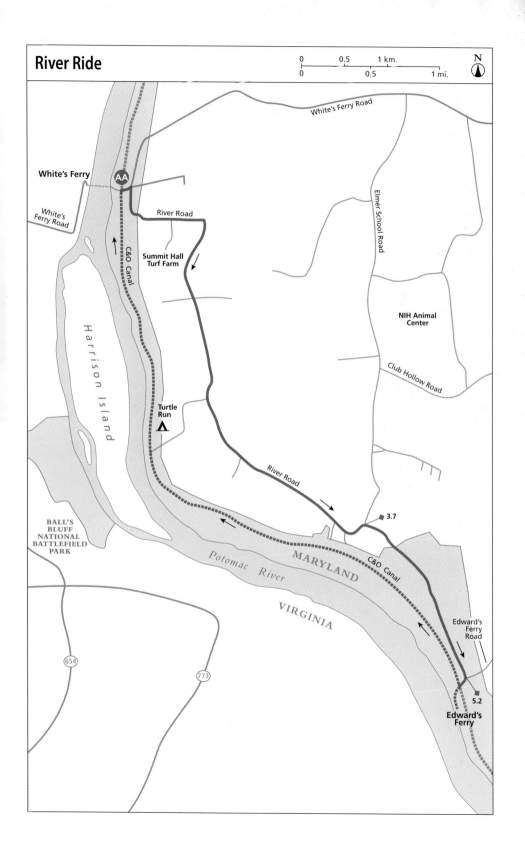

River Ride

0   0.5   1 km.
0   0.5   1 mi.

N

White's Ferry Road

AA
White's Ferry

White's
Ferry Road

River Road

Elmer School Road

Summit Hall
Turf Farm

NIH Animal
Center

Harrison Island

Club Hollow Road

Turtle
Run
⚑

BALL'S
BLUFF
NATIONAL
BATTLEFIELD
PARK

River Road

C&O Canal

MARYLAND

3.7

C&O Canal

Potomac River

VIRGINIA

Edward's
Ferry
Road

654

773

5.2

Edward's
Ferry

This ride, rich in history, is meant for the lighter side of mountain biking, as it travels along flat dirt roads and the C&O Canal Towpath. You won't have to worry much about traffic and should enjoy pedaling past an enormous replica of what many homeowners work a lifetime to achieve—a perfect lawn. The Summit Hall Turf Farm, along River Road, grows a magnificent 380-acre "lawn," carpeted in thick green zoysia, bluegrass, bent grass, and mixtures of blue and rye grass. The sod is then harvested and sent to area golf courses, local landscapers, and some very fortunate homeowners.

Miles and Directions

0.0 Start at the White's Ferry parking lot on the Maryland side of the Potomac River. Approximately 50 feet north of the parking lot, turn right off White's Ferry Road on River Road (unpaved). This runs parallel to the C&O Canal Towpath to the right.

3.7 At the three-way intersection, continue right on River Road.

5.2 Turn right on Edward's Ferry Road. Cross over the C&O Canal and arrive at Edward's Ferry. Return along the C&O Towpath back to White's Ferry.

10.0 Arrive at the White's Ferry parking lot.

Ride Information

Local Information

White's Ferry
Dickerson, MD
(301) 349-5200
www.facebook.com/WhitesFerry

Summit Hall Turf Farm
(301) 948-2900

Montgomery County Visitors Bureau
Germantown, MD
(301) 428-9702

Loudoun Tourism Council
(800) 752-6118

Local Events and Attractions

Leesburg Calendar of Events: www.leesburg online.com

Waterford Homes Tour and Crafts Exhibit: October, (540) 882-3085, www.waterfordva.org

Accommodations

Loudoun County Guild of Bed-and-Breakfasts
(800) 752-6118

Rocker Inn
Poolesville, MD
(301) 973-3543

BB Sugarloaf Scenic Circuit

Privately owned, the trails in Sugarloaf Mountain used to be a popular mountain-biking destination. In the past few years, however, overused trails prompted the managers of the Sugarloaf Trail system to close the area to bikes during the weekend. Today, portions of the Saddleback Trail remain open to mountain biking but only during specific times. The Sugarloaf Scenic Circuit is an alternative to the otherwise excellent but off-limits trails up on the mountain. This circuit of dirt, gravel, and paved roads surrounding the mountain will allow cyclists to experience all the beauty and serenity this Maryland countryside has to offer. For information about the Saddleback Trail and when it is open to mountain bikes, contact the Stronghold Corporation directly.

Start: Sugarloaf Park entrance in Stronghold
Length: 12.5 miles
Ride time: About 1.5–2 hours
Difficulty: Moderately challenging length, with rolling hills along dirt, gravel, and paved roads
Trail surface: Paved and unpaved roads
Lay of the land: Rolling scenic countryside
Land status: Public roadways circumnavigating private land trust

Nearest town: Frederick, MD
Other trail users: Horseback riders and automobiles
Trail contacts: Stronghold Corporation, (301) 869-7846; Sugarloaf Mountain Staff, (301) 874-2024
Schedule: Sugarloaf Mountain Park and Stronghold Corporation are open daily from early morning to sunset, year-round.

Getting there: From the Capital Beltway (I-495): Take I-270 north approximately 21 miles to the Hyattstown exit (exit 22). Circle under I-270, heading southwest on MD 109 (Old Hundred Road). Follow Old Hundred Road 3 miles to the town of Comus, then turn right on Comus Road. You will see Sugarloaf Mountain from here. Follow Comus Road straight into Stronghold to the entrance of the mountain. There is parking, but it is extremely tight. So get here early.

From the Baltimore Beltway (I-695): Take I-70 west approximately 38 miles to Frederick. From Frederick, follow I-270 south 9.5 miles to the Hyattstown exit (exit 22). Get on MD 109 (Old Hundred Road) and continue as above. GPS coordinates: 39.251529, -77.393375.

The Ride

Named after the sugar loaf by early pioneers because of its shape, Sugarloaf Mountain stands at an elevation of 1,282 feet, more than 800 feet above the Monocacy Valley. The mountain dominates the landscape for miles in all directions and has attracted its share of attention throughout history. The earliest known map of Sugarloaf was sketched by a Swiss explorer in 1707, when the American colonies were still part of Great Britain. General Edward Braddock marched past the mountain in 1755 during the French and Indian War. Later in American history, during the Civil War, the

The Sugarloaf grinder offers some great local scenery.

mountain was a matter of contention between the North and South, as its summit and overlooks provided ideal observation of the valleys below.

During the very early part of the 20th century, the mountain's main peak and surrounding land were purchased by Gordon Strong, who in 1946 organized Stronghold, Incorporated, a nonprofit organization designed for "enjoyment and education in an appreciation of natural beauty." Strong's original plan was for a vacation retreat. He built the Strong Mansion atop the mountain and a number of homes at the foot of the mountain in what is now Stronghold. Since Strong's death in 1954, Stronghold, Inc. has continued to manage the 3,250 acres of land on and around Sugarloaf Mountain as a place of natural beauty and wildlife, with a commitment to maintaining its natural state.

This loop travels on both paved and unpaved roads. Sugarloaf Mountain is always looming above you as you pedal past magnificent horse farms and along the rushing waters of Bennett Creek. This ride is not recommended for a regular road bike, since many roads are gravel and dirt. As you climb back over the mountain toward Stronghold on Mount Ephraim Road, all remnants of pavement disappear, and you are transported deep into a mountain forest.

Geologically speaking, Sugarloaf Mountain is what's called a monadnock. This is a hill or mountain that remains standing high above the surface after much of the surrounding land has eroded away. It took nearly fourteen million years for Sugarloaf to look the way it does today.

This is a great ride for cyclists wanting the adventure and unique scenery often associated with riding off the beaten path but not interested in the severe challenges of singletrack trails twisting up and down the mountain slopes.

Miles and Directions

0.0   Start from the parking area at the intersections of Sugarloaf Road and Comus Road. There is a small parking area with limited spaces in front of the Stronghold area. Head south on Sugarloaf Road.

0.4   Turn right on Mount Ephraim Road. You'll remain on this road for a little more than 4 miles.

0.8   Stay to the left at this intersection. To the right will take you back to the parking area.

4.6   Turn right on Park Mill Road.

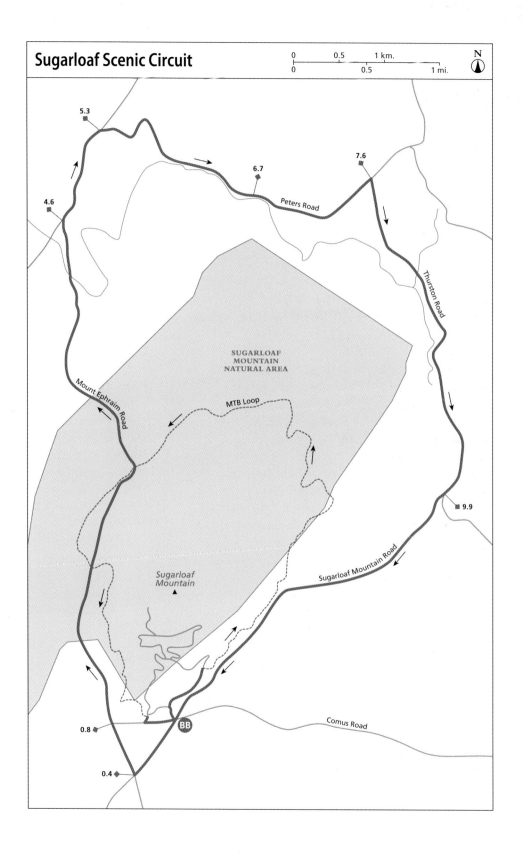

Sugarloaf Scenic Circuit

0   0.5   1 km.
0   0.5   1 mi.

N

5.3

4.6

6.7

7.6

Peters Road

Thurston Road

SUGARLOAF
MOUNTAIN
NATURAL AREA

Mount Ephraim Road

MTB Loop

9.9

Sugarloaf Mountain Road

Sugarloaf
Mountain

Comus Road

BB

0.8

0.4

5.3 Turn right on Peters. Stay on Peters for approximately 2.3 miles.

6.7 A local watering hole; $5 if you swing and jump in.

7.6 Make a sharp right on Thurston Road.

9.9 Turn right on Sugarloaf Mountain Road and continue straight until you reach the parking area.

12.5 The loop is complete.

Ride Information

Local Information

Tourism Council of Frederick County
Frederick, MD
(301) 663-8687

Local Events and Attractions

See Frederick County's online visitors' guide for links about local events and attractions: www .visitfrederick.org

Accommodations

Rocker Inn
Poolesville, MD
(301) 973-3543

CC Middleburg Vineyard Tour

Virginia is quickly becoming renowned worldwide for its wine. And Loudoun County is home to a number of the Old Dominion's finest wineries. This mostly unpaved (gravel and dirt) ride is set up to lead cyclists through the area's beautiful rolling horse country, connecting (or passing nearby) a number of Northern Virginia's most productive vineyards. Make plenty of time for this trip and stop often to taste the latest wine.

Start: Middleburg Elementary School
Length: 23.1 miles
Ride time: About 2–3 hours (not counting stops at vineyards)
Difficulty: Moderate to difficult (due to length)
Trail surface: Unpaved dirt and gravel roads
Lay of the land: Mostly easy rolling
Land status: Public roads
Nearest town: Middleburg, VA

Other trail users: Motorists and wine tasters
Trail contacts: None
Schedule & fees: Meredyth Vineyard 10 a.m. to 5 p.m., seven days a week; Piedmont Vineyard 10 a.m. to 4 p.m., seven days a week; Swedenburg Vineyard, 10 a.m. to 4 p.m., seven days a week; small fees at wineries for wine tastings

Getting there: From the Capital Beltway (I-495): Take I-66 west 8.5 miles to exit 57, US 50 West. Go 23 miles on US 50 West into Middleburg. US 50 (John Mosby Highway) becomes Washington Street within the Middleburg town limits. From Washington Street, turn right on VA 626 (Madison Street). Go 0.1 miles and turn right into the Middleburg Elementary School parking lot. GPS coordinates: 38.970761, -77.735273.

The Ride

This ride travels through some of Virginia's finest wine country, where visits to the vineyards are always welcome and wine tasting is just part of the tour.

You start in the historic town of Middleburg, a small touristy outpost in the middle of hunt country. Horses abound in this magnificent countryside. A town with a rich history, Middleburg has enjoyed its share of good fortune. Established in 1787, this centuries-old town was even graced by a US president when the Kennedy family attended the local Catholic church and built a home just outside town.

The ride starts on a route toward Piedmont Vineyard but breaks off from the main road onto backcountry dirt, perfect for an off-road tourist. This first section rolls comfortably past small estates and low-key horse farms. But when you turn east, the roads lift you into the hills. You'll pass some of the old and new—abandoned stone houses and state-of-the-art homes—then head toward Meredyth Vineyard to lavish in the land of the well-to-do. Gorgeous estates rest on acres of open land, where thoroughbreds graze in the warm sun. What a wonderful place to ride and dream.

Riding the gravel roads of Virginia's wine country is especially beautiful.

But don't forget to stop at the vineyard. (Its hours are from 10 a.m. to 4 p.m.) The rest of the ride rolls up and down below Bull Run Mountain, taking you past one more vineyard, the Swedenburg Estate, before leading you back into Middleburg.

If the wine doesn't get the best of you, enjoy the endless dirt roads scattered throughout this region. This is excellent off-road riding for cyclists looking for a change of pace and scenery.

Miles and Directions

0.0 Start at the Middleburg Elementary School parking lot. Turn left on VA 626, Madison Street (paved).

0.1 Turn right on Washington Street (US 50) (paved).

0.3 Turn left on Plains Road (VA 626). Follow the purple vineyard sign (paved).

1.1 Turn right on VA 705 (paved).

1.2 VA 705 changes to dirt (unpaved).

3.2 Stay straight on VA 705 at this intersection. VA 706 turns right.

3.4 Stay right on VA 705 at this intersection. VA 706 turns left.

4.2 Turn left at the T, continuing on VA 705. VA 708 goes right (unpaved).

5.3 Turn left at the stop sign on VA 702 (unpaved).

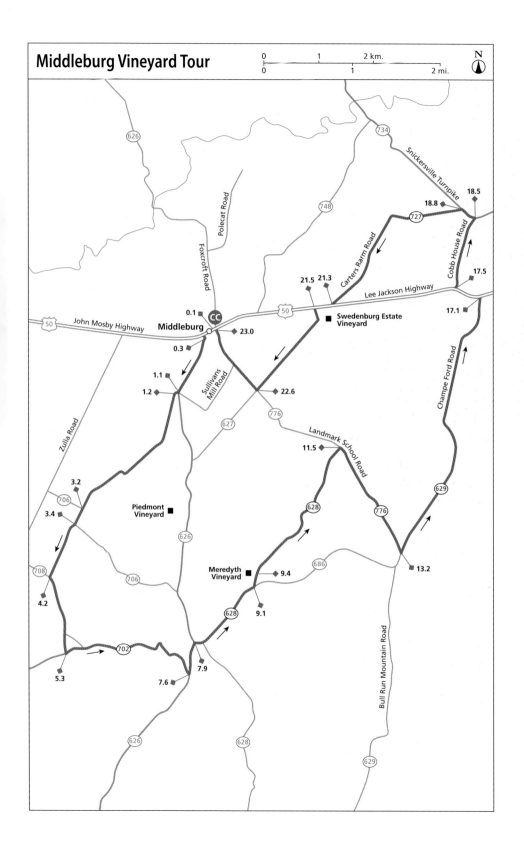

Middleburg Vineyard Tour

0   1   2 km.
0   1   2 mi.

N

626

734

Snickersville Turnpike

Polecat Road

748

18.5

18.8

727

Carters Farm Road

Cobb House Road

21.5 21.3

17.5

Foxcroft Road

Lee Jackson Highway

50

17.1

0.1

CC

Champe Ford Road

50   John Mosby Highway   Middleburg

Swedenburg Estate
Vineyard

23.0

0.3

1.1

Sullivans
Mill Road

1.2

22.6

Zulla Road

776

627

Landmark School Road

11.5

3.2

629

706

Piedmont
Vineyard

3.4

626

628

776

708

Meredyth
Vineyard

9.4

686

13.2

706

4.2

628   9.1

Bull Run Mountain Road

702

5.3

7.9

7.6

626

628

629

7.6 Turn left on VA 626 (paved).

7.9 Bear right on VA 679 at the bottom of the descent. This turns into VA 628.

9.1 Turn left on VA 628 (unpaved). This is slightly hidden. The turn comes after a long rock wall on the left, just past a large brick house with three chimneys.

9.4 Meredyth Vineyard on the left. Stop in for a tour. Hours are from 10 a.m. to 4 p.m.

11.5 Turn right on Landmark School Road (VA 776) (paved). For those who have had enough, you can turn left on Landmark School Road and take the shortcut back to Middleburg (2.4 miles).

13.2 Turn left on Champe Ford Road (VA 629) (unpaved).

17.1 Turn left on John Mosby Highway (US 50). Be careful of traffic (paved).

17.5 Turn right on Cobb House Road (VA 629) (unpaved).

18.5 Turn left on Snickersville Road (paved).

18.8 Turn left at the bottom of the hill on Carouters Farm Road (VA 627) (unpaved).

21.3 Turn right on John Mosby Highway (paved). Pass Swedenburg Estate Vineyard. Stop for a sip of wine before continuing on.

21.5 Turn left on Parsons Road (VA 627) (unpaved).

22.6 Turn right on Landmark School Road (VA 776) (paved).

23.0 Arrive back in Middleburg. Cross Washington Street to Madison Street.

23.1 Turn right into the school parking lot. Drink too much wine?

Ride Information

Local Information
Loudoun Tourism Council, (800) 752-6118

Local Events and Attractions
Middleburg Farm and Wineries
www.middleburgonline.com/wineries.asp

DD Canal Ride/River Grinder

Traveling first in Virginia, the course alternates between paved and unpaved roads, starting out flat, then rolling, before getting very hilly as it crosses over Catoctin Mountain. On the Maryland side, you can relax along the all flat, all dirt C&O Canal Towpath, which meanders along the scenic Potomac River. Along the way, you will cross over the Monocacy Aqueduct, the largest aqueduct along the 185-mile canal. Catch the ferry at White's Ferry to cross back over to the Virginia side and return to the start of the ride.

Start: Loudoun County High School
Length: 36.5 miles
Ride time: About 3+ hours
Difficulty: Difficult, due to length of ride and mountain climb
Trail surface: Dirt roads, canal towpath
Lay of the land: Hilly
Land status: Public roads

Nearest town: Leesburg, VA
Other trail users: Tourists and motorists
Trail contacts: C&O Canal headquarters, (301) 739-4200
Schedule & fees: Open year-round, sunrise to sunset; White's Ferry is open from 6 a.m. to 11 p.m. each day. Small fee to bring a bike on White's Ferry

Getting there: From the Capital Beltway (I-495): Take exit 10, US 7 (Leesburg Pike), west all the way to Leesburg (28 miles). At the Leesburg city limits, stay on US 7 (Market Street) through Leesburg. Turn left on Catoctin Circle. At the third light, turn left on Dry Mill Road. Loudoun County High School is on your right. Park here. GPS coordinates: 39.111696, -77.578882.

The Ride

Following what he believed were instructions from General George McClellan to push south, Union General Charles P. Stone set in motion a series of events on the night of October 20, 1861, that would result the next evening in carnage on the wooded bluff above the Potomac River.

Reconnaissance reported to General Stone an ill-guarded Confederate camp outside Leesburg, Virginia. Eager for the opportunity to destroy it, Stone positioned his men at Conrad's (White's) Ferry, Harrison's Island, and Edward's Ferry. Movement across the swollen Potomac began at midnight, but Stone's men found no camp at the reported site. Instead, they found only a moonlit grove of trees, mistaken by his men the previous night for tents.

They chose to continue toward Leesburg and, early that morning, met resistance from a Confederate outpost just north of Leesburg near Ball's Bluff. After hearing of skirmishes with Union soldiers, four companies of Confederate infantry were sent from Leesburg to the previously small outpost just west of Ball's Bluff, pushing the Union troops back toward the river. Throughout the afternoon, a series of

Loudoun County's gravel roads are perfect for gravel grinding.

advancements and attacks by a continually reinforced Confederate line forced the ill-fated Union troops near the edge of a steep drop to the rocky banks of the Potomac. When Union reinforcement did arrive by climbing a path at the side of the bluff, there was confusion among the officers over who was in command. A decision finally was made to fight their way through Confederate lines, since the only alternative was to retreat off the bluff, 90 feet down to the river below. But just as the Union troops attempted their advance, Confederates launched a murderous attack, blocking both the path that Union reinforcements had previously climbed and any chance for their retreat. Federal troops were suddenly forced to choose between furious Confederate gunfire and a suicidal leap to the rocks far below. Nearly 1,000 Union soldiers were lost that afternoon, dealing a severe blow to the Northern army, which was still reeling from its recent defeat at the first Battle of Bull Run. Ball's Bluff National Cemetery and Battlefield, the country's smallest national battlefield, remains today a quiet testimony to America's most violent era.

Miles and Directions

0.0   We'll begin measuring from the entrance to the high-school parking area along Catoctin Circle Drive and head north toward Old Waterford Road.

0.6   Cross West Market Street.

Canal Ride/River Grinder

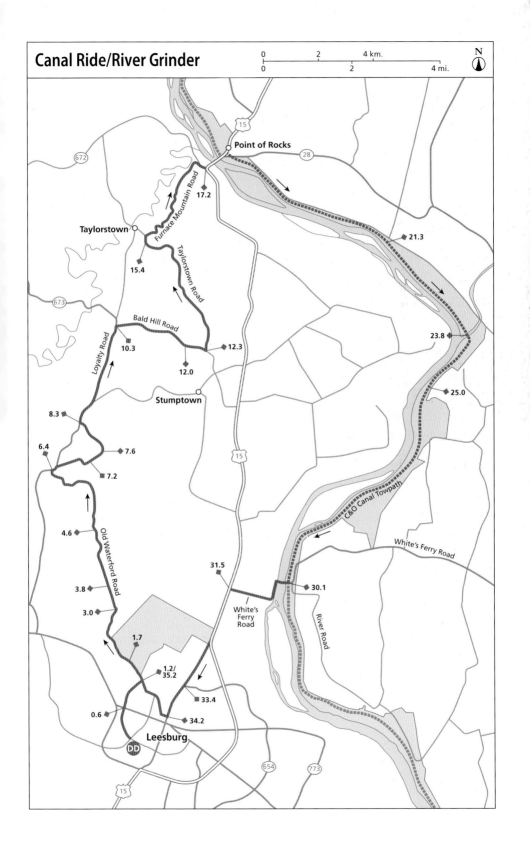

0   2   4 km.
0   2   4 mi.

N

672

Point of Rocks

15

28

17.2

Taylorstown

Furnace Mountain Road

15.4

Taylorstown Road

21.3

673

Bald Hill Road

Loyalty Road

10.3

12.3

12.0

23.8

Stumptown

25.0

8.3

6.4

7.6

7.2

15

C&O Canal Towpath

4.6

Old Waterford Road

White's Ferry Road

3.8

3.0

31.5

30.1

1.7

White's
Ferry
Road

River Road

1.2/
35.2

33.4

0.6

34.2

Leesburg

DD

15

654

773

1.2 Turn left on Old Waterford Road. Gravel and hills await.

1.7 Gravel begins.

3.0 Continue following Old Waterford Road to the left.

3.8 Continue straight at this intersection.

4.6 Continue following Old Waterford Road to the right.

6.4 Gravel ends. Turn right on Loyalty Road.

6.5 Turn right on Browns Lane. Gravel begins again.

7.2 Continue straight.

7.6 Back on pavement, now on Hannah Road.

8.3 Turn right on Loyalty Road. Use caution here as there is more traffic along this stretch.

10.3 Turn right on Bald Hill Road. You are back on gravel.

12.0 You are back on pavement.

12.3 Turn left onto Taylorstown Road. Once again, be careful along this stretch since there is more traffic. You will stay on Taylorstown Road for approximately 3 miles.

15.4 Turn right onto Furnace Mountain Road. This is an easy intersection to miss because you will be enjoying a screaming downhill.

17.2 Turn right on Lovetsville Road and then immediately left onto the James Madison Highway, MD 15. Be extremely careful along this section as you go over the bridge that spans the Potomac River; there is lots of traffic at this point. Immediately after crossing the bridge you will turn right on the ramp for MD 28 and then make an immediate right on Clay Street. This is a perfect point to resupply and take a break. The Deli on the Rocks is just up ahead to the left. You're done with the hills now; it's pretty much flat all the way home. From Clay Street follow the signs to the C&O Canal and Point of Rocks over the railroad tracks and then make an immediate left on the C&O Canal towpath. You'll now stay on the canal for the next 13 miles.

21.3 Alternate starting point. There is a parking area and restrooms to the right.

23.8 Lock 27 will be to your left.

25.0 Substation to the left, and Maryland fire-department training grounds to the right. You can also see a kayak training course to the right.

30.1 Turn right into historic White's Ferry. The protocol here is to ride up to where the first car is lined up to board the ferry and then wait for the attendant to direct you to board, generally after the ferry has been filled with vehicles. At the time of this writing cost to cross the river was $2 per bike. After you disembark the ferry, follow White's Ferry Road toward MD 15.

31.5 Turn left on MD 15.

33.4 Welcome back to Leesburg, Virginia.

34.2 Turn right on North Street.

34.4 Turn right on Old Waterford Road.

35.2 Turn left on Fairview Street and head back toward the starting point of the ride.

36.5 The ride is complete.

Ride Information

Local Information

White's Ferry
Dickerson, MD
(301) 349-5200
www.facebook.com/WhitesFerry

Loudoun Tourism Council
(800) 752-6118

Local Events and Attractions

Ball's Bluff Battlefield Regional Park
(703) 779-9372
www.nvrpa.org/park/ball_s_bluff

Civil War Reenactment in Leesburg, VA, August
(703) 777-1368

Accommodations

Tarara Winery and Bed-and-Breakfast
(703) 771-8157

EE Waterford Dirt Ride

With no singletrack in sight, this backcountry ride along quiet dirt and gravel roads makes for a perfect ramble through Northern Virginia's hunt country. Cyclists should bring along a pair of well-conditioned legs to help them through the ride's length and smattering of small climbs. Don't forget the camera, though, as this route takes you through some of the prettiest countryside and most historic towns west of the Beltway.

Start: Loudoun County High School
Length: 27.5 miles
Ride time: About 3-4 hours
Difficulty: Moderate to challenging due to length and many small climbs
Trail surface: Rolling dirt and gravel roads

Lay of the land: Rolling backcountry roads through Leesburg's scenic countryside
Land status: Public roads
Nearest town: Leesburg, VA; Waterford, VA
Other trail users: Motorists
Trail contacts: None available
Schedule: None available

Getting there: From the Capital Beltway (I-495): Take exit 10, US 7 (Leesburg Pike), west all the way to Leesburg (28 miles). At the Leesburg city limits, stay on US 7 (Market Street) through Leesburg. Turn left on Catoctin Circle. At the third light, turn left on Dry Mill Road. Loudoun County High School is on your right. Park here. GPS coordinates: 39.111696, -77.578882

The Ride

When Amos Janney led a small group of Quakers in 1733 from Bucks County, Pennsylvania, to the fertile land just west of the Catoctin Mountain along South Fork Creek, he may never have imagined that someday the land he sought out would become some of Virginia's most beautiful horse country. And more significantly for bicyclists, the land would become an ideal setting for some exceptionally scenic off-road bicycle rides.

But then again, perhaps he did. Janney and his group of Quakers yearned to be free from the persecutions of the Old World and wished to escape Pennsylvania's ever-increasing population. They sought the solitude and peace of this expansive valley between Catoctin and the Blue Ridge Mountains.

Today, unpaved roads climb along Catoctin Mountain, then roll leisurely along the valley floor. Panoramic views of the green countryside and the mountains beyond are a wonderful backdrop to the horse and dairy farms spread throughout the valley. The Waterford-Hamilton-Leesburg area, just as Amos Janney and his group of settlers discovered, is still the perfect location to escape the masses, to be free of the oppressive daily grind of our "new world," and to discover an undisturbed, peaceful haven.

Waterford Road is particularly scenic.

This route is comprised primarily of unpaved dirt and gravel roads, perfect for the off-road tourist looking for more than ballistic singletrack and rugged trails. Stop in the historic town of Waterford and have a look around. Amos Janney settled this Virginia town and called it Milltown. An Irish cobbler whose hometown was Waterford, Ireland, later renamed it. Cross the Washington & Old Dominion Trail into the town of Hamilton for a break, then be on your way, heading south toward Mount Gilead before riding north again to Leesburg. Be sure to notice the spectacular homes along Loudoun Orchard Road and Mount Gilead Road, and be careful not to bump into the deer residing in force throughout this area.

This route is comprised primarily of unpaved dirt and gravel roads, perfect for the off-road tourist looking for more than ballistic singletrack and rugged trails.

Miles and Directions

0.0   Start at the Loudoun County High School parking lot off Dry Mill Road. Turn left on Dry Mill Road. Follow the yellow bike route signs (paved).

0.3   Cross over Washington & Old Dominion trail. Continue straight.

0.5   Cross Loudoun Road.

0.6   Cross Market Street.

0.7   Turn right on Cornwall Street (paved).

0.8   Turn left on Memorial Drive. Memorial Drive stays to the right side of Memorial Hospital, heading toward Gibson Street (paved).

0.9   Turn right on Gibson Street (paved).

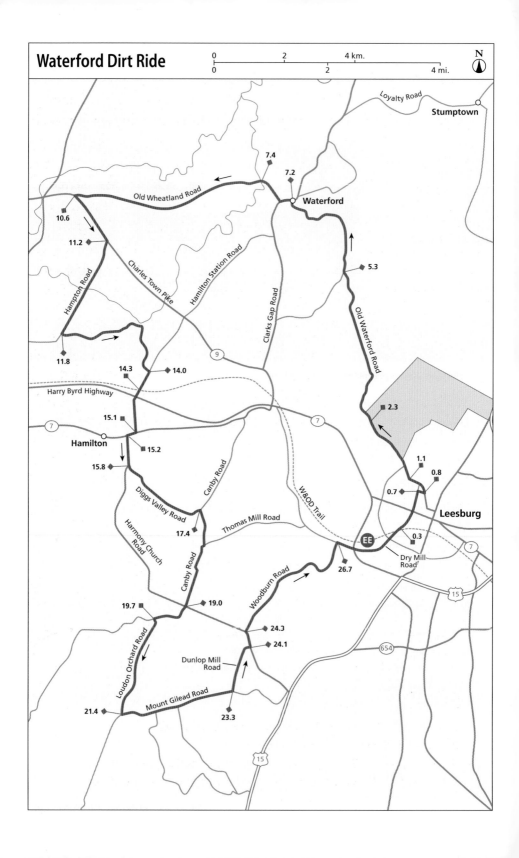

Waterford Dirt Ride

0   2   4 km.

0   2   4 mi.

N

Loyalty Road

Stumptown

Old Wheatland Road

7.4

7.2

Waterford

10.6

11.2

Charles Town Pike

Hamilton Station Road

5.3

Clarks Gap Road

Old Waterford Road

Hampton Road

11.8

9

14.3

14.0

Harry Byrd Highway

2.3

15.1

7

7

Hamilton

15.2

1.1

0.8

15.8

0.7

Canby Road

W&OD Trail

Leesburg

Diggs Valley Road

Thomas Mill Road

0.3

Harmony Church Road

17.4

EE

26.7

Dry Mill Road

7

Canby Road

Woodburn Road

15

19.7

19.0

24.3

24.1

654

Loudon Orchard Road

Dunlop Mill Road

21.4

Mount Gilead Road

23.3

15

YOU MAY RUN INTO: PETE BEERS

The day I met Pete, my life changed, as I'm sure it has for everyone that has had the pleasure of meeting him. The guy is a human-powered vehicle, and is one of the very few people I know who practices what we all preach. "I live to show people that they can leave their car home," he told me. "I'm not a talker. I never have been. I never will be. I'd much rather let my legs do the talking." And he does. Pete rides his bike everywhere, to and from work, for errands, for fun, and even to haul things he used to tuck in the trunk of his car. He rides to our rides. When we all plan a 20-mile loop around a given park, Pete rides the 25 miles to get there, and then the 25 miles to get home. Last year alone he logged more than 13,000 miles. Yes, you read that right, more than 13,000 miles! In the process he spared the environment nearly 13,000 pounds of CO_2. He's also active with Bike Arlington and has helped others find safe routes to and from work.

Pete's been riding nearly all his life. "I started out when I was very young, and it was all downhill from there," he kidded with me the other day. "Seriously, I made a conscious choice. Cycling became a way for me to go places. When I was young and on my bike I was free to go where I wanted. Even when I learned to drive, the bicycle was still a huge part of my life. I simply love to ride."

I'm certain that you'll spot him on the trail or road one day. This route is one of his favorites. He's easy to find. He'll either be riding a fixed-gear bike with an enormously large front tire, or a custom-made bright orange mountain bike tandem with a willing stoker behind him. Or, he'll be riding for the glory of the motherland (Mexico) and while doing it, practicing his "danger panda" maneuver: taking self-portraits as he spins. When you do run into him, say hello, and ask him to tell you all about his Mexican National Team experience. . . . (Or you can follow him on Twitter @I_am_Dirt.)

PHOTO COURTESY OF PETE BEERS

1.1 Turn left on Old Waterford Road (paved). Graveyard on the right.

2.3 Old Waterford Road turns to gravel (unpaved).

5.3 Stay right on Old Waterford Road at the intersection with Hurley Lane (unpaved).

7.2 Turn left on Main Water Street (paved). Arrive in the historic town of Waterford.

7.4   Turn left on Old Wheatland Road (paved).

7.7   Old Wheatland Road turns to gravel (unpaved).

10.6   Turn left on Charles Town Pike (VA 9) (paved). Be careful along this road. The speed limit for cars is 55 miles per hour.

11.2   Turn right on Hampton Road (unpaved).

11.8   Turn left on Piggott Bottom Road (unpaved).

12.2   Bear left at the stop sign, continuing on Piggott Bottom Road.

14.0   Turn right on Hamilton Station Road (paved).

14.3   Cross Washington & Old Dominion trail.

15.1   Turn right on Colonial Highway (paved). Arrive in the historic town of Hamilton.

15.2   Turn left on Harmony Church Road (paved).

15.8   Bear left on Diggs Valley Road (unpaved).

17.2   Diggs Valley Road comes to a four-way intersection. Turn left, continuing on Diggs Valley Road (unpaved).

17.4   Turn right on Canby Road (unpaved). Stay on Canby all the way to Harmony Church Road.

19.0   Cross Harmony Church Road on Loudoun Orchard Road (paved).

19.7   Bear left, continuing on Loudoun Orchard Road (paved).

20.1   Loudoun Orchard turns to gravel (unpaved).

21.4   Turn left on Mount Gilead Road (unpaved).

23.3   Turn left on Dunlop Mill Road (unpaved).

24.1   Turn left on Harmony Church Road (paved).

24.3   Turn right on Woodburn Road (unpaved).

26.7   Turn right on Dry Mill Road.

27.5   Arrive at Loudoun County High School.

Ride Information

Local Information

Loudoun Tourism Council
(800) 752-6118

Waterford Foundation
www.waterfordva.org

Local Events and Attractions

Leesburg calendar of events
www.leesburgva.gov

Waterford Homes Tour and Crafts Exhibit, October
(540) 882-3085
www.waterfordva.org

FF Prince William Forest Park

Down here in Prince William County lies a relatively large park, preserved as one of the few remaining piedmont forest ecosystems in the National Park Service. Within its 18,000 acres are 35 miles of hiking trails, hundreds of acres open to primitive camping, a scenic paved road looping through the park (incidentally named Scenic Drive Road), and a plethora of wildlife and plant life for city folks to enjoy. Four miles of the Scenic Drive have a dedicated bike lane providing a paved, relatively flat surface ideal for beginning bicyclists. More experienced cyclists have the option of off-road biking on any of the ten fire roads in the park.

Start: Lake Montclair Shopping Center
Length: Varies, depending on route chosen. (There are 8.2 miles of unpaved roads open to cyclists.)
Ride time: Varies, depending on route chosen
Difficulty: Moderate
Trail surface: Paved and unpaved park roads
Lay of the land: Hilly piedmont and coastal plains
Land status: Administered by the National Park Service

Nearest town: Dumfries, VA
Other trail users: Hikers, motorists, nature lovers, and pyrite collectors
Trail contacts: Prince William Forest Park Visitor Center, (703) 221-7181; National Park Service, (703) 759-2915
Schedule & fees: Open daily from dawn to dusk. Registered campers and cabin campers have access twenty-four hours. Visitor center is open between 8:30 a.m. and 5:00 p.m. Small fee for a three-day pass for vehicles or cyclists.

Getting there: From the Capital Beltway (I-495): Take I-95 south toward Richmond for 20 miles. Take exit 152B, VA 234 (Dumfries Road) north toward Manassas. Continue on 234 for approximately 3.2 miles and turn right onto Waterway Dr. Lake Montclair Center will be on your right. GPS coordinates: 38.6086716, -77.3604226.

The Ride

At one time, Prince William Forest Park's thousands of acres of forestland were extensively farmed for tobacco. Then, when the hills eroded and the earth could no longer support their crops, farmers turned to dairy farming, already well established throughout the county. But for those living in the Quantico Creek area, this business also failed. The Civil War was equally taxing for those already struggling here. The Confederates blockaded the Potomac, requiring large numbers of troops for support. Those living in the vicinity of the blockade were required to provide the troops with timber and food and found that what little they had before the war was no longer enough.

In 1889, mining operation near the confluence of the north and south branches of Conduce Creek provided a much-needed boost to the area's economy. But a strike over wages closed the high-grade pyrite ore mine in 1920, bringing down with it any

Cold autumn days are best to enjoy this regional grinder.

hope for the area's recovery. It was soon thereafter that the US government bought the land, resettling nearly 150 families. With the help of the Civilian Conservation Corps, they began the effort to "return the depleted land to an ecological balance."

Originally established as the Chopawamsic Recreational Demonstration Area by an act of Congress in August 1933, Prince William Forest Park, a unit of the National Park Service, is mandated to "conserve the scenery and the natural and historic objects and the wildlife therein and to provide for the enjoyment of the same in such manner and by such means as will leave them unimpaired for the enjoyment of future generations." The park contains the largest example of an eastern piedmont forest ecosystem in the National Park System and is a sanctuary for native plants and animals in the midst of this rapidly developing metropolitan area.

All kinds of outdoor activities, including bicycling, are available within the park. Riding on park trails, unfortunately, is prohibited. However, there are many unpaved, dirt roads throughout the park that can be used by cyclists. Many of these roads are separate out-and-back fire roads, in which case you may need to ride along the paved Scenic Drive Road to create loops. Scenic Drive Road is very well maintained and even has its own dedicated bike lane. Road cyclists from all around often come to Prince William Forest Park just to ride this paved loop through the forest, getting quite a workout from its hilly terrain.

FALL LINE

Prince William Forest Park lies along the border between two physiographic zones: the piedmont and the coastal plain. Many of the faulted rocks represent the fall line, a unique geological feature. Streams form falls or rapids as they leave the harder rocks of the piedmont and enter the softer rocks of the coastal plain.

To witness the progress the forest has made in reclaiming what was once depleted and eroding farmland is a wonderful experience. And riding your mountain bike along the forest roads through the park gives you an up-close look at this process in action.

Folks looking to do more than just bike can explore as many as 35 miles of hiking trails along ridges, into valleys, and beside the two main creeks in the park. Scenic Drive Road provides access to all of the trails and features within the park. Bicycles are not allowed on any of the park's hiking trails.

Miles and Directions

0.0 From the parking area at the Lake Montclair Shopping Center: Cross VA 234 at the Waterway crosswalk and hop on the 234 bike trail. Turn left to head south.

0.5 Turn right into the park road. Follow the signs for cabins 1 and 4. The road will turn to gravel.

0.9 Turn right on Burma Road and go through the park gate.

1.6 Continue bearing left at this intersection, onto Old Spriggs Road. You can bail to the right. This will be our exit point from the park.

2.3 Cross Scenic Drive Road. You are now on Taylor Farm Road.

2.9 Turn right on Old Blacktop Road.

3.9 Turn left on Scenic Drive. You are now on the road.

4.8 Turn right on Oak Ridge Road. At this point you will head into the campground area and do a counter-clockwise loop of the entire site and return to this intersection.

5.4 Reach the campground. Follow the directional arrows and make your way around the camp loop.

6.4 You've competed the campground loop. Double back along Oak Ridge Road to the Scenic Drive.

7.6 Turn left on Scenic Drive and ride along the bike path. We'll stay on the bike path for 3 miles until our next dose of gravel.

8.0 Old Blacktop Road is to your right; continue straight on Scenic Drive.

8.8 You reach the intersection of Burma and Taylor Farm. Continue straight along the bike path.

10.3 Turn left onto North Orenda Road immediately after the parking area to the right. Get ready for a fun descent!

Prince William Forest Park

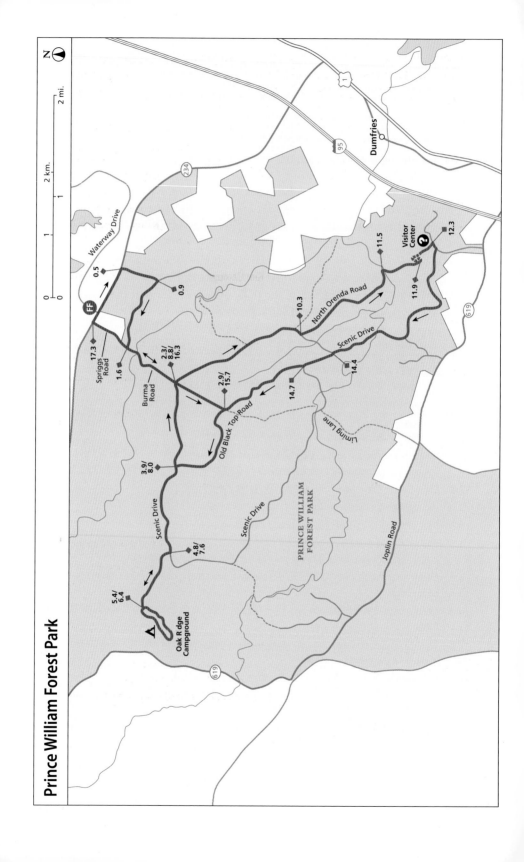

N

2 mi.

2 km.

Waterway Drive

Spriggs Road

Burma Road

17.3

1.6

0.5

0.9

FF

2.3/
8.8/
16.3

3.9/
8.0

Scenic Drive

4.8/
7.6

5.4/
6.4

Oak Ridge
Campground

Scenic Drive

Old Black Top Road

2.9/
15.7

14.7

Liming Lane

PRINCE WILLIAM
FOREST PARK

Joplin Road

North Orenda Road

10.3

Scenic Drive

14.4

11.9

11.5

Visitor
Center

12.3

619

234

95

1

Dumfries

11.5 Turn right and walk your bike over the bridge. The trail ahead is closed to bikes! Immediately after crossing the bridge look for the sign for South Orenda Road and follow it. Get ready to pay the bill for that last descent.

11.8 Continue to the right on South Orenda.

11.9 Turn left onto the singletrack. This is the IMBA trail, conceived by my good friend Scott Scudamore after years of work.

12.1 Turn left on the gravel path and then immediately right onto the pavement. You are now on the far end of the Pine Grove area; continue straight through the parking area to the stop sign.

12.3 Make a right at the stop sign. Please take a little detour to the left and head to the park office to pay your day-use fee. If you plan on coming to Prince William Forest Park often, I recommend the annual pass, which pays for itself in four visits.

12.4 Turn right onto Scenic Drive.

14.4 Turn left and follow the signs for Turkey Run Campground. You can bail and continue straight to shorten the ride.

14.7 Turn right on Turkey Run Road. We're almost back on the gravel!

15.1 Back on gravel. You are now on Old Blacktop Road.

15.7 Turn right onto Taylor Farm Road. At this point you will be doubling back for a short period of time.

16.3 Cross Scenic Drive and hop back on Old Burma Road. The next section is a super fast descent—use caution!

16.6 You're at the intersection of Old Burma and Old Spriggs. Continue straight and get ready for a short climb.

17.3 You are at the 234 bike path. Turn right to complete the loop.

17.5 The loop is complete.

Ride Information

Local Information

Prince William County Convention and Visitors Bureau
(800) 432-1792
www.nps.gov/prwi

Friends of Prince William Forest Park
www.fpwfp.org

Local Events and Attractions

Lazy Susan Dinner Theater
(703) 550-7384

Waterworks Water Park
www.waterworkswaterpark.com

Historic Town of Occoquan
www.historicoccoquan.com

Harbor River Cruises in Occoquan
(703) 385-9433

Historic Occoquan Spring Arts & Crafts Show
(703) 491-2168

Accommodations

Oakridge Campground
Turkey Ridge Run Campground
Cabin Rental, (703) 221-5843

Gravity-Assisted Mountain Biking

Ski resorts offer a great alternative to local trail riding. During the spring, summer, and fall, many resorts open their trails for mountain biking and, just like during ski season, sell lift tickets to take you and your bike to the top of the mountain. Lodging is also available for weekend mountain-bike junkies, and rates are often discounted

LIFT-ASSISTED RIDING

One of my favorite destinations is the new downhill trail system at Bryce Resort in Basey, Virginia. The resort's general manager, Rob Schwartz, recently came to the area with a vision to transform this small Virginia mountain into a regional downhill destination. Since his arrival, Rob has added several downhill runs to the mountain that cater to the novice and advanced rider alike. For a very reasonable fee, you can spend an entire day riding the lifts up to the top of the mountain to enjoy one of the half-dozen lines to the bottom.

I was very lucky to spend a day with Rob and his staff enjoying those trails, and the experience was phenomenal. The level of detail and attention paid to the trail and sleek rental fleet of bikes by Rob's team is critical to that experience.

Rob's vision is simple: "Our primary goal is to provide a complete riding experience, and having immaculate bikes for renters to enjoy is the first step in that direction," he told me. "I want a rider to come and get top-notch equipment so that they can have the full experience," he added. "I've often seen places that have great trails but their bikes are in horrible condition and give renters no confidence." Along with the rentals, Bryce also provides full armor. I highly recommend it, so that you can feel safe on the slopes. The shop will also hook you up with a GoPro so you can capture the entire experience and relive it in the future.

Having visited several other destinations in the region, I can attest that Bryce is by far one of the better ones, and it's conveniently close to the D.C. area. I often take my nine-year-old daughter and we spend hours going down the easy Sundowner trail. She simply loves not having to pedal uphill.

Bryce's location also gives you the opportunity to sample other types of riding. There are lots of rural roads to craft either a road or gravel-grinding loop. Plus, you're a stone's throw away from Harrisonburg and the Shenandoah system of trails, a regional mountain-biking favorite. My good friends over at Shenandoah Mountain Touring (www.mtntouring.com) will be happy to take you on some of the most incredible rides in the region. Be sure to give them a call. Nothing beats their local knowledge, and their supported rides are legendary.

from the normal ski-season prices. Some resorts even rent bikes and lead guided mountain-bike tours. Call ahead to find out just what each resort offers in the way of mountain-bike riding, and pick the one that best suits your fancy.

The following is a list of many of the ski resorts near the Washington, D.C./ Baltimore area that say *yes!* to mountain biking when the weather turns too warm for skiing.

Massanutten
Harrisonburg, VA
www.massresort.com

Wintergreen
Waynesboro, VA
www.wintergreenresort.com

The Homestead
Hot Springs, VA
www.thehomestead.com

Bryce
Basey, VA
www.bryceresort.com

Wisp
McHenry, MD
www.wispresort.com

Timberline
Davis, WV
www.timberlineresort.com

Canaan Valley
Davis, WV
www.canaanresort.com

Snowshoe
Marlinton, WV
www.snowshoemtn.com

Seven Springs
Somerset, PA
www.7springs.com

Fat-Tire Vacations

Bicycle Touring Companies

There are literally dozens of off-road bicycling tour companies offering an incredible variety of guided tours around the world for mountain bikers. A quick Internet search will yield dozens of outfitters nationwide willing to cater to your every whim. On these pay-as-you-pedal, fat-tire vacations, you will have a chance to go places around the globe that only an expert can take you. Your experiences will be much different than those you can have sitting in a tour bus.

From hut to hut in the Colorado Rockies or inn to inn through Vermont's Green Mountains, there is a tour company for you. Whether you want hard-core singletrack during the day and camping at night or scenic trails followed by a bottle of wine at night and a mint on each pillow, someone out there offers what you're looking for. The tours are well organized and fully supported with expert guides, bike mechanics, and "sag wagons" that carry gear, food, and tired bodies. Prices range from $100 to $500 for a weekend to more than $2,000 for two-week-long trips to far-off lands such as Perú, New Zealand, or Ireland.

Locally we recommend the following outfitters. Each of these companies will gladly send additional information to whet your appetite.

Selected Touring Companies
Elk River Touring Center
Slatyfork, WV
www.ertc.com

Shenandoah Mountain Touring
Harrisonburg, VA
www.mtntouring.com

The Art of Mountain Biking

Everything you need to know about off-road bicycling in the Washington, D.C./ Baltimore area can be found in this book. This section explores the fascinating history of the mountain bike itself and discusses everything from the health benefits of off-road cycling to tips and techniques for bicycling over logs and up hills. Also included are descriptions of the types of clothing that will keep you comfortable and riding in style; essential equipment ideas to keep your rides smooth and trouble-free; and explanations of off-road terrain, which will prepare you for the kinds of bumps and bounces you can expect to encounter.

The mountain bike, with its knobby tread and reinforced frame, takes cyclists to places once unheard of—down rugged mountain trails, through streams of rushing water, across the frozen Alaskan tundra, and even to work in the city. There are few limits on what this fat-tired beast can do and where it can take us. Few obstacles stand in its way, few boundaries slow its progress. Except for one—its own success. If trail closure means little to you now, read on and discover how a trail can be here today and gone tomorrow. With so many new off-road cyclists taking to the trails each year, it's no wonder trail access has become a contentious issue. A little education about the issue and some effort on your part can go a long way toward preserving trail access for future use. Nothing is more crucial to the survival of mountain biking itself than to read the examples set forth in this book and practice their message.

Without open trails, the maps in this book are virtually useless. Cyclists must learn to be responsible for the trails they use and to share these trails with others. This guidebook addresses why trail use has become so controversial and what can be done to improve the image of mountain biking. We also cover how to have fun and ride responsibly, and the worldwide-standard rules of the trail.

Mountain Bike Beginnings

It seems the mountain bike, originally designed for lunatic adventurists bored with straight lines, clean clothes, and smooth tires, has become globally popular in the time it takes to race down a mountain trail.

Like many things of a revolutionary nature, the mountain bike was born on the West Coast. But unlike in-line skates, purple hair, and the peace sign, the concept of the off-road bike cannot be credited solely to imaginative Californians—they were just the first to make waves.

The design of the first off-road-specific bike was based on the geometry of the old Schwinn Excelsior, a one-speed, camel-back cruiser with balloon tires. Joe Breeze was the creator behind it, and in 1977 he built ten of these "Breezers" for himself and his Marin County, California, friends at $750 apiece—a bargain.

Breeze was a serious competitor in bicycle racing, placing thirteenth in the 1977 US Road Racing National Championships. After races, he and friends would scour local bike shops, hoping to find old bikes they could then restore.

It was the 1941 Schwinn Excelsior, for which Breeze paid just $5, that began to shape and change bicycling history forever. After taking the bike home, removing the fenders, oiling the chain, and pumping up the tires, Breeze hit the dirt. He loved it.

His inspiration, though prescient, was not altogether unique. On the opposite end of the country, nearly 2,500 miles from Marin County, East Coast bike bums were also growing restless. More and more old beat-up clunkers were being restored and modified. These behemoths often weighed as much as eighty pounds and were so reinforced they seemed virtually indestructible. But rides that take just forty minutes on today's twenty-five-pound featherweights took the steel-toed-boot- and blue-jean-clad bikers of the late 1970s and early 1980s nearly four hours to complete.

Not until 1981 was it possible to purchase a production mountain bike, but local retailers found these ungainly bicycles difficult to sell and rarely kept them in stock. By 1983, however, mountain bikes were no longer such a fringe item, and large bike manufacturers quickly jumped into the action, producing their own versions of the off-road bike. By the 1990s, the mountain bike had firmly established its place with bicyclists of nearly all ages and abilities. Mountain bikes now command nearly 90 percent of the US bike market.

There are many reasons for the mountain bike's success in becoming the hottest two-wheeled vehicle in the nation. They are much friendlier to the cyclist than traditional road bikes because of their comfortable upright position and shock-absorbing fat tires. And because of the health-conscious, environmentalist movement of the late 1980s and 1990s, people are more activity minded and seek nature on a closer front than paved roads can allow. The mountain bike gives you these things and takes you far away from the daily grind—even if you're only minutes from the city.

Mountain Biking into Shape

If your objective is to get in shape and lose weight, then you're on the right track, because mountain biking is one of the best ways to get started.

One way many of us have lost weight in this sport is the crash-and-burn-it-off method. Picture this: You're speeding uncontrollably down a vertical drop that you realize you shouldn't be on—only after it is too late. Your front wheel lodges into a rut and launches you through endless weeds, trees, and pointy rocks before you come to an abrupt halt in a puddle of thick mud. Surveying the damage, you discover, with the layers of skin, body parts, and lost confidence littering the trail above, that those unwanted pounds have been shed—permanently. Instant weight loss.

There is, of course, a more conventional (and quite a bit less painful) approach to losing weight and gaining fitness on a mountain bike. It's called the workout, and bicycles provide an ideal way to get physical. Take a look at some of the benefits associated with cycling.

Cycling helps you shed pounds without gimmicky diet fads or weight-loss programs. You can explore the countryside and burn nearly 10 to 16 calories per minute or close to 600 to 1,000 calories per hour. Moreover, it's a great way to spend an afternoon.

No less significant than the external and cosmetic changes of your body from riding are the internal changes taking place. Over time, cycling regularly will strengthen your heart as your body grows vast networks of new capillaries to carry blood to all those working muscles. This will, in turn, give your skin a healthier glow. The capacity of your lungs may increase up to 20 percent, and your resting heart rate will drop significantly. The Stanford University School of Medicine reports to the American Heart Association that people can reduce their risk of heart attack by nearly 64 percent if they burn up to 2,000 calories per week. This is only two to three hours of bike riding!

Recommended for insomnia, hypertension, indigestion, anxiety, and even recuperation from major heart attacks, bicycling can be an excellent cure-all as well as a great preventive. Cycling just a few hours per week can improve your figure and sleeping habits, give you greater resistance to illness, increase your energy levels, and provide feelings of accomplishment and heightened self-esteem.

Be Safe—Know the Law

Occasionally, even hard-core off-road cyclists will find they have no choice but to ride the pavement. When you are forced to hit the road, it's important for you to know and understand the rules.

Outlined below are a few of the common laws found in Virginia, Maryland, and D.C., as well as some common-sense ideas.

- In Virginia, Maryland, and D.C., you can pedal on any paved public road except urban freeways.
- Follow the same driving rules as motorists. Be sure to obey all road signs and traffic lights.
- Wear a helmet and bright clothing so that you are more visible to motorists. Bright colors such as orange and lime green are highly visible at night.
- Equip your bike with lights and wear reflective clothing at night. When riding at night, the bicycle or rider must be equipped with a white light visible at least 500 feet to the front and a red light or reflector visible at least 600 feet to the rear.
- Pass motorists on the left, not the right. Motorists are not expecting you to pass on the right, and they may not see you.
- Ride single file on busy roads so motorists can pass you safely.
- Use hand signals to show motorists what you plan on doing next.
- Ride with the traffic, not against it.
- Follow painted lane markings.

- Make eye contact with drivers. Assume they don't see you until you are sure they do.
- Ride in the middle of the lane at busy intersections and whenever you are moving the same speed as traffic.
- Slow down and announce your presence when passing pedestrians, cyclists, and horses.
- Turn left by looking back, signaling, getting into the left lane, and turning. In urban situations, walk your bike across the crosswalk when the pedestrian walk sign is illuminated.
- Never ride while under the influence of alcohol or drugs. Remember that DUI laws apply when you're riding a bicycle.
- Avoid riding in extremely foggy, rainy, or windy conditions.
- Watch out for parallel-slat sewer grates, slippery manhole covers, oily pavement, gravel, wet leaves, and ice.
- Cross railroad tracks at a right angle. Be especially careful when it's wet out. For better control as you move across bumps and other hazards, stand up on your pedals.
- Don't ride too close to parked cars—a person opening a car door may hit you.
- Avoid riding on sidewalks. Instead, walk your bike. Pedestrians have the right-of-way on walkways. By law, you must give pedestrians audible warning when you pass. Use a bike bell or announce clearly, "On your left/right."
- Slow down at street crossings and driveways.

The Mountain Bike Controversy

Are off-road bicyclists environmental outlaws? Do we have the right to use public trails?

Mountain bikers have long endured the animosity of folks in the backcountry who complain about the consequences of off-road bicycling. Many people believe that fat tires and knobby treads do unacceptable environmental damage and that our uncontrollable riding habits are a danger to animals and other trail users. To the contrary, mountain bikes have no more environmental impact than hiking boots or horseshoes. This does not mean, however, that mountain bikes leave no imprint at all. Wherever people tread, there is an impact. By riding responsibly, though, it is possible to leave only a minimum impact—something we all must take care to achieve.

Unfortunately, it is often people of great influence who view the mountain bike as the environment's worst enemy. Consequently, we as mountain-bike riders and environmentally concerned citizens must be educators, impressing upon others that we also deserve the right to use these trails. Our responsibilities as bicyclists are no more and no less than any other trail user. We must all take the soft-cycling approach and show that mountain bicyclists are not environmental outlaws.

Etiquette of Mountain Biking

When discussing mountain-biking etiquette, we are in essence discussing the soft-cycling approach. This term refers to the art of minimum-impact bicycling and should apply to both the physical and social dimensions of the sport. But make no mistake—it is possible to ride fast and furiously while maintaining the balance of soft cycling. Here are a few ways to minimize the physical impact of mountain-bike riding.

- Stay on the trail. Don't ride around fallen trees or mud holes that block your path. Stop and cross over them. When you come to a vista overlooking a deep valley, don't ride off the trail for a better vantage point. Instead, leave the bike and walk to see the view. Riding off the trail may seem inconsequential when done only once, but soon someone else will follow, then others, and the cumulative results can be catastrophic. Each time you wander from the trail you begin creating a new path, adding one more scar to the earth's surface.

- Do not disturb the soil. Follow a line within the trail that will not disturb or damage the soil.

- Do not ride over soft or wet trails. After a rain shower or during the thawing season, trails will often resemble muddy, oozing swampland. The best thing to do is stay off the trails altogether. Realistically, however, we're all going to come across some muddy trails we cannot anticipate. Instead of blasting through each section of mud, which may seem both easier and more fun, lift the bike and walk past. Each time a cyclist rides through a soft or muddy section of trail, that part of the trail is permanently damaged. Regardless of the trail's conditions, though, remember always to go over the obstacles across the path, not around them. Stay on the trail.

- Avoid trails that, for all but God, are considered impassable and impossible. Don't take a leap of faith down a kamikaze descent on which you will be forced to lock your brakes and skid to the bottom, ripping the ground apart as you go.

The concept of soft-cycling should apply to the social dimensions of the sport as well, since mountain bikers are not the only folks who use the trails. Hikers, equestrians, cross-country skiers, and other outdoors people use many of the same trails and can be easily spooked by a marauding mountain biker tearing through the trees. Be friendly in the forest and give ample warning of your approach.

- Take out what you bring in. Don't leave broken bike pieces and banana peels scattered along the trail.

- Be aware of your surroundings. Don't use popular hiking trails for race training.

- Slow down! Rocketing around blind corners is a sure way to ruin an unsuspecting hiker's day. Consider this: If you fly down a quick singletrack descent at 20 miles per hour, then hit the brakes and slow down to only 6 miles per hour to pass someone, you're still moving twice as fast as the hiker!

Like the trails we ride on, the social dimension of mountain biking is very fragile and must be cared for responsibly. We should not want to destroy another person's enjoyment of the outdoors. By riding in the backcountry with caution, control, and responsibility, our presence should be felt positively by other trail users. By adhering to these rules, trail riding—a privilege that can quickly be taken away—will continue to be ours to share.

Trail Maintenance

Unfortunately, despite all of the preventive measures taken to avoid trail damage, we're still going to run into many trails requiring attention. Simply put, a lot of hikers, equestrians, and cyclists use the same trails—some wear and tear is unavoidable. But like your bike, if you want to use these trails for a long time to come, you must also maintain them.

Trail maintenance and restoration can be accomplished in a variety of ways. One way is for mountain-bike clubs to combine efforts with other trail users (hikers and equestrians) and work closely with land managers to cut new trails or repair existing ones. This work not only reinforces to others the commitment cyclists have in caring for and maintaining the land, but it also breaks the ice that often separates cyclists from their fellow trail mates. Another good way to help out is to show up on a Saturday morning with a few riding buddies, ready to work at your favorite off-road domain. With a good attitude, thick gloves, and the local land manager's supervision, trail repair is fun and very rewarding. It's important, of course, that you arrange a trail-repair outing with the local land manager before you start pounding shovels into the dirt. Managers can lead you to the most needy sections of trail and instruct you on what repairs should be done and how best to accomplish the task. Perhaps the most effective way to help maintain your local trails is to reach out and join your local mountain bike advocacy group. Organizations like the Mid-Atlantic Off-Road Enthusiasts (MORE), the Frederick Area Mountain Bike Enthusiasts (FAMBE), the Fredericksburg Area Trail Users Group (FATMUG), Eastern Shore IMBA (ESIMBA), and Southern Maryland Mountain Bike (SMMB) have taken the lead to make sure our region's trails are maintained properly. These advocacy and social groups have packed calendars with rides and trail days in which you can easily participate. Check the Local Bicycle Clubs and Organizations section of this guide for contact information for the area's most prominent and active clubs to see how you can help them help you keep riding.

Rules of the Trail

The International Mountain Bicycling Association (IMBA) has developed these guidelines for trail riding. These "rules of the trail" are accepted worldwide and will go a long way in keeping trails open. Please respect and follow these rules for everyone's sake.

- Ride only on open trails. Respect trail and road closures (if you're not sure, ask a park or state official first), do not trespass on private property, and obtain permits or authorization if required. Federal and state wilderness areas are off-limits to cycling. Parks and state forests may also have certain trails closed to cycling.

- Leave no trace. Be sensitive to the dirt beneath you. Even on open trails, you should not ride under conditions by which you will leave evidence of your passing, such as on certain soils or shortly after a rainfall. Be sure to observe the different types of soils and trails you're riding on, practicing minimum-impact cycling. Never ride off the trail, don't skid your tires, and be sure to bring out at least as much as you bring in.

- Control your bicycle! Inattention for even one second can cause disaster for yourself or for others. Excessive speed frightens and can injure people, gives mountain biking a bad name, and can result in trail closures.

- Always yield. Let others know you're coming well in advance (a friendly greeting is always good and often appreciated). Show your respect when passing others by slowing to walking speed or stopping altogether, especially in the presence of horses. Horses can be unpredictable, so be very careful. Anticipate that other trail users may be around corners or in blind spots.

- Never spook animals. All animals are spooked by sudden movements, unannounced approaches, or loud noises. Give the animals extra room and time so they can adjust to you. Move slowly or dismount around animals. Running cattle and disturbing wild animals are serious offenses. Leave gates as you find them, or as marked.

- Plan ahead. Know your equipment, your ability, and the area in which you are riding, and plan your trip accordingly. Be self-sufficient at all times, keep your bike in good repair, and carry necessary supplies for changes in weather or other conditions. You can help keep trails open by setting an example of responsible, courteous, and controlled mountain-bike riding.

- Always wear a helmet when you ride. For your own safety and protection, a helmet should be worn whenever you are riding your bike. You never know when a tree root or small rock will throw you the wrong way and send you tumbling.

Thousands of miles of dirt trails have been closed to mountain bicycling because of the irresponsible riding habits of just a few riders. Don't follow the example of these offending riders. Don't take away trail privileges from thousands of others who work hard each year to keep backcountry avenues open to us all.

The Necessities of Cycling

When discussing the most important items to have on a bike ride, cyclists generally agree on the following four items.

- Helmet. The reasons to wear a helmet should be obvious. Helmets are discussed in more detail in the "Be Safe—Wear Your Armor" section.

- Water. Without it, cyclists may face dehydration, which may result in dizziness and fatigue. On a warm day, cyclists should drink at least one full bottle during every hour of riding. Remember, it's always good to drink before you feel thirsty—otherwise, it may be too late.

- Cycling shorts. These are necessary if you plan to ride your bike more than thirty minutes. Padded cycling shorts may be the only thing keeping your derriere from serious saddle soreness by ride's end. There are two types of cycling shorts. Touring shorts are good for people who don't want to look like they're wearing anatomically correct cellophane. They look like regular athletic shorts with pockets, but have built-in padding in the crotch area for protection from chafing and saddle sores. The more popular, traditional cycling shorts are made of skintight material, also with a padded crotch. Whichever style you find most comfortable, cycling shorts are a necessity for long rides. If you plan on riding longer distances, or for extended periods of time, you will want to invest in some chamois cream. A quality cream will help reduce friction between the points where your body meets the chamois of your shorts and help reduce, or flat-out eliminate, saddle sores.

- Food. This essential item will keep you rolling. Cycling burns up a lot of calories and is among the few sports in which no one is safe from the "bonk." Bonking feels like it sounds. Without food in your system, your blood sugar level collapses, and there is no longer any energy in your body. This instantly results in total fatigue and light-headedness. So when you're filling your water bottle, remember to bring along some food. Fruit, energy bars, or some other forms of high-energy food are highly recommended. Candy bars are not, however, because they will deliver a sudden burst of high energy, then let you down soon after, causing you to feel worse than before. Energy bars are available at most bike stores and seem similar to candy bars, but they provide complex carbohydrate energy and high nutrition rather than fast-burning simple sugars.

Be Prepared or Die

Essential equipment that will keep you from dying alone in the woods:

- Cell phone
- Spare tube
- Tire irons
- Patch kit
- Pump or CO_2 cartridges
- Money
- Spoke wrench

- Spare spokes (tape these to the chain stay)
- Chain tool
- Allen keys (bring appropriate sizes to fit your bike)
- Compass/GPS
- Duct tape
- First-aid kit
- Rain gear for quick changes in weather
- Matches
- Guidebook: In case all else fails and you must start a fire to survive, this guidebook will serve as an excellent fire starter.
- Food and water
- Jacket

To carry these items, you may need a bike bag. A bag mounted in front of the handlebars provides quick access to your belongings, whereas a saddlebag fitted underneath the saddle keeps things out of your way. If you're carrying lots of equipment, you may want to consider a set of panniers. These large bags mount on either side of each wheel on a rack. Many cyclists, though, prefer not to use a bag at all. Some use large hydration backpacks or they just slip all they need into their jersey pockets and off they go.

Be Safe—Wear Your Armor

While on the subject of jerseys, it's crucial to discuss the clothing you must wear to be safe, practical, and—if you prefer—stylish. The following is a list of items that will save you from disaster, outfit you comfortably, and, most important, keep you looking cool.

- Helmet. A helmet is an absolute necessity because it protects your head from complete annihilation. It is the only thing that will not disintegrate into a million pieces after a wicked crash on a descent you shouldn't have been on in the first place. A helmet with a solid exterior shell will also protect your head from sharp or protruding objects. And you can, of course, paste several stickers from your favorite bicycle manufacturers all over the helmet's outer shell, giving companies even more free advertising for your dollar. If you are riding along one of the several downhill locations listed in the book, you may want to also invest in a full face helmet and neck protector to avoid serious injury.
- Shorts. Padded cycle shorts provide cushioning between your body and the bicycle seat. Cycle shorts also wick moisture away from your body and prevent chafing. Form-fitting shorts are made from synthetic material and have smooth seams to prevent chafing. If you don't feel comfortable wearing form-fitted shorts, baggy padded shorts with pockets are available.

- Gloves. You may find well-padded cycling gloves invaluable when traveling over rocky trails and gravelly roads for hours on end. When you fall off your bike and land on your palms, gloves are your best friend. Long-fingered gloves may also be useful, as branches, trees, assorted hard objects, and occasionally small animals will reach out and whack your knuckles. Insulated gloves are essential for winter riding.

- Glasses. Not only do sunglasses give you an imposing presence and make you look cool (both are extremely important), they also protect your eyes from harmful ultraviolet rays, invisible branches, creepy bugs, and dirt. They also hide your glances at riders of the opposite sex wearing skintight, revealing Lycra.

- Shoes. Mountain-bike shoes have stiff soles that transfer more of the power from a pedal stroke to the drive train and provide a solid platform to stand on, thereby decreasing fatigue in your feet. You can use virtually any good light outdoor hiking footwear, but specific mountain bike shoes (especially those with inset cleats) are best. They are lighter and breathe well and are constructed to work with your pedal strokes instead of the natural walking cadence.

- Other clothing. To prepare for Maryland's and Virginia's weather, it's best to dress in layers that can be added or removed as weather conditions change. In cold weather, wear a wicking layer made of a modern synthetic fiber next to your skin. Avoid wearing cotton of any type. It dries slowly and does not wick moisture away from your skin, thus chilling you directly as it evaporates. The next layer should be a wool or synthetic insulating layer that helps keep you warm but also is breathable. A fleece jacket or vest works well as an insulating layer. The outer layer should be a jacket and pants that are waterproof, windproof, and breathable. Your ears will also welcome a fleece headband when it's cold out.

Oh, Those Chilly Metropolitan Days

If the weather chooses not to cooperate on the day you've set aside for a bike ride, it's helpful to be prepared.

- Tights or leg warmers. These are best in temperatures below fifty-five degrees. Knees are sensitive and can develop all kinds of problems if they get cold. Common problems include tendinitis, bursitis, and arthritis.

- Plenty of layers on your upper body. When the air has a nip in it, layers of clothing will keep the chill away from your chest and help prevent bronchitis. If the air is cool, a polypropylene long-sleeved shirt is best to wear against the skin, beneath other layers of clothing. Polypropylene, like wool, wicks away moisture from your skin to keep your body dry. Try to avoid wearing cotton or baggy clothing when the temperature falls. Cotton holds moisture like a sponge, and baggy clothing catches cold air and swirls it around your body. Good cold-weather clothing should fit snugly against your body, but not be restrictive.

- Wool socks. Don't pack too many layers under those shoes, though. You may restrict circulation, and your feet will get real cold, real fast.

- Thinsulate or Gore-Tex gloves. There is nothing worse than frozen feet—unless your hands are frozen. A good pair of Thinsulate or Gore-Tex gloves should keep your hands toasty and warm.

- Keeping your head warm. Sometimes, when the weather gets really cold and you still want to hit the trails, it's tough to stay warm. Ventilated helmets are designed to keep heads cool in the summer heat, but they do little to help keep heads warm during rides in subzero temperatures. Polypropylene and thin merino wool skullcaps are great head and ear warmers that snugly fit over your head beneath the helmet without compromising protection.

All of this clothing can be found at your local bike store, where the staff should be happy to help fit you into the seasons of the year.

To Have or Have Not—Other Very Useful Items

There is no shortage of items for you and your bike to make riding better, safer, and easier. We have rummaged through the unending lists and separated the gadgets from the good stuff, coming up with what we believe are items certain to make mountain bike riding easier and more enjoyable.

- Tires. Buying a good pair of knobby tires is the quickest way to enhance the off-road handling capabilities of a bike. There are many types of mountain-bike tires on the market. Some are made exclusively for very rugged off-road terrain. These big-knobbed, soft rubber tires virtually stick to the ground with magnetic-like traction, but they tend to deteriorate quickly on pavement. Other tires are made exclusively for the road. These are called "slicks," and they have no tread at all. For the average cyclist, though, a good tire somewhere in the middle of these two extremes should do the trick. Realize, however, that you get what you pay for. Do not skimp and buy cheap tires. As your primary point of contact with the trail, tires may be the most important piece of equipment on a bike. With inexpensive rubber, the tire's beads may unravel, or chunks of tread might actually rip off the tire. If you're lucky, all you'll suffer is a long walk back to the car. If you're unlucky, your tire could blow out in the middle of a rowdy downhill, causing a wicked crash.

- Clipless pedals. Clipless pedals, like ski bindings, attach your shoe directly to the pedal. They allow you to exert pressure on the pedals during down- and upstrokes. They also help you maneuver the bike in the air or while climbing various obstacles. Toe clips may be less expensive, but they are also heavier and harder to use. Clipless pedals and toe clips both take a little getting used to, but they're definitely worth the trouble.

- Hydration backpack. These bags are basically backpacks with dedicated compartments to carry large quantities of water. In addition to the hydration component, these bags are ideal for carrying keys, extra food, guidebooks, foul-weather clothing, tools, spare tubes, and a cellular phone, in case you need to call for help.

- Bike computers, GPS receivers. These fun gadgets are much less expensive than they were in years past. They have such features as speedometers, odometers, clocks, altimeter, alarms, and global positioning satellite (GPS) systems. Bike computers will come in handy when you're following these maps or just want to know how far you've ridden in the wrong direction.

Types of Off-Road Terrain

Before roughing it off-road, you may first have to ride the pavement to get to your destination. Don't be dismayed. Some of the country's best rides are on the road. Once we get past these smooth-surfaced pathways, though, adventures in dirt await us.

- Rails-to-trails. Abandoned rail lines are converted into usable public resources for exercising, commuting, or just enjoying nature. Old rails and ties are torn up and a trail, paved or unpaved, is laid along the existing corridor. This completes the cycle, from ancient Indian trading routes to railroad corridors and back again to hiking and cycling trails.
- Unpaved roads. These are typically found in rural areas and are most often public roads. Be careful when exploring, though, not to ride on someone's unpaved private drive.
- Forest roads. These dirt and gravel roads are used primarily as access to forestland and are kept in good condition. They are almost always open to public use.
- Doubletrack. Doubletrack trails are generally old forest roads or gravel roads that have been closed to vehicular traffic and have been "reclaimed" by the environment around them. They are narrower than a forest road but can easily accommodate two cyclists riding by side.
- Singletrack. Singletrack can be the most fun on a mountain bike. These trails, with only one track to follow, are often narrow, challenging pathways through the woods. Remember to make sure these trails are open before zipping into the woods. (At the time of this printing, all trails and roads in this guidebook were open to mountain bikes.)
- Open land. Unless there is a marked trail through a field or open space, you should not ride there. Once one person cuts his or her wheels through a field or meadow, many more are sure to follow, causing irreparable damage to the landscape.

Techniques to Sharpen Your Skills

Many of us see ourselves as pure athletes—blessed with power, strength, and endless endurance. However, it may be those with finesse, balance, agility, and grace that get around most quickly on a mountain bike. Although power, strength, and endurance do have their places in mountain biking, these elements don't necessarily form the framework for a champion mountain biker.

The bike should become an extension of your body. Slight shifts in your hips or knees (body English) can have remarkable results. Experienced bike handlers seem to flash down technical descents, dashing over obstacles in a smooth and graceful effort as if pirouetting in Swan Lake. Here are some tips and techniques to help you connect with your bike and float gracefully over the dirt.

Braking

- Using your brakes requires using your head, especially when descending. This doesn't mean using your head as a stopping block, but rather to think intelligently. Use your best judgment in terms of how much or how little to squeeze those brake levers.

- The more weight a tire is carrying, the more braking power it has. When you're going downhill, your front wheel carries more weight than the rear. Braking with the front brake will help keep you in control without going into a skid. Be careful, though, not to overdo it with the front brakes and accidentally toss yourself over the handlebars. And don't neglect your rear brake! When descending, shift your weight back over the rear wheel, thus increasing your rear braking power as well. This technique will balance the power of both brakes and give you maximum control.

- Good riders learn just how much of their weight to shift over each wheel and how to apply just enough braking power to each brake so as not to "endo" over the handlebars or skid down a trail.

Going Uphill—Climbing Those Treacherous Hills

- Shift into a low gear. Before shifting, be sure to ease up on your pedaling to decrease pressure on the chain. Find the gear that best matches the terrain and steepness of each climb.

- Stay seated. Standing out of the saddle is often helpful when climbing steep hills with a road bike, but you may find that on dirt, standing may cause your rear tire to lose its grip and spin out. Climbing requires traction. Stay seated as long as you can and keep the rear tire digging into the ground. Ascending skyward may prove to be much easier in the saddle.

- Lean forward. On very steep hills, the front end may feel unweighted and suddenly pop up. Slide forward on the saddle and lean over the handlebars. This position will add more weight to the front wheel and should keep you grounded.

- Keep pedaling. On rocky climbs, be sure to keep the pressure on, and don't let up on those pedals! The slower you go through rough trail sections, the harder you will work.

Going Downhill—The Real Reason We Get Up in the Morning

- Shift into the big chain ring. Shifting into the big ring before a bumpy descent will help keep the chain from bouncing off. And should you crash or disengage your leg from the pedal, the chain will cover the teeth of the big ring so they don't bite into your leg.
- Relax. Stay loose on the bike, and don't lock your elbows or clench your grip. Your elbows need to bend with the bumps and absorb the shock, while your hands should have a firm but controlled grip on the bars to keep things steady. Steer with your body, allowing your shoulders to guide you through each turn and around each obstacle.
- Don't oversteer or lose control. Mountain biking is much like downhill skiing, since you must shift your weight from side to side down narrow, bumpy descents. Your bike will have the tendency to track in the direction you look and follow the slight shifts and leans of your body. You should not think so much about steering but rather the direction you wish to go.
- Rise above the saddle. When racing down bumpy, technical descents, you should not sit on the saddle but instead stand on the pedals, allowing your legs and knees to absorb the rocky trail.
- Drop your saddle. For steep, technical descents, you may want to drop your saddle 3 or 4 inches. This lowers your center of gravity, giving you much more room to bounce around. Several manufacturers make "dropper posts" that allow you to do this on the fly.
- Keep your pedals parallel to the ground. The front pedal should be slightly higher so that it doesn't catch on small rocks or logs.
- Stay focused. Many descents require your utmost concentration and focus just to reach the bottom. You must notice every groove, every root, every rock, every hole, every bump. You, the bike, and the trail should all become one as you seek singletrack nirvana on your way down the mountain. But if your thoughts wander, then so may your bike, and you may instead become one with the trees!

Watch Out! Back-Road Obstacles

- Logs. When you want to hop a log, throw your body back, yank up on the handlebars, and pedal forward in one swift motion. This technique clears the front end of the bike. Then quickly scoot forward and pedal the rear wheel up and over. Keep the forward momentum until you've cleared the log, and, by all means, don't hit the brakes, or you may do some interesting acrobatic maneuvers!
- Rocks. Worse than highway potholes! Stay relaxed, let your elbows and knees absorb the shock, and always continue applying power to your pedals. Staying seated will keep the rear wheel weighted to prevent slipping, and a light front end will help you respond quickly to each new obstacle. The slower you go, the more time your tires will have to get caught between the grooves.

- Water. Before crossing a stream or puddle, be sure to first check the depth and bottom surface. There may be an unseen hole or large rock hidden under the water that could wash you up if you're not careful. After you're sure all is safe, hit the water at a good speed, pedal steadily, and allow the bike to steer you through. Once you're across, tap the brakes to squeegee the water off the rims.

- Leaves. Beware of wet leaves. These may look pretty, but a trail covered with leaves may cause your wheels to slip out from under you. Leaves are not nearly as unpredictable and dangerous as ice, but they do warrant your attention on a rainy day.

- Mud. If you must ride through mud, hit it head on and keep pedaling. You want to part the ooze with your front wheel and get across before it swallows you up. Advanced riders will generally speed through mud by lifting their front tire (small wheelie) and letting the rear guide through it. Above all, don't leave the trail to go around the mud. This just widens the path even more and leads to increased trail erosion. Keep singletrack "single."

Urban Obstacles

- Curbs are fun to jump, but as with logs, be careful.

- Curbside drains are typically not a problem for bikes. Just be careful not to get a wheel caught in the grate.

- Dogs make great pets but seem to have it in for bicyclists. If you think you can't outride a dog that's chasing you, stop and walk your bike out of its territory. A loud yell to "Get!" or "Go home!" often works, as does a sharp squirt from your water bottle right between the eyes.

- Cars are tremendously convenient when we're in them, but irate motorists in big automobiles can be a real hazard when you're riding a bike. As a cyclist, you must realize that most drivers aren't expecting you to be there and often wish you weren't. Stay alert and ride carefully, clearly signaling all of your intentions.

- Potholes, like grates and back-road canyons, should be avoided. Just because you're on an all-terrain bicycle doesn't mean you're indestructible. Potholes regularly damage rims, pop tires, and sometimes lift unsuspecting cyclists into spectacular swan dives over the handlebars.

Last-Minute Check

Before a ride, it's a good idea to give your bike a once-over to make sure everything is in working order. Begin by checking the air pressure in your tires to make sure they are properly inflated. Modern mountain bikes are sometimes equipped with tubeless tires so pressures vary from situation to situation. We've found that about forty-five to fifty-five pounds of air pressure per square inch will do the trick for most situations. If your "tubed" tires are underinflated, there is greater likelihood that the tubes may get pinched on a bump or rock, causing the tire to go flat.

Looking over your bike to make sure everything is secure and in its place is the next step. Go through the following checklist before each ride.

- Pinch the tires to feel for proper inflation. They should give just a little on the sides but feel very hard on the treads. If you have a pressure gauge, use it.
- Check your brakes. Squeeze the rear brake and roll your bike forward. The rear tire should skid. Next, squeeze the front brake and roll your bike forward. The rear wheel should lift into the air. If this doesn't happen, then your brakes are too loose. Make sure the brake levers don't touch the handlebars when squeezed with full force.
- Check all quick releases on your bike. Make sure they are all securely tightened.
- Lube up. If your chain squeaks, apply some lubricant.
- Check your nuts and bolts. Check the handlebars, saddle, cranks, and pedals to make sure that each is tight and securely fastened to your bike.
- Check your wheels. Spin each wheel to see that it spins through the frame and between brake pads freely.
- Have you got everything? Make sure you have your spare tube, tire irons, patch kit, frame pump, tools, food, water, and guidebook.

Local Bicycle Clubs and Organizations

MORE: Mid-Atlantic Off-Road Enthusiasts
www.more-mtb.org

FAMBE: Fredericksburg Area Mountain Bike Enthusiasts
www.fambe.org

FATMUG: Fredericksburg Area Trail Management and User Group
www.fatmug.org

ESIMBA: Eastern Shore IMBA
www.esimba.org

SMMB: Southern Maryland Mountain Bike
www.ridesmmb.org

MTB LoCo: Mountain Bike Loudoun County
www.mtbloco.org

Delaware Trail Spinners
www.trailspinners.org

QMTB: Quantico Mountain Bike Club
www.facebook.com/groups/QMTBClub

CAMBO: Culpepper Area Mountain Bike Operators
www.cambomtb.com

National Organizations
IMBA: International Mountain Bicycling Association
www.imba.com

USA Cycling
www.usacycling.org/mtb

Rails-to-Trails Conservancy
www.railtrails.org

Ride Index

About the Authors

When not working with his local IMBA chapter, MORE, **Martín Fernández** is out riding the backcountry trails and roads around the D.C. region looking for routes for one of his guidebooks. A native of Lima, Perú, Martín has lived in the D.C. region for nearly three decades. For two of those, Martín has been actively involved with MORE to ensure we have quality places to ride. Shortly after leaving the Armed Forces, Martín settled in Virginia where he now lives with his wife Courtney and daughter Ari. You may run into Martín at one of his local rides at Fountainhead, Laurel Hill, Meadowood, or the gravel and paved roads of Prince William Forest Park.

PHOTO © TY LONG, NOFILMPHOTOGRAPHY 2014

When not conquering fiery new trails on his mountain bike or racing from town to town on his road bike, **Scott Adams** is hard at work on his next guidebook, cleaning up after his dogs, or exploring the backcountry and unique corners of this planet with his wife, Amy. Scott is a native of Virginia who lives his life to be outdoors but finds much of his time spent behind the monitor of a computer, preparing the next set of maps or arranging for the next book in the series. Few things reward him more than a long hike to the top of a mountain or an early-morning bike ride with no particular place to go.

WHAT'S SO SPECIAL ABOUT UNSPOILED, NATURAL PLACES?

*Beauty Solitude Wildness Freedom Quiet Adventure
Serenity Inspiration Wonder Excitement
Relaxation Challenge*

There's a lot to love about our treasured public lands, and the reasons are different for each of us. Whatever your reasons are, the national **Leave No Trace** education program will help you discover special outdoor places, enjoy them, and preserve them—today and for those who follow. By practicing and passing along these simple principles, you can help protect the special places you love from being loved to death.

THE PRINCIPLES OF **LEAVE NO TRACE**

- Plan ahead and prepare
- Travel and camp on durable surfaces
- Dispose of waste properly
- Leave what you find
- Minimize campfire impacts
- Respect wildlife
- Be considerate of other visitors

Leave No Trace is a national nonprofit organization dedicated to teaching responsible outdoor recreation skills and ethics to everyone who enjoys spending time outdoors.

To learn more or to become a member, please visit us at www.LNT.org or call (800) 332-4100.

Leave No Trace, P.O. Box 997, Boulder, CO 80306